when the solution's straightforward

with 25,000 web addresses registered every day, it's important that you secure your presence on the web - before someone else does. By making your business name your web and e-mail address it's easy for existing customers to communicate with you, and potential ones to access you.

domainnames.com is part of the VeriSign group, a premier Internet company and the authority on web based solutions for businesses and individuals.

our simple approach and customer support make it easy to take the first step. If you don't have a web site, registering your name gives you the breathing space to develop one when it suits your business - perhaps even move into e-commerce.

there's more to our domain names than just a name. Our online solutions also include -

- cost-effective packages to protect your name
- the support to help build your site and register your business on the major search engines
- web mail to check your e-mails anytime, anywhere
- the entire range of web addresses - European endings and those requiring foreign characters

so secure your presence on the web through **domain**names.com straight away, and let our online solutions create even more business opportunities.

Visit us at **www.business.domainnames.com**
or speak to one of our consultants right now on

0800 085 7561

domainnames.com
A VeriSign company

To Malcolm Allan of LS Angus Modelmakers, Glasgow, who gave me my first chance in marketing.

First published in 1985
Second edition 1989
Third edition 1995
Fourth edition 1998
Fifth edition 2001

This book has been endorsed by the Institute of Directors.

The endorsement is given to selected Kogan Page books which the IoD recognises as being of specific interest to its members and providing them with up-to-date, informative and practical resources for creating business success. Kogan Page books endorsed by the IoD represent the most authoritative guidance available on a wide range of subjects including management, finance, marketing, training and HR.

The views expressed in this book are those of the author and are not necessarily the same as those of the Institute of Directors.

Kogan Page Limited
120 Pentonville Road
London N1 9JN

The views expressed in this book are those of the author, and are not necessarily the same as those of Times Newspapers Ltd.

British Library Cataloguing in Publication Data

A CIP record for this book is available from the British Library.

ISBN 0 7494 3524 0

Typeset by Jean Cussons Typesetting, Diss, Norfolk
Printed and bound in Great Britain by Bell & Bain Ltd, Glasgow

Contents

to get past the secretary 194; The presentation 195;
What the buyer worries about 196; Learn to listen 197;
Difficult buyers 198; Buying indicators 198;
Concessions 199; Handling objections 199; Second
sourcing 200; Closing the sale 201; Other products and
other customers 206; The dangers of sale or return 206;
The art of demonstrating 207; Quotations, invoices and
terms of trading 208; Using agents 211; Telephone sales
212; Customer care 216; Sales promotion 217; Price
manipulation 218; Loyalty schemes 218; Competitions
219; Promotional gifts 221; Summary 222

Preface

This fully revised fifth edition remains a *practical* guide to marketing for the small business employing fewer than 20 people. Bigger firms probably have their own marketing director who will not need to be told how to write a press release, design ads that sell, or waste money on arty Web sites that please the chairperson but fail to pull any business.

There must be hundreds of books on running small businesses written by academics and redundant middle managers of multinationals, but few seem to grasp that small firms are different. In 25 years of helping small businesses (and running my own), I can only recall a handful of companies that had written a business plan or had a marketing budget. Yes, writers of the textbooks and lecturers at business schools will wring their hands – but that's the way small firms are.

This may come as a disappointment, but there is more to marketing than setting up your own Web site – much more. The Internet may now make the world seem smaller, but there are thought to be around two billion Web sites out there, all competing for your attention. How are you going to get *your* message across, and to whom? Few dispute that the Internet has changed the way business operates, and we certainly have a long way to go yet. Businesses that don't grasp the opportunities will fall behind. Every aspect of these changes should be examined in relation to how you can adapt and react to the global opportunities and the changing reaction speed of your customers – everything has gone into fast-forward.

But don't get carried away. A consultant's report in January 2000 claimed that new Internet retailers in the UK *lost* £75 million on increased sales of £200 million. Remember that turnover is vanity, profit is sanity. In the same way that the arrival of the office PC was going to produce a paperless office (it hasn't) and that CD ROMs would kill off the book (more titles published last year than ever before), the Internet has not revolutionised every aspect of business – it is another marketing tool that has to be supported by a strategy, research, customer care and value for money.

While the Internet has brought opportunities, it has also introduced a trend towards cheaper prices – a dangerous direction for small businesses with limited capital. More than ever, the small firm has to be aware that marketing is a discipline that needs to be grasped if it is to survive beyond the next change of bank manager.

Don't worry if I talk about 'product' when you are providing a service. The terms are interchangeable. As products become increasingly alike and price-competitive, the difference to the consumer lies in the way the buyer is treated. As call centres and the Internet take over our lives, the firms that succeed will be those that master after-sales service and customer care. It is far more expensive to attract new customers than retain existing ones, so the emphasis must be on improving customer retention. Big firms do get it wrong, as complaints to the various ombudsmen show – this is where the small firm can still have the edge.

Three basic principles

Learn to differentiate

Try to be a little different in the way you present your message, the way you design the product or service. 'Me-too' products that sell off the back of others can only sell by being cheaper – their lives tend to be short and inspire little enthusiasm among stockists. Boring products and tame ads don't inspire much emotion. I was once asked to design a mailshot for servicing dust-extraction equipment – you can't get much more uninspiring than that. So I pictured the message on a gravestone with the implied threat that ignoring the purchase might hasten the reader's end. The mailshot leaflet was certainly read.

Find gaps in the market

Make niche marketing your philosophy. Leave Sainsbury's to swamp the shopper with cornflakes while you seek out hotels that appreciate Dorset blue cheese. Niche segments will not produce volume, but they are less price sensitive, easier to identify once some sales have been made and cheaper to promote. Mass markets are governed by price – full stop.

Think benefits

The consumer only pays when he or she is satisfied with 'What's in it for me?'. Design all your promotion to answer that question. Write sales letters from the reader's point of view. Mobile phone ads I read talk about GPRS, HSCSD and even Serial/IMEI. How many people know what they're talking about? They've confused *benefits* with *features*.

Dave Patten
Merry Marketing
North Curry
Taunton

Acknowledgements

Leach of Muchelney for reining me back on my worst excesses, Tom Insall, super salesman, for sharing his closing techniques and Henry Clark from dear old CoSIRA for the encouragement to start.

1

What is marketing?

Without change nothing is possible. Not to change is a sure sign of extinction.

Sir John Harvey Jones

Marketing has been described as knowing where to go, while selling is the act of getting there. But the discipline of marketing has made the process much more complex. Marketing embraces market research, advertising, public relations, direct mail, exhibitions, design, export and the relatively new discovery of customer care. As running a business becomes more demanding, most recognise that acquiring the skills of marketing is essential to profitable growth. Even those who trumpet the wonders of the Internet acknowledge that turnover may only increase by 5 per cent, and there are reported to be another 7,500 new Web sites appearing *each day.*

Think of some of the recent successful businesses – Virgin, Psion, Dyson. They've all been marketing- and innovation-led. They have not relied on old methods, instead seeking new technology, new ways of doing things that put consumer needs at the forefront. They have *chased* markets rather than expecting clients to come to them to buy what they already have. The accelerating pace of change has been frightening.

Marketing as a management skill has been adopted by such august bodies as the Patent Office, waste disposal teams, the Ordnance Survey and even our local schools that have to compete with one another.

If you are looking for some snappy definitions of what it is, try:

● Marketing matches customers needs with the strengths of the business.

- Good marketing places the customer at the centre of the business.
- Marketing is the link between customer and producer.

Of if you prefer a slick American version – sales with a college education.

Service or product?

A century ago Britain produced 90 per cent of the world's ships, and in them carried many of the manufactured goods that an expanding global market needed. At the close of the 20th century only 20 per cent of the nation's GDP was in manufactured goods, the rest being made up of services – tourism, retailing, insurance, and that catch-all phrase 'financial services'. Only 1 in 10 of new businesses now manufactures anything. And 90 per cent of our export trade is carried out by just 40 companies.

The process of marketing a product and a service is basically the same, but having sold both in a varied business career, I can tell you that services are much harder. A product can at least be seen, handled and judged on performance. Selling an intangible relies more on promise, faith and integrity. Many businesses – retailing, for example – are a combination of both. The traditional high-street greengrocer and butcher are in danger of extinction under pressure from the supermarkets unless they can find a way of satisfying customers. Vegetable prices are dearer in the supermarket and of the same quality, but convenience seems to rule. The alert greengrocer will have to go for flavour and variety allied to keen prices to survive. The only butchers who survive in my town have done so by emphasising top-quality local herds (adding the quality of traceability) and product knowledge. Attention to top-class service may ensure that some small produce outlets survive the all-embracing greed of the supermarkets. In addition, the alert manufacturer has come to realise that, though he may have the product that everyone needs, the service element – looking after the customer – is just as important.

So for the sake of simplicity I will talk about the product – and imply this covers services – except where a strong distinction needs to be made.

Figure 1.1 Marketing is all about objectives and knowing where you're going – as simple as this sign

Who is the customer?

Central to marketing is identifying the customer. Without a flow of prospects who need your product you haven't got a business. Most of your waking hours should be spent in:

- thinking of what your market segment needs;
- finding ways to reach that segment at an effective cost;
- dreaming up more products that your existing customers need;
- looking for fresh customers who will buy from your existing range;
- innovating new products to replace those that are beginning to falter.

As business becomes more competitive and many sectors contract to fewer major players, customers also demand and expect more for their money. Standards and expectations have risen all round. Thanks to television consumer programmes, travel abroad and – for those in employment – a higher standard of living, we have become a more sophisticated buying audience. Greater standardisation and brand power mean that the same product can be bought at many outlets. The problem for the small firm is how to capture and retain the customer, and here the service element must be paramount. If many firms sell the same product the only way of differentiating your supply is by excellent customer service.

A recent survey found that the number of customer complaints to big organisations has risen, despite the rise of call centres and ombudsmen. It is the image of faceless remoteness that many large firms portray that seems to antagonise so many of us. However, this is the small firm's opportunity.

It cannot be over-stressed that the needs of the customer must become paramount in running your business. Word of mouth will always remain the best advertisement and unhappy customers soon tell their friends of bad experiences. Managing customers starts with managing and motivating your own staff, for unhappy and disillusioned staff will never create the right environment. Low staff morale inevitably means a high staff turnover and probably theft or fraud of one sort or another. Far cheaper in the long run is to treat your employees as human beings and individuals with worries and aspirations, rather than just another business cost to be hired, fired or manipulated.

A happy work environment will imbue your customers with goodwill and make dealing with you a memorable experience and one to be repeated. The customer pays your bills, staff, profit and future growth. Customers can be a nuisance sometimes, but without them you haven't got a business; being pleasant to people is better in the long run.

One of the reasons that the concept of marketing has got an indifferent image among small businesses is that many large firms have been wasteful in their advertising, injudicious in how they have run their PR campaigns, and failed in many cases to grasp the essentials to success in direct mail. More attention to identifying the prospect, closer targeting and not indulging in promotion unless you can measure the response are all vital ingredients of small firms' growth.

With a forward order book your bank manager should be willing to provide the working capital to finance purchases, pay for stock, and cover the running costs in anticipation of cash sales. Running a business becomes much simpler when you have a foreseeable steady demand for your product.

Parting people from their money

The psychology of buying is fascinating. I often think that the ambitious businessman should attend a course on motivation before getting to grips with marketing. On the premise that people usually only buy things for a good reason let's think for a moment about why a civilised society buys a product or a service.

- *Fulfil a need*: we all have to eat and wear clothes.
- *Fashion*: less important as we get older, vital to the smart set.
- *Image*: a GTI means more than a base model.
- *Salesmanship*: the wonders of double glazing.
- *Advertising*: the power of the media.
- *Peer pressure*: schoolchildren must have the 'right' trainers.
- *Impulse*: supermarket sweet displays by the checkout.
- *Price*: many buy the cheapest but it can be suicide for a small firm always to aim to be the cheapest in town. Fortunately, some buyers prefer to pay more: let's call it snobbery.
- *Location and convenience*: ease of parking, or nearness to a bus stop can be very helpful.
- *Value*: perceived to be the best value for money, not the same as being the cheapest.
- *Security*: mobile phones are sold to women drivers on the platform of reassurance.
- *Fear*: what happens if you don't take out my policy?
- *Legislation*: the law may demand purchase – safety equipment for example.
- *Specification*: what does it do? Performance standards.
- *Quality and reliability*: cheap and inferior goods are poor value in the long run.
- *Reputation*: usually where a big firm will score over a small firm except in their immediate locality. Personal recommendation is a powerful inducer.
- *Guarantees and after-sales service*: vital for expensive and any new products.
- *Gift*: the buyer is not always the user. Offering a wrapping service (as the French do so well) will attract custom.

There are many more reasons and you should think hard about your clients, what they are looking for, and pitch the appeal accordingly. It is the emotional trigger that will unlock the best deals. The psychology of buying is complex, once you get away from the basic needs of hunger, shelter and that three-letter word. Human nature has probably stayed the same down the ages but life has become more complicated. The gap between rich and poor, those in receipt of a regular salary and those on means-tested benefits, has widened the gulf. It is a truism to say that children grow up earlier and demand a different lifestyle from their parents. At the same time, the average level of debt per household has put fresh pressure on the wage earners – and resort to the black economy to make ends meet.

Marketing must take account of these continual changes in society and the way we apportion our resources. Some point out that the only affluent section left of any size is the retired or those who have paid off their mortgage and got their kids off their hands (are they ever?). These are the folk who take several holidays a year, buy health care products, go to restaurants, leave the complications of the car and DIY to paid experts and generally seem to have a good time. Saga Holidays was one of the first to spot and specifically cater for this group.

But there are dangers in this. Dealing with the older age group requires delicate phraseology. Few regard themselves as old and it is easy to be patronising.

Price is king?

When I meet a small firm for the first time my usual opening gambit is to ask, 'Why do your customers buy from you?' If the answer is 'price', meaning cheapness, then I usually fear for the widow and orphans. While many firms may think that their business is founded on a highly competitive pricing policy, in practice there are probably more significant reasons. Location, range of stock or product knowledge may be more important, allowing greater price flexibility. All too often I come across firms that have undersold their product, have worked extremely hard, and are still wondering why they never seem to make any money. There is no virtue in being a busy fool. One of the less welcome aspects of the Internet (from the supplier's point of view) is that it has become easier to compare prices. HMV sells records at a third cheaper on its Web site than in its stores. There are even Web sites set up specifically to monitor certain goods and work out the cheapest brands. Basing your marketing strategy on selling cheap is not a good tactic for a small firm. More on pricing later in this chapter.

Features and benefits

It is important to recognise that we buy a product or service for what it will do for us. We look for the benefits. A feature is what the manufacturer has designed. You may say this is semantics but look at almost any computer magazine and for first-time buyers the jargon is often inpenetrable. A large potential audience is cut off from buying a computer because the industry has swathed itself in computerspeak, instead of explaining in simple English what it will do for the user. The manufacturer has paid for the features – the customer pays for the benefits. Or to put it another way, the drill salesperson is not selling bits but more holes. Kodak does not sell films, it sells nostalgia. On a more mundane level the window cleaner's insurance policy is of no interest: we just want to know that if he or she falls through the conservatory someone else will pay up.

The active marketeer must never lose sight of the politician's old cliché, 'What's in it for me?'

When you can answer that question from the prospect, you have made a sale. Every time you compose a sales letter, write an ad, design a trade stand, you must get to the heart of the matter. Why should a client purchase your wares? What benefit will it bring him or her?

All your marketing efforts should be viewed from the prospect's point of view, not your own. One businessman mailed out a few thousand letters and was disappointed that the response was so poor. By mistake one had been returned and the envelope sat on the desk looking at him. Although he knew what it was, he actually opened it and straight away realised why it was so awful. The tables had been turned.

Try to be objective: take a detached view. Research a little – ask someone who will give an honest answer, not a relative or sycophant.

Isolate the segment

Marketing is all about segmentation – talking to a precise, identifiable section of the market. Segmentation can be by sex, age, income, occupation, interest, location, buyer, prospect, job title or whatever is germane to your product. It is a common mistake for small firms to think of supplying a mass market, of trying to compete with Marks & Spencer or Woolworths. You have to find a niche where the need can be directly exploited and developed and is not already covered by a mass manufacturer. You can never compete on price with the big boys or Far Eastern imports.

If you are in the construction industry and deal with, for example, architects but also surveyors, project managers, land agents and planners, you must appreciate that they all will expect to receive a slightly different treatment. Their jargon, professional interest and trade associations are different. They read different journals, attend separate conferences and exhibitions and have their pecking order within the building hierarchy.

Developing your segment will lead to finding out what else you can provide to satisfy that market. It may lead to more stock in depth or better training and knowledge for staff. Stretch the service beyond the popular times, be it tourism or late-evening opening, to capitalise on existing customer wants. Servicing the needs of the elderly or housebound means adjusting to the slower mentality of a previous age. Your values may not be theirs. The tone of your letters must not be patronising, and must show an understanding of their fears and needs. Top service is vital, with immediate response and integrity. You will get strong loyalty and recommendation to others. The older age group has also been found to make more complaints. As we get older, we get fussier – but learn to please this segment and you will enjoy loyalty for life.

I could not sell to teenagers. I may kid myself that I am still young at heart, but the culture is a mystery, so I would have to employ someone much younger and more in tune with the motivations of the age group.

Analysing your customer base is essential to finding out more about what makes them buy, where they are, how often they purchase and, most important of all, who are the *heavy* users. You can learn a lot from getting closer to these wonderful, enlightened customers. Why do they buy so much? Are they re-sellers? Do they have another use for your product that you haven't stumbled across? If Mrs X uses so much, go

Figure 1.2 A nice example of segmentation and specialisation. Stock in depth will attract buyers from some distance. Word of mouth and journalistic novelty should do the rest

and look for more Mrs Xs with the same needs and problems. Match her profile with others. Try to draw up a profile of your typical customer and keep it ever before you. You are looking for a snapshot of your average customer needs, interests and buying patterns. What do your customers read, where do they meet, how do they get their information, what do they belong to? You are then in a better position to decide how to reach them most cost effectively with your irresistible sales message.

One example to ponder. The snack food market is huge, yet like most food products profit hinges on cost-effective distribution. It is very difficult for a small-volume producer to break in. I have worked with a healthy fruit flapjack manufacturer to develop a niche market for the product, where advertising and brand promotion has had of necessity to be nil. We found that producing a larger size opened up a less price-sensitive segment for outdoor types to munch on the hoof – and became a gift product to take home to Mum. Point-of-sale material emphasised the benefits.

Growth segments in the consumer market

Apart from Lottery winners, at the time of writing the significant growth area to devote most attention to seems to be the Woofties (Well-Off Over Fifties). This group consists of individuals who have probably paid off most if not all of their mortgages, are in stable relationships, have seen their children settled, may have reaped building society windfalls and possibly have taken early retirement. They are still fit, active and have money to spend and the time to indulge in their long-repressed wants. This is also the age when their parents die and leave large unencumbered properties to rent or sell off at values undreamt of when first bought.

The needs of this group include long-haul holidays to exotic destinations, good wines, healthy eating and fitness clubs, financial planning and investment, motoring, home improvements and even home computers; price does not seem to be a consideration. In every case value and perceived benefits take precedence over price. The vagaries of interest-rate rises, commuter train fare increases and the price of butter are of little significance. This group is motivated by enjoyment, catching up on past dreams and spoiling the grandchildren. This group is mature enough to see through slick and pretentious advertising and is generally unmoved by fads or fashion and the brand image manipulation so important to the teenage and twenty-something market.

The segment splits down further as we get older. Whichever government is in power it would seem increasingly unlikely that the old age pension will be anywhere near sufficient to meet people's needs. Those who have been fortunate enough to make private provision will have more disposable income, the rest – several millions – are likely to spend their declining years in poverty.

Statisticians tell us that one-third of the UK population is over 50 and this figure will rise to half in 30 years, so this enormous slice of the population needs close attention; make sure that you direct the right message to each segment.

Growth segments in the business market

The hunger at the moment is for competent Web site designers – or anyone who knows how to fix software problems. One of my firms is currently using a 17-year-old whizzkid who has yet to take his A levels. Without doubt, the only people making real money from the predicted explosion in e-commerce are Web site designers, e-commerce advisers with experience (ie those who've been at it for more than 18 months) and venture capitalists vetting hopeful e-millionaires (99 per cent are declined, but what about the upfront fees?).

Mobile communications are another obvious vein worth mining, from retail to designing fancy phone cases. As products are designed and produced so quickly around the world nowadays, there is scope for personalisation for businessmen who want to stamp their own identity on their belongings – I think they call it a style statement. Nokia may make thousands of phones a day, but you can now buy covers for them in your own colours or logo. The mass manufacturers produce the bulk of these, but the small firms can make accessories and service equipment when it goes wrong.

As I write, there seems no end to the boom in house prices – at least in the south-east. Service trades can feed off this frenzy by providing house extensions, landscape gardening, security lighting and statuary. If the money is flowing, chase the market.

Make your product different

As markets become more developed, you have to work harder to *differentiate* your product. There is little point in small firms on low promotional budgets making 'me-too' products and relying on a budget price to survive. They will invariably get squeezed out. You must constantly be striving to think up fresh ways of adding value, tuning the service, improving the range and getting closer to the customer's needs. One of the hardest tasks of marketing is to make sure that you are remembered. If your product is the same as everyone else's only heavy promotion will draw punters to your door. Not a game for the faint-hearted.

Driving schools have been around since Henry Ford, so new starters are up against stiff competition. There are two neat solutions in my home town. One claims to cater for 'the young driver' and the other – yes, for 'the mature driver'. The logic is beautifully simple. Each end of the scale has different problems. Youngsters learn quickly but cause most accidents and I would guess that most fees are paid by the parent, who would be attracted by a school that claims to give a solid, accident-free grounding to a driving career. Older people, perhaps wives learning to drive for the first time or those who have let their skills get rusty, will appreciate being taught by an older, more sympathetic teacher. The school cars emphasise the advantages.

The point is that *all* driving schools can and do teach all ages – but these two have set out to make their service that little bit different and have targeted a specific segment of the market. Price then becomes of less importance, because drivers are attracted for different reasons.

Avoid lone products

I can only recall one successful small firm that flourished on producing a single product. It discovered a gap in the market for fixing road signs on poles. By designing a one-man device, producing a unique machine to make it and at the same time deter competition, the firm now exploits worldwide markets and has made a considerable business. That is the exception.

For most businesses you need a range. The hard part of marketing is to identify profitable customers and avoid forever hunting for more.

Once you have sold them something find another line that will fit alongside. Treasure their allegiance, turn that goodwill into profit.

Think of Black & Decker. The power drill is a wonderful tool, but is only the start of a complete home workshop. The only limit is the depth of your purse. Drills, saws, polishers, sanders – the list is added to every year. Franklin Mint adopt the same philosophy. It rarely tries to sell you one plate. It tries to tempt you with a series, and a free display stand for the first one. Magazine 'part works', manuals on car maintenance and DIY use the same strategy.

A mobile carpet cleaner should not be looking for just the lounge carpet but for car valeting, upholstery and commercial work as well. Travel agents now actively market skiing and spring holidays to capitalise on past customer satisfaction. Hire shops started life as predominantly trade outlets to builders but now encompass a wide range of more domestic kit.

Positioning

Along with targeting and segments, *positioning* is another of those gruesome words, beloved by marketing academics, whose principles need to be firmly grasped. For a holiday job, my student son worked in a local meat factory that supplied three of the major supermarkets. The identical burger was packed in three different boxes with differing prices to match the positions that the chains have created for themselves. Marks & Spencer was inevitably the most expensive, followed by Sainsbury's and Tesco. A Marks & Spencer shopper could save money by buying burgers in Tescos, but they wouldn't be M&S burgers, would they?

Where a product or service is positioned governs all the messages that the supplier needs to achieve: price, value, image, performance. There is a dry-cleaning service in London's West End that fits out its delivery drivers in livery. Naturally, it is much more expensive than a corner shop. Customers *expect* to pay more and no doubt hope their neighbours will notice the regular van delivery.

Some premium lagers make the expensive price a virtue. They say nothing about the flavour, for goodness' sake. Lagers, and especially whiskies, are sold on image, reflected glory. Some shops in Bond Street don't display a price: if you need to ask you can't afford it. But positioning doesn't just relate to high-value items. Before the term 'fast food' was invented, there was and still is a shop in Edinburgh called Gobble 'n' Go. Now, many educated people would regard that as horrendous, but I think it is rather clever. In one phrase it has summed up quite explicitly the nature of food and service available. If it is right for that area and attracts custom, who are we to criticise?

Positioning governs the standard of service, quality of staff and expectations of customers. If you are a market trader, gift wrapping would be quite out of place. Move that business to the high street, and it may steal a march over the competition. Price is obviously a strong consideration. We have a view or opinion on the value of an article once we see the price. We form a judgement. As markets develop and more competition is attracted, where you position your business on that ladder of competing businesses governs everything that follows thereafter. Customer expectations reflect the price and position that you manage to achieve.

Figure 1.3 Positioning: both are baked beans, but are deliberately pitched at opposite segments of the market. A multi-coloured label and the brand attracts the affluent or selective eater. The plain label will be bought by the student and others on a low income. Assumptions – or prejudices – will be formed just by the outer appearance

Positioning is most important when it comes to advertising in a developed market with many competing journals or papers. Think of the readership of the *Daily Telegraph* or the *Guardian*. Ignoring the jibe that the *Telegraph* is supposed to be read by those who think they still run the country (*The Times* is read by those who do, etc), both are quality broadsheets, but with quite distinct political slants, one right wing, the other read by teachers, social workers, media people. Advertisers need to take account of the spending power and moral stance of these readers. The local and regional press can rarely afford the luxury of anything other than an apolitical viewpoint.

Positioning is a vital ingredient of branding, with Virgin carrying it to extremes. Based entirely on the so far untainted image of Richard Branson, the prime mover, Virgin has spread from airlines and record shops to the complex world of financial services. More on branding on page 18.

Hunt for gaps

The footwear market is of course dominated by imports and the high-street shops, but one Somerset firm called Cosyfeet has become market leader in the niche sector of supplying to the elderly housebound. The proprietor saw that these people could never get to a high-street shop, and also suffered from bunions and other ailments, with the result that they could never find shoes or slippers wide or deep enough to fit. Cosyfeet's business is done almost entirely by mail-order catalogue following enquiries generated by page advertising. The nursing homes and hospitals provide trade and volume business, as the company's main problem is that names need to be constantly updated and new customers found to replace those who die.

The distribution chain

Unlike the service provider, the product manufacturer often has to go through various intermediaries to reach the eventual user. Wholesalers, distributors, maybe an agent and the retailer are in business just like you, and need paying for the service that they provide.

A wholesaler will invariably be a specialist supplier in a narrow field, probably regionally based. Take the hardware/housewares/DIY market. Twenty-five years ago every town had its corner hardware store selling screws, paint, brushes, curtain track and pots and pans. Today we all know what has happened. Out-of-town 'sheds' as the trade calls them – your B&Q, Texas, Homebase, Do It All – have decimated the small family business and everything is pre-packaged, with advice from assistants nominal. Convenience and accessibility have overridden everything. To the small manufacturer with a new product, the way into this market is fraught with peril. Most of these giants will not touch a lone product from a small firm. They want Mr Dulux, Black & Decker, Crown, etc, to merchandise 50 feet of shelf space and not be bothered with opening a new account for a small line.

The small firm is left with the shrinking field of independents, served by specialist wholesalers, who will carry paints, timber, electricals or whatever, but who are probably already listing between 5 and 20,000 lines. Very difficult. The Internet comes into its own for specialisms, as in this field availability not price should be the reason for purchase. It's a grand place to search for obscure lines, but Web sites still need to be promoted. The trick is to make it interesting and up to date so that buyers keep on coming back. More on this in Chapter 3.

This story can be repeated in many sectors – food especially, where the market is again dominated by a handful of giants. Distribution in the food industry is crucial to the success of the venture. Fortunately, stricter hygiene regulations now mean carriage by temperature-controlled vehicles for many lines, but in rural areas, and those remote from major markets, these specialist carriers are scarce. Small drops are uneconomic.

In one way the food industry is fortunate: we all have to eat. But food is a mass market where, with a few luxury exceptions, volume is the only way to get the price to an acceptable level. Mass advertising, brand support, discounts and dealer incentives are all expected from today's grocer, making it difficult for small firms to supply anything other than a local market.

Take bottled water. Twenty years ago it would have been laughable to suggest that the British would copy the French habit of drinking water that we bought in a supermarket and lugged home, when it is there in the tap. Working in Somerset, as I do, there was hardly a week went by when a struggling farmer did not contact me, insisting that his water was purer than anyone else's. They all missed the point. It was the access to market and distribution channels that counted.

Transporting bulky, low-value items is difficult to compete against. Give or take a bubble or two, all bottled British water is the same. When you are up against Schweppes with access to every store in the country, then you have your work cut out.

Margins and mark-ups

Everyone in the distribution chain takes a cut and, before getting excited about working from the price you see in the shops as a basis for setting *your* price, you must establish the margins that these maligned but essential people work to. You need to establish a *price structure*.

First, let's establish what these terms mean, for many simple costing errors have started from misinterpretation of these fundamentals. The *mark-up* is what your buyer adds on to sell on. The *margin* (or profit) is what the buyer enjoys. They are not the same thing at all. Take a rustic craft potter who produces a pot for £10 (including a miserable profit) that is sold on to a wholesaler. He may mark up (add on) 33⅓ per cent to arrive at his selling price on £13.33. But his margin (profit) will be 25 per cent. The wholesaler may sell to a kitchen shop which could well add on 100 per cent, giving an eventual price of £31.32 – including VAT.

When doing your research and negotiating with buyers it is most important to discover whether the buyer is talking about margin, mark-up or discount. To help you remember use Table 1.1.

Table 1.1 The relationship between margin and mark-up

Margin *per cent*	Mark-up *per cent*
10.00	11.11
15.00	17.65
20.00	25.00
25.00	33.33
30.00	42.86
33.33	50.00
40.00	66.67
50.00	100.00

And don't forget that to find the VAT element of the selling price, you need to deduct 14.893 per cent, not 17.5 per cent (or, if you prefer, × 7 then ÷ 47). If you run your business on an across-the-board gross margin, this *aide-mémoire* will be useful.

Some trades have their own jargon; for example, the food trade talks about POR – price off retail, rather than discounts or mark-ups. Every trade has its industry standard or accepted practice, but as a guide, fast-moving everyday consumables enjoy lower mark-ups than luxury or strongly seasonal items.

You will be fortunate to find any gift retailer that marks up less than 100 per cent, while the more exclusive gallery will be looking at much more than that. Location also plays a major part. Expensive boutiques will work on bigger mark-ups than department stores. At the other end of the scale, cigarettes are down to about 7 per cent – simply because it is a fast-moving, addictive product widely available.

Another example. The pet trade works on a 50 per cent mark-up over wholesale, while the wholesaler will add on between 25 and 30 per cent over the price at which he will buy from you.

Mail order operators are something else. Even though you may be selling direct to one of the burgeoning home mail catalogues, the difference between your ex-works price and the catalogue is often a factor of four. Be warned.

Brand identity

Nestlé paid millions for Rowntree to get its hands on the brand names, Kit-Kat among others. Kit-Kat is one of the oldest UK chocolate biscuits and goes back to 1935. Cadbury's Dairy Milk was the first chocolate bar (1921). Not many small firms can go back that far, but it illustrates the point that a strong brand image is important to retain customers, develop the range of products and add value to the balance sheet.

I am often disappointed how few small firms actually put their name on the product or on the side of the van. It is as simple as that. Branding includes names on shop overalls, sweaters at a show, stationery and graphics. It is your corporate image (more on that on page 114).

Start with a good name, memorable and preferably illustrative of what you do. My own trading style is Merry Marketing. It invariably brings a smile to whomever I am addressing and people remember it. As I try to run my business with a little quirk of humour it seems an apt title. If your father was called Smith, then try to tag on a descriptive phrase. (Yes, I have heard of WH Smith, but they've been around a few years.)

The image and identity of the product or service should be carried through the range of whatever you do. We are talking about the personality of what you do. If you are a happy, outgoing person the image and service of your staff should be in the same vein.

Branding is very much tied to the position where you place your business. Upmarket goods will demand elaborate presentation and premises to match. Market traders pile it high, sell it cheap.

Everyone strives to be brand leader in their field. This is obviously difficult for small firms, but it may happen in a niche market. Brand leaders set the pace, not just with price but with innovation, product development, profits and calibre of staff. All the bright people want to work for them. Staff training and commitment, customer care policies, solid reputations and no-quibble guarantees are invariably the hallmarks of brand leaders.

Price levels are invariably set by the brand leader. Where they go, others follow.

Establishing a strong brand identity will take years, but you have to start somewhere. As your reputation becomes recognised you can add more products or services to capitalise on your good name. Some lines can be bought in and rebadged, bearing in mind that the new additions must equal or exceed the quality you already offer. Such *brand extension*, as the pundits call it, could damage the whole enterprise if there is a failure, and some would argue that, if overdone, it could weaken the brand impact and credibility. Virgin, Sainsbury's and Marks & Spencer have gone into banking and mortgages: a far cry from what they were set up to do. Maybe it will all work out...

Hunt the heavy users

After a time every business finds that a proportion of its customers is spending a disproportionate amount of money.

I know a firm that is a major player in educational software. When it examined the buying list it found that a few people were buying a lot more software than the average. They turned out to be semi-retired teachers now doing home tutoring for dyslexic children.

It can be very illuminating to identify your heavy users, the major purchasers of what you provide. Why do they buy so much? What do they find so beneficial? Can you find more with the same profile? Time spent isolating and then talking to these wonderfully enlightened people will be time well spent. These heavy users are your *key accounts*. They will control the profitability and direction of your business. Keep them happy and find more of the same and your business will expand.

Heavy users can be identified by age, income, gender, interests or industry sector. You are looking for what they have in common.

One danger. Do not get too dependent on one customer. If you have more than 30 per cent of turnover from one customer, it could prove fatal if you lost him or her. Below that and you can generally scramble through, depending on whether you have any bad debts from that customer, or just simply lose the future turnover.

Pricing for profit

How do you set your price? Copy what Charlie does down the road minus 5 per cent, add X per cent on to your bought-in price or run a continuous sale?

While this is a book on marketing, not accounting, setting the correct price is one of the most vital aspects of staying in business. In my experience small firms tend to underprice rather than overcharge. New firms in particular both underestimate the costs of running a business and undervalue their own worth. Back to basics. Why do people buy from you? Do you provide a quality, knowledgeable service where they never have to return for more information or are you one of those who jump from one topic to another without ever mastering any? Do you always keep your promises and never let clients down?

Never forget the old saw 'turnover is vanity, profit is sanity'. Avoid products that require huge volumes to generate a profit. A high turnover may look good on the profit and loss account, but your banker is more interested in the bottom line. Many firms in the 1980s found turnover shooting up but lost money on bad debts, high borrowing and expansion costs.

Golden rule: price what the market will bear. Easier said than achieved, but that should be your yardstick. The costs of production are almost irrelevant, it is what the customer is prepared to pay that is important. I can remember *Which?* doing a study on face cream, and the cost of ingredients of one of the brand leaders (largely egg white) was pence. The price to the Christmas shopper was measured in pounds.

Genuinely new products in particular need careful calculation and market testing to arrive at the right price. As a generality, a new line with no comparison and many benefits should be launched dear and reduced as competition intrudes. It is easier to reduce a price – and be able to give a discount on quantity – than to put the price up.

Naturally, you must known what your product or service *costs* you to provide, but that need bear little relation to what you charge. You must have the figures to ensure you are at least ahead of break-even to be able to form a *pricing policy*, unless some lines are sold as a loss-leader (traditionally, milk and the white sliced loaf are loss-leaders in supermarkets).

Pricing policy

At various stages in the life of your business you will undoubtedly change your pricing policy – sometimes due to market opportunities, sometimes through the threat of competition. Let's look at some:

1. *Your marketing objectives.* New products can be launched significantly below the competition to buy a large chunk of the market. It may be important to 'get the product out into the market'. Car makers usually do this as there is no better way of getting cars on the road. It has been rumoured that irresistible staff discounts are offered to achieve the same ends and push the car up the best-selling lists. Alternatively, it could be argued that a product with notable differences – an extra perceived benefit – deserves a higher price, regardless of the costs of production.
2. *The competition.* Though I hope through this book to show ways of differentiating your product or service from the herd, inevitably the consumer makes price comparisons, and certainly in the early stages of most small firms' development

you are bound by what the prevailing competitive price level is. 'Unique' is a word bandied about by some advertisers to no purpose. There are extremely few genuinely unique products around, and if you value your integrity – let alone the preservation of the English language – you will be sparing in the use of the term.

It is also important to define what the competition is. My local coach operator to London seems locked in a price war with National Express, but I would contend that his service is so superior that he is capturing people from the train, not the immediate rival, and the train fare is dearer by a factor of five.

3. *Chain of distribution.* Service providers who sell direct will have a different price structure from manufacturers who must go through intermediaries. Theoretically I could have published and distributed this book myself, but as there are over 3,000 booksellers in the UK, most of whom will never take more than a couple of any title at one time, the solution is painfully obvious. The method of selling is the main influence on your pricing strategy. Going direct by selling 'off the page adverts' (see Chapter 5) to avoid middlemen will incur heavy advertising costs.

4. *Location and overheads.* It is almost impossible now for an independently owned shop to exist in the high street due to the cost of rates and rent. All our main thoroughfares are full of building societies, travel agents, shoe and fashion shops. The grocers and ironmongers (does anyone under the age of 40 use that word?) have disappeared to out-of-town supermarkets and DIY superstores. The independent has to survive in secondary positions where the pedestrian traffic flow is a twentieth of that a few yards away. Those that have survived are being squeezed or have some unusual edge over neighbours.

5. *The volume of production and purchase cycle.* Tyre manufacturers caught a cold when radial tyres became common – they lasted longer. The increase in tyre-depth regulations has, however, helped to bring in more frequent business. Swings and roundabouts. If your product is so well made that it never wears out you will have to continually promote to find more customers. The conservatory supplier will need a high advertising budget – not many of us will buy twice. Dry-cleaners know that smart dresses come back time after time.

Two immediately seasonal activities spring to mind: November the fifth and Christmas. I know a firm that has built a very successful business importing and distributing Christmas tree lights, but they would rather like to find a summer activity. Fireworks are becoming less seasonal with stage-managed extravaganzas, so the focus is not so pronounced.

6. *Discount structure.* Money given away here is a straight deduction from the profit. Discounts are usually given for three reasons: to encourage a larger order, to secure prompt payment or to retain customer loyalty.

   When customers are scarce it is always tempting to lower your quantity steps and give everyone the bulk rate. Do this as a sales ploy if you must but make sure you really know the costs of distribution. Big firms are notorious for being slow payers, but still take the early settlement discount when finally paying the invoice. There is not a great deal you can do about this if you wish to continue to enjoy their custom, short of writing to point out the error of their ways. Some firms can build in an inflated figure to knock off as a discount to encourage cash flow. Cash and Carries operate on low margins and no credit.

7. *Differential pricing* is common among service trades to encourage usage at unpopular times or target different segments of the market. Hairdressers often have a cheaper prices for OAPs as do B&Q on a mid-week day. Travel operators offer free or reduced prices for children. It is usual for coach operators to give the party leader a free seat if the numbers exceed 12.

   Swimming pools and other leisure activities use differential pricing widely to attract ladies only, youngsters, learners and season-ticket holders.

   Differential pricing is also practised among manufacturers to target trade and consumer products. The ingredients can often be identical, but the packaging, presentation and positioning allow widely different prices to be realised.

8. *Commission.* Those running a sales force will come up against the commission element endemic in most organisations.

   The effect of high unemployment levels always seems to be to shift salary to commission-related pay, so we see double glazing, advertising and life assurance salespeople struggling to make ends meet. Overgenerous commission payments to salesmen in the 1980s have cost the life assurance industry millions in correcting the mis-selling of pension schemes.

If commission needs to be paid to sellers you must make allowances in your price strategy.

9. *The product life cycle* affects every product and every business (see page 28). If it is a new product with little competition you can probably charge more. As sales grow and it is seen to be in demand, almost inevitably you will get pressure from similar products that will tend to undercut you. You either build in more benefits or reduce the price to match.

10. The law of diminishing returns says that ever-increasing turnover is unlikely to lead to a profit rise in tandem. The only exception I can recall at present is Microsoft, which is currently enjoying a one-third ratio profit to turnover – the most profitable company in the United States. Maybe the recent anti-trust legislation is the only method of stopping it.

For the rest of us, the continued drive for growth leads to increased problems – strains on liquidity, management time, premises, plant and people. It is a rare business that does not make mistakes when the pressure is on, reducing the profitability. Your pricing strategy should be continually tweaked to attain a level of maximum profitability – watching cash flow at all times. Many of the high-street chains have to make *daily* cash returns to head office. It is that important.

The special problems of marketing services

In the good old days before marketing became fashionable, there were products and services: you were a provider of either one or the other. It was somehow thought demeaning simply to provide a service rather than manufacture a product to sell. The early 1980s were the watershed for the UK economy.

It seems clear the the market sector will continue to generate more jobs than manufacturing, generally because you need less capital to set up. Premises and plant requirements are usually less, while many small manufacturing firms are subcontractors or component suppliers subject to demand often beyond their control.

Marketing for manufacturers is often through intermediaries – wholesalers, agents, retailers – with all the problems of slow payment, bad debts and tight margins. Products can be touched, dropped and tested against agreed standards.

Services are bought much more on personal recommendations, by repute. The image and standing of the premises, and the confidence and integrity of the seller, help to raise customer confidence. Service providers are more likely to deal with the end user, the buyer, the client. They are more often closer to the marketplace and better able to adjust prices, volumes and the sales message. It is this sharper focus that needs attention. When you are marketing intangibles – or as the Treasury says, 'invisibles' – it is a much more personal creation.

The people business

The service trade is a people business. Customers are very much the king and do expect to be treated as individuals, with all their quirks and foibles.

I've always admired those who have the gift of seeming to give you their entire attention as if nothing else mattered in the whole world. They make you feel very special.

Not only must you believe in what you are doing, but you must carry that conviction to all your staff. They are all ambassadors for your business. This means listening to them, not just telling them, asking what they think and making them feel involved in the venture. Your own motivation is different. You are the boss, perhaps with your name over the shop. If your colleagues are only working for the pay packet at the end of the week, it will be a fairly soulless existence.

Paying the proper wage and thanking them for their efforts is often overlooked. Try to avoid always telling them off: catch them doing something right – and tell them so. There is so much more to motivating people than wages.

Delegation is often difficult for small firm owners, but delegate or die. Proper training and occasional absences with deputies in charge help to build confidence. It's so important it's worth a book on its own (Julian Richer has – see p 216).

The ideal is to grow your own managers from within so you have a recognised career structure and goals for the bright to aim for.

Inevitably some fresh blood will be needed to bring an outside view, but don't disappoint your own staff without good reason.

The image

Because services are intangible, close attention needs to be given to creating and maintaining a strong image of your operation. By image, I am including reputation and after-sales service, as well as the more obvious presentation of the business.

It is wearying to repeat the old adage that you never get a second chance to make a first impression, but it is true. Running a service business is like that. The total image of your activity could so easily be marred by slipshod appearances, casual staff or failing to keep a promise. This is all wrapped up in that much abused creation *PR*, which most of us would say is plain common sense. More of that later in Chapter 7.

If you invite patrons on to your premises much of the atmosphere will be engendered by the decor, furnishings, colour, lighting, and perhaps the Muzak – to say nothing of the air conditioning. My nearest record store always seems to be playing loud rock music, but there are shelves of classical titles. I don't visit there often. There is some evidence that the sense of sound is more emotive than the sense of sight.

Pubs, hotels and hairdressers are very conscious of striking the right tone. Little things like price labels are important. The graphical image you present can range from the tasteful and discreet to greengrocer's Day-Glo. Even your carrier bag (Harrod's green and gold) not only has entered the classic folklore, but is, to slink into the jargon, a fashion statement about yourself. It is all reflected glory.

We are really talking about the total environment in which you operate. It is the personality you can create and manage that positions your business in the market and attracts, repels or selects the type of customer who is good for your business. You need more of them.

The quality

Quality has become the current obsession. BS 5750, or as has now become ISO 9001, seems to have become the darling of the consultants. Originally set up as a defence requirement quality standard, it spread in the 1980s to encompass much of the manufacturing industry and is now spreading its tentacles into the service sector.

Why do I sound jaundiced? Well, for my audience of small firms, it can tend to develop into a paper machine of endless complexity, increased overheads, and, for the efficient firm, no change in quality. Conferment of the certificate does not mean that your standards have been raised. It just means that your existing standards of performance will be maintained. Nursing homes and solicitors among others are now clambering to get ISO 9001 – I'm not quite clear why. In my experience the most common reason for a small firm to feel the need is because a major customer has insisted it obtains it. Stores like B&Q will not deal with any supplier without it. It will also cost you about £1,500 minimum depending on the size of your business, excluding your time to write the manuals and procedures. There are additional fees for the annual audit.

But you don't need an outside body to convince you that quality matters. The Japanese won their world markets by three things – market identification, innovation and quality. The quality of your service will lift your business out of the herd of also-rans. The readiness with which you settle any complaints, meet unusual requests and act in a thoroughly professional manner are some of the obvious parameters.

The personal message

Service businesses are much more personal than product providers – or they should be. Success comes from the willingness and flexibility to meet or even anticipate customer needs on an individual face-to-face basis. Tailoring a service, be it a kitchen design, a holiday, fitness course, or restaurant meal, will make the customer feel wanted and special.

It is the attention to detail that counts. The bow on the gift wrapping, the flowers on the back seat of a new car, sweeping up after a building job or just making the customer feel welcome.

I know one self-catering cottage owner who leaves milk in the fridge, local bread and farm eggs in the kitchen, and fresh flowers in the lounge. When you're talking of perhaps over £300 a week rental, the cost of these little extras is irrelevant, but it sets the tone for how you approach your customers. The most powerful advertising medium is recommendation – word of mouth – where a contented customer can be a strong advocate for your business. And all at no extra charge.

For those of you engaged in a service trade, a large part of your success will come down to *training*: motivated and knowledgeable staff who believe both in you and what they are doing can overcome all manner of difficulties. A long time ago US industrial psychologist discovered that people's greatest motivator was not money but self-satisfaction in doing a job well – and being appreciated by their superiors. We all need a little love now and again.

Finally, it has to be said that the distinction between a service and product provider is often blurred. The better manufacturer realises that accentuating the service provided will win a better relationship. As most businesses have found the last 10 years' trading exceedingly hard, the survivors have learnt to make their service more important and reduce dependence on price cutting. Small firms have had to learn that the only way to compete with bigger firms is by beating them on quality of service.

The product life cycle

While I have tried to keep theory to a minimum there is one immutable law of business that you should be aware of: the product life cycle. Every product – and business – has a birth, life and eventual death. A chart of its progress in terms of sales and profit is shown in Figure 1.4 and, while the angle of slope will be different for each business, many will broadly follow that pattern. It is up to you to keep the downward slope gradual for as long as possible.

While the detail is largely the preserve of academics, the inevitable theory should always be borne in mind. Twenty years ago, who would have thought that the mighty IBM – many times larger than all the other hardware manufacturers put together – would ever be threatened? But miniaturisation and complacency together shattered their market.

Prolonging the product's life means being alert to the competition, investing in new designs, and anticipating changes in legislation, fashion and consumer demand. It is the pace of change that can be frightening these days. As the world shrinks, it will only be the progressive business that survives.

Extending the product life cycle

It is debatable whether the first or the second in the market makes the most profit. Often the first signposts the way, allowing the second to

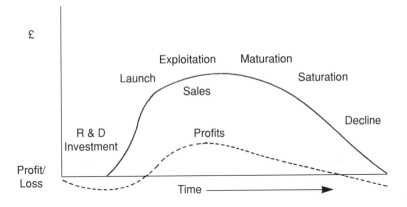

Figure 1.4   The product life cycle

learn from the other's mistakes. It is often expensive to be the trail-blazer. It all depends how ready the consumer is to take up the offering.

In my town the cinema was dying. It was privately owned and needed money spent on it. Along came a multi-screen edge-of-town national chain that has scooped the market and is doing a roaring trade despite the plethora of video hire shops. Going to the cinema in the right surroundings is still regarded as a good night out. In this case the timing and location were right.

Relaxing Sunday trading laws has exacerbated the decline of city centre trading and the traditional small shopkeeper. They have to decide whether to open even longer hours, become more specialised or find gaps in the market that the multinationals are ignoring.

Innovation and product management

Businesses committed to innovation will survive, but it takes an agile mind and resources to keep ahead. Your range of products and services must continue to be seen to offer more benefits than your rivals'. Effective product management entails keeping a close eye on the profit contribution that each line makes. Don't be fooled by overall prof-itability. Examine each line sold and form a judgement. Long-range plans should always be updated to keep a strategic view on where the business is going. We live in a changing world. Attending your trade show, reading the magazines, and asking your customers should all be mandatory.

A service trade could emulate one florist I have helped. I suggested putting a reply-paid card in each arrangement that was posted. The recipient was only too pleased to respond, appreciating that the supplier had not drawn a line when the goods left the shop. Apart from checking on delivery times by the Post Office, it reassured the customer that the florist cared about the service – and it also brought extra business.

The staff suggestion box may be a joke in some businesses, but it shouldn't be. Honda has an entire shadow factory set aside for staff to engineer new products that may have no connection with motors.

Asking staff for improvements or ideas should be part of the activities of every progressive firm. Involve everyone and carry them with you.

Product management may involve licensing in new technology or developing new products yourself. The tangled web of intellectual property is covered in Chapter 10.

The marketing mix

Every book on marketing somehow manages to bring in this, one of the earliest holy grails of marketing theory. Read it once – then get on with running your own business.

The concept of marketing can be broken down into four variables – the product, price, place and promotion (the four Ps). Getting the right balance (mix) of these will create the best appeal to the customer. It is 'the means by which a firm defines and supports the competitive position it seeks to occupy in the target market' (Philip Kotler, leading US marketer). Delving further we can list the four Ps as:

Product
  Technical specification
  Features
  Design
  Quality
  Packaging
  Guarantee
  After-sales service

Price
  Retail
  Trade
  Special offers
  Instalment terms

Place
  Channels of distribution
  Stockists
  Location

Promotion
  Advertising
  Sales promotion
  Selling
  Trade shows
  PR
  Internet

Price in these terms should not be taken too literally, as we should all realise that *value* is far more important. The way that this is presented to the consumer will largely determine the success of the enterprise. A price cut could well reduce sales for some quality goods, as we still often associate price with quality (what's wrong with it?). In other words, the right goods in the wrong shops will sell less. The right goods at the wrong price, or poorly advertised, will also stick on the shelves.

Location

Businesses relying on the Internet, or pure mail-order operators, do not have to worry about Conrad Hilton's diktat. Any business that has to attract passing trade (shops, hotels, craft businesses, garages) may sink or swim depending on their location and visibility. Picking the right spot is an art in itself. As I write the high streets in most towns are in flux, with the drift becoming a stampede to out-of-town centres. This leaves what may seem cheap opportunities in vacant lots. Some things you can alter, but where trends in public shopping behaviour are concerned, I fear the facts are against you. You need to evaluate:

1. Where are the main traffic flows, by foot or by car? What may be due for pedestrianisation? Where are the yellow lines, car parks?
2. What effect does the rush hour have?
3. Are the premises visible? What signs can you put up?
4. What is loading and delivery access like?
5. Where are the main draws – Sainsbury's, Marks & Spencer, etc?
6. What developments are afoot? Visit the planning office, talk to neighbours.
7. What is the minimum lease you can sign?

8. What is the minimum capital you need to spend on smartening the property and fixtures and fittings as opposed to the stock that can be turned into cash?
9. What was the previous business, and what are your prospective neighbours engaged in?

Marketing plans

Part of your business plan that you will be preparing both for those with a financial interest in your success and your own peace of mind should be marketing. I have to say that few include it. It defeats me why it has now become accepted wisdom to prepare at least an annual financial projection but ignore how and where the sales are coming from.

Part of the preparation of your marketing plan is to carry out a SWOT analysis.

Strengths: what you are good at (production, marketing, finance, motivating people, etc).
Weaknesses: unashamedly list what you are not so good at, for which you may need to hire in the expertise.
Opportunities: the gaps in the marketplace, where competition is weak or fresh demand is appearing.
Threats: what the competition is up to.

This is also known as a *marketing audit* and attempts to list all facets of the business in the same way that a financial audit looks after the monetary side of the business.

Marketing *objectives* are then tackled in terms of market segment, positioning of the products, expanding the customer base and market share. These must be specific, reasonably attainable and capable of being monitored.

The *strategy* needed to reach these objectives spells out pricing policy, channels of distribution, promotional methods, after-sales service, etc. Each market segment will need a different outline of strategy because each will respond to different stimuli and appeals. The marketing mix will have to be adjusted.

So your marketing plan will need to cover the following:

1. Market information: what the customer is looking for, existing suppliers, price and satisfaction levels, trends.
2. Segments: where are the gaps, where lies the profit, how big is the customer base.
3. SWOT analysis: how you can match the needs of the customer with the strengths of the business.
4. Main objectives: pinpoint targets to be achieved.
5. Strategy: plan how to reach those objectives.
6. Audit results to monitor progress. No plan is worth drawing up unless some means is set up to review progress and make changes where necessary.

You don't have to write a tome, but the headings should at least encompass the following:

1. The objectives.
2. A sales forecast.
3. Strategy to achieve it, listing action, dates and costs.

The objectives

These should be readily measurable, specific and realistically attainable. You need to look at the short term (the next financial year) and the medium term. Some City institutions and applications for the few government grants ask for the next three years' projections – a somewhat unfathomable task. The objectives can be an increase in turnover, more sales per employee, increase in market share or, most importantly – an increase in profit. The hardest and first job is to prepare the sales forecast.

The sales forecast

Existing businesses have a distinct advantage. They have records on which to base their predictions, broken down into market segments, product classifications, geographical areas, distribution channels and other important strata. New businesses are groping in the dark. However, for both parties there are similarities. Much the same influences on demand will be common to both and the same sources of information will need to be assessed.

The market

What segment of the market are you aiming for? Where are the gaps? Are they likely to grow or reduce? How can they be defined – age, sex, socio-economic, area, industrial or consumer?

The trends

What are the influences that could affect demand? What are the trends? Is there new technology in the pipeline, government legislation, taxation changes, fashion, seasonal influences, undue trade restrictions?

The competition

What is the competition doing? Are new competitors being attracted into your segment? Will you have to offer more discount, sales promotion, sales staff etc, to maintain your market share?

Products

What changes are planned in the product range? Obsolescent products dropped or new ones introduced? Which make the most profit? Can existing lines be revamped or promoted with increased benefits or added value to appeal to a wider audience? Where are they on the product life cycle?

Strategy considerations

How fast do you want to grow? What other resources and constraints must be taken into account – finance, premises, staff, etc? While the experienced businessman may know his own capabilities very well, many circumstances outside his control or knowledge may render any serious attempt at forecasting unreliable. Changes in bank rate or taxation can throw investment decisions awry in whole industries.

It should be quite feasible to plan a short-term sales forecast within the existing productive and distributive capabilities of the company. Beyond that, many industries are subject to cycles of demand. The CBI regularly produces surveys of its members that predict future confidence in order books that have a strong bearing on all members of that sector. In the longer terms, forecasting is inevitabily less accurate with predictions on trends rather than real figures.

Compiling the sales forecast

There are two main areas to look at – desk research and field or commissioned research.

Desk research

1. Look at existing company records, planned production and strategy, available statistics, trade and technical publications and possible market surveys already done. Where to find these sources is set out more fully in the next chapter. Visiting reps are often a rich and reliable sources of marketing information.
2. Because of inflation it is often more realistic to compare your own year-end results on a unit basis rather than monetary values. The effects of price discounts and other manipulations will give a distorted picture.
3. For multi-product companies it may be simpler to remember the Pareto 80/20 rule: 80 per cent of your sales tend to come from 20 per cent of your stock. Concentrate on your best and most profitable lines.
4. The influence of the product life cycle is a dominant factor in all your forecasting. New products may require more promotion, have less acceptability, meet stiffer resistance than maturer lines. Profitability will certainly be different depending on where the product stands on the curve.

Time is the greatest enemy of more sophisticated analysis. Few small firms have the time available to devote to detailed examination of statistics or will have broken down their own records into the requisite number of headings. Ideally, these should be product lines (turnover and profit contribution), timescale (to pinpoint seasonal fluctuations), area (penetration by sales force or concentration of marketing effort) and distribution channels (wholesalers, retailers, agents or direct response).

What influence a good Web site will have on turnover is difficult to determine at this early stage of its development. Trade figures suggest that you may get between a 5 per cent and a 20 per cent turnover from e-commerce, but every business is different and the shopping world is in some turmoil. Accurate figures are impossible to obtain.

Field research

Big companies spend large sums on continual marketing research into their customers' attitudes and on evaluating the competition. Occasionally a second-hand report is available at a reduced cost that is not too out of date and is relevant to smaller concerns. How to track down these studies is detailed in the next chapter.

In this area of sales forecasting you will want to ask samples of your target audience basic questions covering future order levels, timing, value and response to price incentives, fresh packaging or changing promotional methods. By getting closer to your market segment and by regular updating you should not be caught unawares by any changes in market conditions.

The strategy

This section of the marketing plan will be your working tool where you list the actions to be taken through the year with expenditure, and monitoring for results. You can list leaflets to be printed, shows to attend, adverts designed and placed – all the marketing expenditure that will be incurred.

What's my marketing going to cost?

To many businesses marketing is an immeasurable and elastic activity, impossible to cost or budget. What do you include under the heading? The Christmas goodwill calendar? The salesman's car? To some outside the business world, marketing is a confusing miasma of junk mail and PR sleaze – or as I was told recently, 'Marketing is a con.' Very uplifting for your ego. Most firms will only invest if they can quantify the rewards with a fair degree of accuracy and expectation. Buy a truck today and a look at *Glass's Guide* will give you a fair estimate of the trade-in value in three years' time. Place an ad in a new magazine, and no one can be sure what results will be achieved.

Marketing is not an exact science – part of its appeal and challenge – but some of the variables can be eliminated or at least reduced. It will be argued later that advertising should not be undertaken except where the response can be directly measured. Direct response marketing can and must be tested before launching any significant campaign.

So how much should you spend? Every business is different. The market trader will spend a minute amount, relying on position and repeat custom. The high street motor trader will have to promote his continuously changing stock to attract casual punters. I have yet to see a satisfactory formula for equating costs with returns, but for what it's worth, there are supposed to be about 15 different methods, the most popular of which are:

1. The same as last year.
2. Last year plus X per cent (and X can be anything).
3. A percentage of past sales, forecast sales, gross profits or unit costs.
4. The ratio to your share of the market (if you know it).
5. What the competition is thought to spend.
6. What you (or the bank manager) think you can afford.

Accepting that generalities will help few people, it may be some guide if I say that it would not be extraordinary for a new enterprise to devote 5 per cent of gross sales to marketing, settling back to half that when more established. Other influences to take into account are:

1. Well-developed, crowded markets need more promotion to accentuate what are often minute differences between brands.
2. Infrequent purchases need more promotion to remind prospects.
3. Selling a general consumer product is invariably ruinously expensive to a small firm, unless you can slot it into someone else's catalogue.
4. Sales and cut-price offers need frequent promotion to alert prospects.
5. High-quality, purpose-made items sold in a small area rarely need high promotion. Personal recommendation fills the gap.
6. Specialist markets that can be readily identified should need less promotion. (This is the ideal slot for small firms.)
7. If the market is expanding with fresh competition you'll need to keep your name visible.
8. If your product lasts a long time you will have to keep hunting for new customers.

Just isolating advertising, the Advertising Association publishes a table that shows advertising spend as a percentage of turnover. Top of the list at 6 per cent is medical and toiletries. Drink and tobacco spend 1.12 per cent while industry spends 0.47 per cent.

The obvious moral from this is that different products are marketed in different ways. Industry relies much more on face-to-face selling and trade shows. Insurance has changed to more direct mail. Consumer products are heavily advertised on TV and in the glossy magazines.

Summary

- Aim to be a market rather than a production-led venture.
- Make your customers the centre of the business.
- Think about needs and benefits. Most purchases are made to satisfy a definite requirement. Try to understand the motivation of your prospect.
- Stress the value, rarely the price. Isolate the main reasons why people should buy from you. Answer the MP's question, 'What's in it for me?'
- Try to appeal to a distinct segment of the market – you can't sell to everyone. Speak in the tone that strikes a chord with where you position your product.
- Look for the gaps and exploit them. Try to spot trends. Where is the competition falling down?
- How can you reach that segment most profitably? Establish the price structure for your sector – take account of any middlemen's margins.
- Find the heavy users and establish the purchasing cycle. How often will people buy?
- Plan your objectives and work out your strategy.
- Aim to provide the best service and try always to keep your promises.
- Remember, the Internet is just another marketing channel – it is not a cure for all the world's problems.

2   *Market research*

> We encourage customer complaints. Feedback is free market research.
>
> *Virgin Trains*

Never take anything for granted – least of all the claims of advertising salespeople. One of my clients was close to a county border and took ads in both the local papers for years – till I convinced the company to monitor where the enquiries came from. It found that one paper out-pulled the other by a ratio of seven to one. The company saved a lot of money by cancelling the less effective.

For another client, my company ran identical ads in two well-known farming magazines, alternating the copy dates. One has twice the circulation of the other, it out-pulled response by such significant margins that we cancelled the other ad as soon as we could.

One more example. Caravanners use a level to adjust the legs when on uneven ground. A new bubble device came on the market that looked smart but was too big and three times dearer than existing levels that are imported from China. A simple investigation at a specialist wholesaler might have saved a few thousand pounds.

Market research is simply a matter of finding out as much as you can before committing yourself to an irretrievable step. It is a process that should never stop, as you must never assume that the market is standing still. Customer preferences alter, new fashions appear and competitors lure away regular buyers.

Your research should set out to discover:

1. What does the customer need?
2. What is the target audience and how much can you find out about them?

3. What is the competition?
4. Are there any gaps in the market?
5. The acceptability of the product by test marketing.

Market research is a major area of expensive and exhaustive activity for big companies. Large departments are continually combing the world markets testing product awareness, customer reaction, advertising recall and buying preferences. Sophisticated statistical analysis predicts sales demands allowing for competitive interaction. Surveys are frequently commissioned by outside agencies with teams of roving interviewers posing carefully weighted questionnaires.

Even the simplest research study seems to cost well into four figures if performed by a specialist agency, and I will assume that the small firm reader is more interested in learning what can be achieved with limited resources.

Your research can really be divided into two: local and national. If you intend purely to serve your neighbourhood then it will not take long. More ambitious horizons will take more time.

Investigations into the existing market – products, customers and the competition – can be tackled by visits to libraries, trade shows and studying the relevant specialist journals. And by combing the Internet. Specialist directories are a good source of information, starting with the ubiquitous Yahoo!, then Google and HotBot. Pursue the links.

Where the big firm scores is in its ability to commission what I tend to call *attitude* surveys – scientific predictions of future demand and trends based on qualitative sampling. The expertise required to draw up several questionnaires and evaluate the results is beyond the scope of the amateur. Actual test sampling of a limited production run is often the only way to carry out a trial, involving a higher proportionate risk to the small firm.

On the other hand, the small firm is invariably closer to its customers and market and able to take advantage of shifts in consumer choice more swiftly. Big firms tend to be far more hierarchical and bureaucratic when it comes to speed of decision taking.

Taking into account your limitations, where do you start? It is a constant puzzle to me why businessmen know so little about the best sources of ready information in most towns.

Model Railway Club (MRC) 1910
■ Keen House, 4 Calshot St, London, N1 9DA.
    0171-837 2542 fax 0171-837 2542 (hq)
    Hon Sec: F H Smith
▲ Company Limited by Guarantee
O *G; interest in the hobby of model railways
● Mtgs – Exhib – Lib – VE
M 240 i, 70 org, UK / 10 i, 5 org, o'seas
¶ Bulletin – 6; AR; both ftm only.

Model Yachting Association (MYA) 1911
■ 11 College Lane, Hatfield, Herts, AL10 9PB.
    01707 265791 (hsp)
    Sec to Council: Henry Farley
▲ Un-incorporated Society
O *G, *S; the promotion of the design, construction & racing of
    model yachts; to act as the model yacht racing authority for the UK
● Mtgs – Comp – Settling conditions, venues & dates for national &
    international competitions
< Intl Yacht Racing U (model yacht racing divn); R Yachting Assn;
    Cent Coun of Physical Recreation (water recreation divn)
M 44 i, 72 clubs, UK / 5 i, o'seas
¶ Acquaint – 7; ftm only. Ybk – 1; ftm, donation nm.

Modern Churchpeople's Union (MCU) 1898
■ St Martin's Vicarage, 25 Birch Grove, London, W3 9SP.
    0181-992 2333 fax 0181-993 5812 (hsp)
    Hon Sec: Revd N Henderson
▲ Registered Charity
O *R; a Church of England society for the advancement of liberal
    Christian thought
● Conf – Mtgs
M 1,200 i, UK / 400 i, o'seas
¶ Modern believing – 4; £12 yr m, £4 each nm.

Modern Humanities Research Association (MHRA) 1918
■ Birkbeck College, Malet St, London, WC1E 7HX.
    0171-631 6103 fax 0171-383 3729 (hsb)
    Hon Sec: Prof D A Wells
▲ Registered Charity
Br Washington, DC
O *L, *Q; advanced studies & research in modern & medieval
    languages & literature (incl English)
● Res – Inf
< Intl Fedn Modern Languages Literatures
M i
¶ Modern Language Review – 4; ftm. Bulletin – 1; ftm.
    Year's Work in Modern Language Studies – 1.
    Slavonic & East European Review – 4.
    Portuguese Studies – 1.
    Yearbook of English Studies – 1.
    Annual Bibliography of English Language & Literature – 1.
    MHRA Style Book.   Dissertation series.
    Publications of the MHRA.

Modern Studies Association (MSA) 1972
■ 71 Dalmahoy Drive, Dundee, DD2 3UU.
    01382 814887 (v-chmn/editor)
    14 Fontstane St, Monifieth, Dundee, DD5 4LE. (sec).
    Vice-Chmn: Gordon Black,   Sec: Irene Morrison
O *E; *P; to promote & enhance teaching of modern studies
● Conf – Mtgs – Res – Comp
M 468 i
¶ Most (Jnl) – 1; ftm, £5 nm. NL – 2; ftm only.
    MSA Ybk; ftm, £5 nm.

Monarchist League 1943
■ BM Monarchist, London, WC1N 3XX.
    01892 835899 fax 01892 835899
    e-mail nicklaw@cix.compulink.co.uk (mail/address)
    Sec–Gen: Donald Foreman
▲ Un-incorporated Society
Br 12; Australia, USA
O *G; to promote, support & defend the monarchical system of
    government in the UK & abroad
Gp Bulgaria; Romania; Portugal; Poland; Heraldry; Legitimism
● Mtgs – Inf – Lib – LG
< cooperates with c 100 monarchist organisations worldwide
M 750 i, UK / 400 i, o'seas
¶ Monarchy (NL) – 4; ftm only.
    Note: The Constitutional Monarchy Association is part of the
    League.

Money Advice Association (MAA) 1984
■ Gresham House (1st floor), 24 Holborn Viaduct, London,
    EC1A 2BN.
    0171-236 3566 (hq)
    Administrator: Jane Guy
▲ Registered Charity
O *P, *W; for professionals giving advice on debt & bankruptcy
    management for individuals; to use members experience to
    comment on social policy as it affects people in debt
● Conf – Mtgs – ET – Stat – Inf – LG
< National Debtline
M 500 i, 60 f, 10 org
¶ Quarterly Account – 4; ftm. NL. AR.

Monmouthshire Show Society Ltd 1790s
■ Parclands House, Raglan, Monmouthshire, NP5 2BX.
    01291 691160 fax 01291 691161 (hsb)
    Management Sec: Mrs K Spencer
▲ Registered Charity
O *F; agricultural show; welfare of animals
● Mtgs – ET – Exhib – Comp
M 300 i

Montessori Society (AMI) UK (AMI) 1935
■ 26 Lyndhurst Gardens, London, NW3 5NW. (hq)
    Chmn: Mrs E A Hood,   Sec: Miss N Berry
▲ Un-incorporated Society
O *E; promotion of the philosophy of Dr Maria Montessori with
    regard to child development
Gp Assn Montessori Directors & Directresses in the UK (AMDD UK)
● Conf – Mtgs – ET – Res – Exhib – SG – Inf
< Assn Montessori Intle
M 400 i
¶ Montessori Review – 2; Communications – 3/4;
    Montessori Directions – 2/3; all ftm only.

Monumental Brass Society 1887
NR c/o Society of Antiquaries, Burlington House, Piccadilly, London,
    W1V 0HS. (mail address)
    Hon Sec: W Mendelsson
Br 12; 2 in USA
O *L; study & preservation of monumental brasses, indents of lost
    brasses & incised slabs
● Conf – Mtgs – Res – Stat – Inf – VE – Advice & assistance to Church
    authorities on care & repair of brasses
M 600 i, 50 org
¶ Portfolio – irreg; ftm only.
    Transactions – 1; ftm only.
    Bulletin – 3; ftm.

Moorland Association 1987
■ 16 Castle Park, Lancaster, LA1 1YG.
    01524 67171 (hsb)
    Sec: R M N Gillibrand
▲ Un-incorporated Society
O *K; to conserve heather moorland in England & Wales
● Conf – Mtgs – ET
M 130 i, 10 f
¶ . NL – irreg; AR; both ftm only.

Moorland Gamekeeper's Association
NR Stable Edge, Newbiggin in Teesdale, Barnard Castle, Co Durham,
    DH12 0UG.
    Sec: Lindsay Waddell
O *K; campaigning against illegal poisoning

Morris Federation (MF) 1975
■ 36 Foxbury Rd, Bromley, Kent, BR1 4DQ.
    0181-460 0623 (hsp)
    Hon Sec: Beth Neill
▲ Un-incorporated Society
O *D, *G; to encourage & maintain interest in Morris dancing
Gp Notation; Archive; Publicity; Step-dance
● Conf – Mtgs – Res – Inf – PL – Public dance displays
< Engl Folk Dance & Song Soc
M 30 i, 310 org, UK / 2 i, 3 org, o'seas
¶ NL – 4; ftm only.

314

Figure 2.1   Specimen entries from Directory of British Associations
(Courtesy: CBD Research Ltd)

The reference library

While the Internet is potentially a vast source of information, the much-ignored local reference library – if it's good – can still contribute a great deal. It depends on how much detail you are after. In my 25 years of researching for small firms I have found that I use a surprisingly small handful of reference works to start that then lead me on to more detailed areas. These favourite standbys are:

- *BRAD* (*British Rate & Data*), which lists 8,000 UK papers and specialist magazines;
- *Current British Directories*, which lists some 4,000 trade directories.
- *Directory of British Associations*, useful for finding the trade association for a sector (these are the fount of all knowledge though they will not have everyone as members).
- *Exhibition Bulletin*, the best source for finding what exhibitions and shows are coming up, sometimes a year in advance.

Librarians the world over take a pride in sleuthing down bits of odd information. Enlist their help and you will save a lot of time. Make friends of the reference staff and they will be a godsend for years to come.

First, the library service is free, which should excite any small firm. Second, most assistants are only too pleased to get a genuine commercial enquiry as a break from kids and their school projects. They know the reference sources and will go to great lengths to hunt out the information.

Counties vary enormously in what they spend on the system. Away from the conurbations, in the shire counties, you may have to travel to the main county library to find the best selection.

Well, what's in the library? In the better ones a gold mine of information on companies, products and statistics produced by government and private sources. Just one day spent going through a dozen trade reference books will yield perhaps a score of names for you to pursue for catalogues and leaflets to *build up a picture* of your sector of business.

Most trade associations have not put their membership lists on the Web, so there is no substitute for sitting down and poring over names to contact. The Web is very good for finding individual companies and products quickly (try www.scoot.co.uk first, then www.yell.co.uk), but if you want more detail, or to examine a whole sector, then the written page in front of you still scores.

Most of the broadsheet newspapers have excellent Web sites if you want to use them for a topic or cuttings search. Start with www.guardianunlimited.co.uk.

To a small firm, probably of least interest will be the government statistics and regional surveys that show long-term trends. They do need skilled interpretation.

Using the Internet

In the forlorn hope that the following information may be some relevance by the time you read it, let me list some Web sites worth tackling. I assume you have a working knowledge of how to use the Web. If not, a must is Jim McClellan's *Guide to the Internet* (published by the *Guardian*). No one search engine can cover all that's on the Net, so at present my favourite is Google, which compares results from the other search engines.

Strathclyde University has compiled an invaluable starting point. Try www.dis.strath.ac.uk/business and then *Business Sources on the Internet*.

Some other sources are as follows:

- *The Biz* is a well-planned business-to-business directory with many links to useful sites: www.thebiz.co.uk. It also has a well-written suite of guides and tutorials.
- BIRD (Business Information Resource Directory) is a database of UK business Web sites: www.bird-on-line.co.uk.
- Dun & Bradstreet lists 2 million UK companies, 19 million worldwide on www.dunandbrad.co.uk.
- Companies House has its Web site at companies-house.gov.uk. Search for current or dissolved names and proposed. A fee is payable.
- Trade directories can be searched at www.datagold.co.uk.
- If you're keen on statistics you will want to click ons.gov.uk, the Office for National Statistics Web site. And in the same vein, dealing with HM Government is helped by turning to www.open.gov.uk. The Stationery Office site for publications is

at www.hmso.gov.uk, which is quick to put Acts and Select Committee reports on view.

- Another large site worth tapping into is www.infoseek.co.uk, which has links to advertising, banking, directories, employment, news, organisations, etc.

Products and companies

Almost every trade association produces a *yearbook* listing members and their specialities. Trade and product names are often also listed. As some yearbooks consist only of paid entries they may not be as comprehensive as their title suggests. A reputable publisher will say in the foreword how the entries were compiled. To find what is available look at *Current British Directories*. This lists around 4,000.

The *Directory of British Associations* is another standard work in every reference library. You can track down thousands of trade and special-interest associations. The scope will surprise you. Details given include size and type of membership, secretary's name and whether a newsletter or other publication is available.

These directories and the *Aslib Directory of Information Sources*, which combines the merits of the two, but in a different format, should provide a good start to your needs. *Aslib* comes in two volumes listing 6,000 organisations that can make information available covering science, technology, commerce, social science, medicine and the humanities.

On the Internet I have found the Scoot site fast and comprehensive in tracking down companies, those offline as well as online. While you're on its page why not register your own business: it's free. Scoot also claims to have 17 million individual names listed as well, presumably the UK electors roll. In the same vein try www.yell.co.uk (the *Yellow Pages* data base) and www.192.com, which though primarily a directory enquiries source is always adding more reference sources. I also like the applegate.co.uk site for tracking down industrial sectors as it is clear to use and well classified. Directors' names are also identified.

If you can't find your answer on the Internet after 15 minutes, I suggest your try more conventional sources – a good reference library. There are many annual publications of impressive thickness that will help in tracking down companies and who makes what. Some of these standard works are listed here. Inevitably there is some overlap.

Start with *Kompass*. This comes in four volumes, each about three inches thick. Some libraries may stock it on CD ROM. It is produced in association with the Confederation of British Industry (CBI) and, like the others, inevitably lists the larger companies. There is quite a clear method of cross-referencing. *Key British Enterprises* claims to cover 90 per cent of the UK manufacturing capacity. It is produced by Dun & Bradsheet, the well-known credit agency. There is a lot of information shown that will enable you to determine the size of company you may be dealing with. The top 20,000 UK companies are shown in two volumes. *Kelly's Manufacturers and Merchants Directory* is probably the oldest trade directory still used but the coverage is now patchy and its usefulness has been largely superseded by the more detailed *Dial Industry* series relating to specific sectors. These are produced by the same publishers.

Other general trade directories

There are half a dozen standard reference books worth browsing through depending on your interests. *Stubbs' Buyers' Guide* (Dun & Bradstreet) gives 130,000 names across the country. *Sell's Directory* lists 65,000 firms. It has a trade names section that will allow you to trace the maker of a particular product: 25,000 products and services are cross-indexed.

The Retail Directory (Newman) is useful for attacking the consumer market as it lists buyers and the business of several thousand department and multiple stores. There is a separate volume for London giving 27,000 names and addresses.

UK Trade Names (published by Kompass) is helpful in tracking down a company from its product name: 60,000 names. Includes imported goods. If you are selling to local authorities you need the *Municipal Year Book*, which gives exhaustive coverage of every District and Chief Officer by name. Don't forget the public sector covers an enormous field – education, health, libraries, refuse collection, etc. It is a massively detailed book. It even tells you which authorities use bins and which sacks.

RIBA Directory of Practices covers selling to the architectural profession, and gives every practice and partner by name.

A good reference library should also stock a selection of the major trade magazines – those not normally on display in newsagents.

Marketing information

Moving from products and companies, it is helpful to track down what is happening in your sector of activity. Much of what follows, I must admit, may be of limited interest while you are starting up, but should grow in importance as you expand. Some of the source books will be in the better libraries while the more expensive volumes will have to be borrowed either from the specialist repositories mentioned or perhaps from your trade association. Don't forget that any book published should be available through the inter-library lending scheme. It may take a week or two and reference books will generally have to remain in the library. If in doubt ask the assistants.

Marketsearch is an annual directory of (currently) 19,000 published market research studies of worldwide markets. Around 5,000 wholly new reports are added each year. Published in association with the BOTB by Arlington Management Publications, 1 Hay Hill, Berkeley Square, London W1X 7LF; 020 7495 1940.

Mintel covers the consumer goods market each month with examinations of new product performance and expenditure. Contact Mintel Publications, 18–19 Long Acre, London WC1A 9HE; 020 7606 4533. Mintel reports are expensive, though occasionally you may come across one in the bigger libraries.

Keynote Publications produces an in-depth analysis of over 200 UK industry sectors from pharmaceuticals to milk and dairy products. Reports follow a standard format, examining industry structure, consumers, industry supply, market size and trends, recent developments and future prospects. There are also 'Company Profiles' on the industry's main players, and a further sources section for taking research further. They're not terribly thick but could provide a good introduction. Keynote's address is Field House, 72 Oldfield Road, Hampton, Middlesex TW12 2HQ; 020 8783 0755.

The government publishes a wealth of statistics on what the country gets up to, ranging from coal and steel production to what the average family in the north-east spends on sliced bread. The Stationery Office *Guide to Official Statistics* is your starting point.

Business Monitors are the main barometer of what is happening to the economy. There are three main series – production, service and distribution, and miscellaneous. The quarterly summary is the most useful. Major libraries will stock them.

For European research you need to study *The Guide* produced by Keynote, which lists what information is available from over 2,000 established information sources covering 18 countries (430 pages).

Where to find specialist libraries

Apart from your main library there are 20 or so specialist business information libraries around the country. Any should be worth making a trip. In London the *Westminster Reference Library* (behind the National Gallery), the *City Business Library* in Basinghall Street and the *Holborn Reference Library* in Theobalds road, WC1, are particularly good.

The *British Library Science Reference Library* is in a class of its own. Go here for science and technology, designs, patents and trade marks. Something like 20 million patents are held here on file. Address: 25 Southampton Buildings, Chancery Lane, London WC2A 1AW; 020 7412 7469. For those not within reach of London there are a few outlying centres (Patent Information Network libraries) that can access data online.

Trade associations, industry and the professions. Trade associations usually have very comprehensive libraries on their own subject. Non-members are rarely barred but a fee is sometimes charged. I have found that many queries are quite happily answered on the phone. The better Chambers of Commerce – London, Birmingham, Bristol, etc – also have extensive resources. Some of the smaller chambers are often useful if they have retained their traditional industries, eg Manchester for textiles. They seem to know every little railway-arch firm. A huge area is industrial and commercial libraries. Every big company has its own internal library and if you ask nicely I'd be surprised if you were refused a browse around.

Don't ignore the professions either. Some years ago I had to do some research on a historical model that appeared in the 1851 Great Exhibition. A trip to the Victoria and Albert Museum library and Institution of Mechanical Engineers' library was most rewarding.

The Chartered Institute of Marketing deserves a place here as the premier professional body for anyone with pretentions to marketing. A number of publications and seminars is available. If you're keen, join as a student member. As you'd expect, it is the repository for a wealth

Directory of Community Development Organisations in Scotland
■ Scottish Council for Voluntary Organisations
031-556 3882
Hist 1984–
Freq Irregular
>> 3rd edition 1989
Cost £4.00; £3.50 (to members)
Size 83 pages
Cont Community development organisations; Independent information, advice & resource centres; Volunteer bureaux; Community business advisory agencies, each AZ (pa, t, contact, aims).
Area UK – Scotland

Directory of Community Health Councils
■ Association of Community Health Councils
071-609 8405
>> Jul 1991
Cost £5.00
Size 38 pages
Cont Councils geog (pa, t, secretary). Geog index; AZ index.
Area UK

Directory of Community Interpreting Services & Resources in the Greater London Area
■ London Interpreting Project
>> Dec 1989
Cost £8.50
Size 80 pages
Cont Resources geog (pa, t, languages offered, availability, resources offered, description). Other translating & interpreting organisations (s.i). AZ index of languages. Demographic listing of languages. Racial organisations (pa, t).
Area UK – London

Directory of Community Organisations in Scotland
■ Scottish Council for Voluntary Organisations
031-556 3882
>> 4th edition 1992
Cost £7.50; £6.00 to members
Size 116 pages
Area UK – Scotland

Directory of Companies
see CRO Directory of Companies

Directory of Computer Conferencing for Libraries
■ Meckler Ltd
Hist 1991–
Freq Annual
>> 2nd edition 1992
Cost £37.50
Size c 250 pages
Area UK

Directory of Computer Training
see Directory of Training

Directory of Construction Industry Consultants
■ John Wiley & Sons Ltd
>> 1992
Cost £84.00
Area UK

Directory of Consultants and Researchers in Library & Information Science
■ British Library, R & D Department
>> 1st edition 1987
Cost £19.00
Size 182 pages
ISSN 0269-1809
Cont Consultants AZ (company / organisation, pa, t, tx; yr began consultancy, business biography / special expertise). Personal name index; corporate name index; subject index.
Area UK
Note Latest edition as at May 1992

Directory of Consulting Practices in Chemistry & Related Subjects
■ Royal Society of Chemistry
071-437 8656
>> 1991
Cost £15.00
Size c 165 pages
Cont Independent consulting practices AZ (pa, t, fax, principals, fields of practice). Subject index.
Area UK

Directory of Consumables Distributors in Western Europe
■ PAPIS Ltd
>> Feb 1991
Cost £300.00
Cont All major distributors of printing consumables ie inks, plates, films & chemicals, AZ under countries (pa, t, fax, tx, contact, turnover, n/employees, ownership & subsidiaries, tonnage of papers sold, product range, main mill & own brands stocked, geog coverage, sales offices & warehouses).
Area W Europe – Austria, Belgium, Denmark, Finland, France, Germany, Greece, Ireland, Italy, Luxembourg, Netherlands, Norway, Portugal, Spain, Sweden, Switzerland, UK

Directory of Consumer Health Information Services in the UK
see CHIC Directory

Directory of Continence Aids
■ Association for Continence Advice
071-266 3704
>> 1991
Cost £17.00
Cont Mfrs & suppliers of continence aids cfd (pa, t).
Area UK

Directory of Continuing Education for Nurses, Midwives and Health Visitors
■ Newpoint Publishing Co Ltd
Hist 1989–
Freq Annual
>> 1990
Cost £4.95
Size 208 pages
Cont Organisations which conduct post registration clinical courses, specialist courses, HE courses, teacher preparation courses, management courses, other courses ie open & distance learning, primary health carers etc, AZ (pa, t, contact, description); AZ index. Soc & inst.
Area UK

Directory of Contraceptives
see Directory of Hormonal Contraceptives

Directory of Contractors
see LET Directory of Contractors

Directory of Contractors and Public Work, Annual
see European Directory of Contractors

Directory of Convalescent Homes Serving Greater London
see National Directory of Hospitals

Directory of Corporate Archives
■ Business Archives Council
071-407 6110
Hist 1985–
>> 2nd edition 1987
Size 75 pages
Cont Cos & organisations AZ (pa, t, contact, history, access to outsiders, description of organisation, search aids ie computer / manual, location of records, publications, other divisions with pa, t, etc).
Area UK

94

Figure 2.2 An extract from *Current British Directories* (courtesy: CBD Research Ltd)

382

Business Press – Brushes & Brushmaking

Brushes & Brushmaking

Brush and Allied Trades Directory

Publisher Turret Rai plc, Armstrong House, 38 Market Square, Uxbridge, Middlesex, UB8 1TG Switchboard: Tel 01895 454545. Fax 01895 454647. Publisher Peter de Lacey. Advertisement Manager Tony Marchant.
Frequency Annual – Nov
Circulation Uncertified
Rates Effective 1 January 1997 Agency Commission 10%
Standard Rates

colour page	£950
mono page	£650

Mono Rates Mono: Page rop £650, Half rop £350
Colour Rates Full colour: Page rop £950 rop £300 extra 1 standard spot colour: rop £175 extra
Special Positions Mono: rop by negotiation
Inserts by arrangement
Production Specifications Type area page 190 x 125, half portrait 190 x 60, half landscape 90 x 125, quarter landscape 40 x 125, quarter portrait 90 x 60. Trim size page 210 x 150. Screen Mono: 40. Colour: 48. Sheet fed litho. Mono: film, positive, right reading emulsion side down. Colour: film, positive, right reading emulsion side down
Deadlines Copy - Date: Nov

Entry amended

Brushwork

Est 1988
Publisher Airstream Communications Ltd, Suite L, The Priory, Haywards Heath, Sussex, RH16 3LB Switchboard: Tel 01444 440188. Fax 01444 414813. Editor Brian Hall. Advertisement Manager Josie Wadd. Circulation Manager Linda Barker.
Frequency 7 issues per year – Jan/Feb, Mar/Apr, May/Jun, Jul/Aug, Sept/Oct, Nov/Dec. Plus catalogue in Apr
Price Per year £85
Special Features

1 May 1998	Houseware & Hardware Brushes. ABMA Review. Cologne Show Review
1 June 1998	World Brushwork Catalogue (Buyers Guide Worldwide)
1 July 1998	Brush Broom & Mop Filling. Materials Special
1 September 1998	Machinery Special. Chicago Hardware Show Report
1 November 1998	Christmas Edition. Handles, Ferrules and Brush Backs

Circulation Uncertified
Publisher's statement Date received 29 September 1997. Avg Circulation 2,200
Rates Effective 1 January 1997 Agency Commission 10%
Standard Rates

colour page	£1225
mono page	£750

Mono Rates Mono: Page rop £750, Half rop £425, series 7 – £400, Quarter rop £300, series 7 – £250, Eighth rop £175, series 7 – £150

Business & Managemei

Contents

Business & Management

Business – General

BCC National Review

The magazine for members of British Chambers of Commerce
Est 1995
Publisher Dennis & Beyond Ltd, Hogarth Studios, 64 Charlotte Street, London, W1P 1LR Switchboard: Tel 0171 637 7931. Fax 0171 636 8103. Publisher Duncan Grant. Managing Editor Tina Simms. Advertisement Manager Mark Wilkins. Production Manager Ken Holt.
Frequency Alt months – Feb/Mar, Apr/May, Jun/Jul, Aug/Sep, Oct/Nov, Dec/Jan
Price Single copy £2.50 Free to qualifying individuals
Editorial Profile Business and policy editorial of interest to small to medium sized businesses and issues of political significance affecting British business
Regular Features (by BRAD Classification) Exporting & Importing
Special Features

1 April 1998	Working capital. Exporting opportunities in Latin America. Surfing the internet
1 June 1998	Distribution/transport. Exporting opportunities in China. Employee benefits
1 August 1998	Security issues for SMEs. Exporting opportunities in South Africa. Intranets explained

Circulation Uncertified
Target Readership Directors and senior managers within 55,000 member organisations of Approved and Accredited Chambers of Commerce throughout the UK
Rates Effective 1 January 1997 Agency Commission 10%
Standard Rates

colour page	£4000
mono page	£3750

Mono Rates Mono: Page rop £3750, Half rop £1950, Quarter rop £1200
Cover Rates Full colour: outside back £4600, inside front £4400
Colour Rates Full colour: Page rop £4000, Half rop £2400, Quarter rop £1400
Production Specifications Type area page 275 x 185. Bleed size page 303 x 216. Trim size page 297 x 210. Screen mono: 54/133. Colour: 60/150. Litho, web fed, heat set. Mono: film, positive, right reading emulsion side down
Deadlines Copy - 15 days preceding publication date Cancellation - 56 days preceding publication date

BJC Today

The Official Magazine of British Junior Chamber
Est 1990
Publisher Erin Associates, 43 Leigham Vale, London, SW16 2JQ Switchboard: Tel 0181 296 9264. Managing Director Paul Bunn.
Frequency Quarterly – Feb, May, Aug, Nov
Price Single copy £3
Circulation Uncertified
Rates Effective 1 January 1996 Agency Commission 10%
Standard Rates

colour page	£3950
mono page	£3950

Mono Rates Mono: Dps rop £4950, Page rop £3950, Half rop £2950, Quarter rop £1950
Cover Rates Full colour: inside front £4950, outside back £5950, inside back £4500
Colour Rates Full colour: Page rop £3950
Inserts Accepted loose £2,950 total
Production Specifications Type area page 254 x 178, half portrait 254 x 86, half landscape 124 x 178, quarter 124 x 86. Bleed size page 303 x 216. Trim size page 297 x 210. Screen 80. Litho. Mono: film, positive or negative, PMT or camera ready artwork. Spot colour: film, separated, positive. Colour: film, positive, right reading emulsion side down
Deadlines Copy · 60 days preceding publication date Cancellation · 60 days preceding publication date

Bristol Businessman Magazine

Est 1996
Publisher Media West Ltd, 30 Drakes Way, Portishead, Bristol, BS20 9XA Switchboard: Tel 01275 817585. Fax 01275 845846. Publisher Harry Childs. Advertisement Manager Rob McCabe.
Frequency Monthly – 1st of the month
Price Free to qualifying individuals
Editorial Profile Information to help him or her at work and in their leisure time. Provides a means of communication between providers of relevant services and MDs of local businesses
Circulation Uncertified
Publisher's statement Date received 19 May 1997. Avg Circulation 6,000
Target Readership Managers of small to medium sized Bristol businesses and MDs of businesses which regularly provide products and services to other local businesses
Rates Effective 1 January 1997 Agency Commission 10% Series discount: 3 - 10%, 6 - 15%, 12 - 20%
Standard Rates

colour page	£750
mono page	£500

Mono Rates Mono: Dps rop £850, Page rop £500, Half rop £320, Quarter rop £165
Colour Rates Full colour: Dps rop £1000, Page rop £750, Half rop £430 Quarter rop £235
Special Positions 10% extra
Inserts Accepted loose £58 per 1000
Production Specifications A4 format. Type area dps 272 x 392, page 272 x 186, half landscape 134 x 186, half portrait 272 x 90, quarter 134 x 90. Screen: 48. Litho, offset, sheet fed. All: Camera ready artwork or film, positive, right reading emulsion side down
Deadlines Copy - 2 weeks preceding publication date Cancellation - 2 weeks preceding publication date

BusinessAge

Business Age

Est 1996
Publisher Business Age Magazine Ltd, 3rd Floor, Newspaper House, 8-16 Great New Street, London, EC4A 3BN Switchboard: Tel 0171 583 9797. Fax 0171 583 7676. Email abhoyrul@aol.com Editor Anil Bhoyrul. Advertisement Manager Richard Partridge. Production Manager Trudi Roche.
Frequency 11 issues per year – 1st of month
Price Single copy £2.75 Per year £25
Editorial Profile Informative, imaginative and entertaining, Business Age profiles leading figures from politics, business and sports
Circulation Uncertified
Target Readership CEOs, company directors and entrepreneurs across a wide range of industries. 90% ABC1 readership, 70% aged 35-55
Rates Effective 1 January 1998 Agency Commission 10%
Standard Rates

colour page	£5450
mono page	£4950

Mono Rates Mono: Dps rop £7864, Page rop £4950, Half rop £2875, Quarter rop £1465
Cover Rates inside front dps £12296, outside back £8274
Colour Rates Full colour: Dps rop £9676, Page rop £5450, Half rop £3150, Quarter rop £1876 1 standard spot colour: 10% extra
Inserts Accepted loose, £75 per 1,000
Production Specifications American A4 format. Type area dps 250 x 390, page 250 x 180, half landscape 123 x 180, half portrait 250 x 90, quarter 123 x 90. Bleed size dps 286 x 426, page 286 x 216. Trim size dps 280 x 420, page 280 x 210. Screen: 54. Web fed. Mono: bromide or film, positive, right reading emulsion side down. Colour: film, separated, positive, right reading emulsion side down
Deadlines Copy · 14 days preceding publication date Cancellation · 14 days preceding publication date

● Advertisement – Duplicate Listing

Business Connections

Bi-monthly business buying guide
Est 1989
Publisher Business Connections (Publishing) Ltd, Lady Grove Court, Hitchwood Lane, Preston, Nr Hitchin, Hertfordshire, SG4 7SA Switchboard: Tel 01462 438866. Fax 01462 440111. Publishing Director Alex Swindells, Tracey McInnes. Advertisement Manager Bill Smith.
Frequency 6 issues per year – Winter, March Direct, Spring, Summer, Sept Direct Autumn
Circulation Uncertified
Target Readership Reaching a targeted business audience via management and industry publications
Rates Effective 1 January 1996 Agency Commission 10%
Standard Rates

colour page	£15900

Cover Rates Full colour: outside back 10% extra front cover picture £795
Colour Rates Full colour: Panel rop £7950 Page rop £15900
Special Positions additional 4 page supplement by negotiation
Conditions and notes RES available
Production Specifications Type area panel size 86 x 137. Web Offset
Deadlines Copy · 4 weeks preceding publication date Cancellation · 8 weeks preceding publication date

● Advertisement – Cross Listing

Business Equipment Digest

Affiliations ABC/Profile BBP PPA
Publisher IML Group plc, Blair House, High Street, Tonbridge, Kent, TN9 1BQ, Ad Doc DX 5521 Tonbridge Switchboard: Tel 01732 359990. Fax 01732 770049. Email imlgroup@dial.pipex.com
For complete listing see entry under Business Press · Business & Management · Office Supplies

Business Express

Est 1993 **Affiliations** ABC BBP PPA
Publisher The Practical Publishing Company Ltd, 1 High Street, Maidenhead, Berkshire, SL6 1JN Switchboard: Tel 01628 784000. Fax 01628 780806. Publisher Tom Kay. Advertisement Manager Rodina Hafiz-Alam. Production Manager Alistair Hargrove.
Frequency 6 issues per year – Last week of Jan, Mar, May, Jul, Sept, Nov
Price Free to qualifying individuals
Editorial Profile A5 direct response buyers guide to business products and services, topics covered per issue · sales promotion, incentives, conferences, office equipment, communications, information technology presentation equipment, direct marketing
Circulation 01 Jul 1996-30 Jun 1997 ABC 50,021 (UK 50,021 Total net circulation for audit issue 49,996 (UK 49,996)

	Total	UK	OS&Eire
Avg Newstrade Sales			
Controlled free	49,996	49,996	
Exhibition/Conference/			

Distribution date on audit issue 25 Jun 1997 Cover identification on audit issue May/Jun 1997
Controlled circulation terms of control-Personnel involved in the Decision Making Process of Purchasing and Selected Marketing, Sales and Business Development Executives. Duplication 4.0% for audit issue Number of issues distributed in period 6 Number of issues with a variance 0
Target Readership Chairman/managing directors, marketing directors, sales director/manager, marketing/brand/product manager, advertising management, market research management, public relations, promotions/conference organisers, new business/business development, account directors/managers, other directors/managers
Rates Effective 1 September 1995 Agency Commission 10%
Standard Rates

colour page	£4450
mono page	£4450

Mono Rates Mono: Page rop £4450, Half rop £2800, Quarter rop £1810
Cover Rates Full colour: outside back £5340, inside front £5340, inside back £5340
Colour Rates Full colour: Page rop £4450, Half rop £2800, Quarter rop £1810
Inserts Accepted loose or bound-in by arrangement
Production Specifications Type area dps 190 x 280, page 190 x 130, half landscape 90 x 130, half portrait 190 x 62, quarter landscape 90 x 62, quarter portrait 43 x 130, third 60 x 130. Trim size page 210 x 130. Screen Mono: 34. Colour: 40. Lithographic, offset, mini-web fed, cold set. Mono: PMT or film, positive, right reading emulsion side down. Colour: film, positive, right reading emulsion side down
Deadlines Copy - 4 weeks preceding publication date Cancellation - 8 weeks preceding copy date

Business and Finance

Est 1964
Publisher Belenos Publications Ltd, 50 Fitzwilliam Square West, Dublin 2, Republic of Ireland Switchboard: Tel 00 3531 6760869. Fax 00 3531 6619781. Executive Chairman William Ambrose. Managing

Figure 2.3 Part of that invaluable book *BRAD*, to show the amount of detail given (courtesy: British Rate and Data)

of marketing information. Address: Moor Hall, Cookham, Maidenhead, Berkshire SL6 9QH; 01628 427500.

Business Link is HM Government's attempt to provide a one-stop shop for small and medium enterprises, which should be able, theoretically, to provide marketing consultants on a part grant-aided basis depending on the feasibility of your project and whether their grant budget allows. Some have libraries and will undertake limited research. There are over a hundred Business Link offices around the country but as I write the service is under review (again).

If you can afford it you can commission a market research survey from a member of the *Market Research Society*, 15 Northburgh Street, London EC1V 0AH; 020 7490 4911. The Society will provide details of its member consultants' experience and turnover.

The trade press

Britain is blessed with a wealth of trade and technical press to cater for every interest. Some 7,500 journals, papers and magazines are published every year on subjects from bee-keeping to boxing, craft teaching to catering. Many sectors have two levels of print – consumer and trade. The popular journals are aimed at the man on the Clapham omnibus and many are readily available at newsagents; alongside is the trade press aimed at the suppliers of those goods. For example, *Autocar* is written for the family driver, but if you're trying to attract the motor stockist for that petrol-saving gadget then you need *Autotrade*. The circulations of some specialist journals are quite modest, only a thousand or two, but they go to a select readership and that is what matters.

There are several directories on what is available. Undoubtedly the most comprehensive and accurate is *BRAD* (*British Rate and Data*), the invaluable monthly guide to the media. This is the ad-person's bible as it lists the cost of advertising, circulation figure, and often a claimed readership profile. You will have to find a library that stocks it or make friends with an advertising agency, for it is expensive to purchase. Advertexpress.com is a good attempt to provide a buying medium that can also be used to track down the media.

If you can't track down *BRAD* there are alternatives: a copy of *Willing's Press Guide* and the *Advertiser's Annual* will probably be in even quite small libraries. These give a bare title listing of journals, etc. *Benn's Media Directory* gives a little more detail.

On the Net look up www.mediauk.com, a very good site that lists all the papers with links to their own Web sites. With many you can also e-mail the paper from the site. Some of the broadsheets are now archiving their back issues, so use their search tools to good effect.

Your market research must include looking through the relevant trade magazines. I suggest you write to the advertising manager who will probably send you the current issue and a rate card for advertising.

You should always take out a subscription for your trade journal. How else are you going to keep track of what's going on? It will tell you of future trade shows, seminars, legislation changes, firms going out of business, mergers and new products. Many trade papers that carry a lot of advertising are free circulation to those who meet their requirements, usually specifiers of what the company will buy.

Scan the ads and use the reader's reply service to write off for product literature. Add new firms and faces to mailing lists. If you have difficulty tracing a product, ring the editor. Editors invariably have been in the trade for years and know everybody.

Trade fairs and exhibitions

Many new products are first exposed at trade fairs. The manufacturers are test sampling the market to get reaction. There is a trade show for everything. Everyone knows of the massive Ideal Home and Motor Shows either in London or the National Exhibition Centre (NEC) in Birmingham. These are consumer shows, ie open to the general public. There are over 3,000 speciality shows reserved for trade only, to which buyers are invited. They vary in size from major international fairs such as the Offshore International Exhibition at Aberdeen, the oil capital of Europe, to small gift shows at hotels in Bournemouth.

You will find regional shows catering for a particular area, and mini Ideal Home shows that tour the provinces. Some sectors are well covered. For example, the gift field has over 20 trade fairs, from the major NEC show in February to the regional West Country one in Torquay in January. Engineers can go to Materials Handling Automation or Powder Technology, both deserving a show in its own right.

There are several sources of advance information available. The most comprehensive is *Exhibition Bulletin* published monthly by the London Bureau, 291 Kirkdale, Sydenham, London SE26 4RZ; 020 7778 2288. It costs £54 for an annual subscription, or you can buy a single copy for £15. Most shows are advised six months ahead. For agricultural shows and country fairs the best source is *Showman's Directory* by Lance Publications of 45 Bridge St, Godalming, Surrey GU7 1HL; 01483 422184. Priced at £15, it runs to an impressive 400 pages. It also lists steam rallies, airshows, horse shows, etc.

Don't worry about getting *into* trade fairs. Most are free, or relatively inexpensive, and all they want to see is a business card. The more specialist shows are not crowded compared with rib-crushers like the Ideal Home, but the stands are manned by the people who matter – sales managers, managing directors and so on. Often they're glad of a chat. Shows are expensive to mount and are taken very seriously. Come away with lots of leaflets, prices and ideas.

Trade marks, patents and registered designs

If you come across a trade mark and don't know the maker, look up the Patent Office Web site (www.patent.gov.uk).

For a complete search you should use the Patent Office Search and Advisory Service at the main office: Cardiff Road, Newport, Gwent NP9 1RH, 01633 814000; or one of the 14 Patent Information Network libraries around the country. The Central Enquiry Point is 0645 500505.

Many of the more recent patents are now held on a computer database. *The Science Reference Library* (see page 47) will help, as will specialist patent searching agencies listed in Chapter 10.
A *design* can also be registered to preserve its unique outward appearance. For more on patents, designs and inventions, see Chapter 10.

Assessing the competition

As a new starter you must assess what is already available. Rival store

UNITED KINGDOM—continued

BIRMINGHAM 1999—continued

Jan. 17 - 19 TROPHEX — Trophies Engraving & Personalisation — NEC — Hill Media Ltd, 119 High Street, Berkhamsted, Herts, HP4 2DJ
Tel 01442 878787 Fax 01442 870888

★ Jan. 24 - 27 Lighting Trade Show — NEC — Miller Freeman, 630 Chiswick High Road, London, W4 5BG
Tel 0181 742 2828 Fax 0181 747 3856 aielo

★ Jan. 24 - 27 DECORATIVE INTERIORS — Interior Design Trade Sh £99 Sp £85 — NEC — Miller Freeman, 630 Chiswick High Road, London, W4 5BG
Tel 0181 742 2828 Fax 0181 747 3856 aielo

★ Jan. 24 - 27 KBB — Kitchens Bedrooms & Bathrooms Trade V 9200 St 98 — NEC — Miller Freeman, 630 Chiswick High Road, London, W4 5BG
Tel 0181 742 2828 Fax 0181 747 3856 aielo

★ Jan. 24 - 27 THE FURNITURE SHOW — Furniture Trade V 25142(A) St 700 — NEC — Miller Freeman, 630 Chiswick High Road, London, W4 5BG
Tel 0181 742 2828 Fax 0181 747 3856 aielo

Jan. 25 - 28 Hospitality Week V 22444(A) St 321 Sh £189 Sp £150 — NEC — Reed Exhibition Co Ltd, 26 The Quadrant, Richmond, Surrey, TW9 1DL
Tel 0181 910 7910 Fax 0181 940 2171 aielo

Feb. 7 - 11 Int Spring Fair (Gift Trade) V 85666 St 3927 Sh £143 Sp £108 — NEC — Trade Promotion Services Ltd, 6 Warren Lane, London, SE18 6BW
Tel 0181 855 9201 Fax 0181 855 3506 aielo

Mar. 2 - 4 FLEXO INTERNATIONAL — Int Flexographic Event — NEC — Reed Exhibition Co Ltd, 26 The Quadrant, Richmond, Surrey, TW9 1DL
Tel 0181 910 7910 Fax 0181 940 2171 aielo

Mar. 2 - 4 RAC — Refrigeration & Air Conditioning Exbn V 6285(A) St 177 Sh £166 Sp £145 — NEC — EMAP Business Communications, 19th Floor, Leon House, 233 High Street, Croydon, CR0 9XT   Tel 0181 277 5000 Fax 0181 277 5105 aielo

Mar. 9 - 11 Powder Coating Supply Industry V 1973 St 62 — NEC — Hill Media Ltd, 119 High Street, Berkhamsted, Herts, HP4 2DJ
Tel 01442 878787 Fax 01442 870888

Mar. 23 - 25 CLOTECH — Clothing Industry Machinery & Technology V 8000 St 146 — NEC — Focal Event Management, The Old Bakery, Albion Road, New Mills, Derbys, SK22 3EX   Tel 01663 746100 Fax 01663 746920 aielo

★ Apr. 17 - 19 OPTRAFAIR — Ophthalmic Trade Fair V 10745 St 188 Sh £117 Sp £100 — NEC — Ophthalmic Exhibitors Association, 37/41 Bedford Row, London, WC1R 4JH
Tel 0171 405 8101 Fax 0171 831 2797

Apr. 20 - 22 AVEX — Int Vending Exbn V 5950 St 143 — NEC — Automatic Vending Assoc, 1 Villiers Court, Upper Mulgrave Road, Cheam, Surrey, SM2 7AJ   Tel 0181 661 1112 Fax 0181 661 2224

Apr. 20 - 22 TRAFFEX — Traffic Engineering & Road Safety Exbn V 10000 St 310 Sh £200 Sp £175 — NEC — Brintex Ltd, 32 Vauxhall Bridge Road, London, SW1V 2SS
Tel 0171 973 6401 Fax 0171 233 5054 aielo

Apr. 25 - 28 Automotive Trade Show V 17063(A) St 326 Sh £170 Sp £140 — NEC — Society of Motor Manufacturers & Traders Ltd, Forbes House, Halkin Street, London, SW1X 7DS   Tel 0171 235 7000 Fax 0171 235 7112

Apr. 27 - 29 THE CLEANING SHOW — Cleaning & Support Services Exbn V 5304 St 154 — NEC — Turret RAI plc, 38 Market Square, Uxbridge, Middlesex, UB8 1TG
Tel 01895 454545 Fax 01895 454588 aielo

May 11 - 13 PE 99 — Process Engineering V 6600 St 50 Sh £210 Sp £180 — NEC — Miller Freeman, 630 Chiswick High Road, London, W4 5BG
Tel 0181 742 2828 Fax 0181 747 3856 aielo

Jul. 13 - 15 ACPO — Int Police & Security Expo — NEC — Labelex Exhibitions Ltd, 131 Southlands Rd, Bromley, BR2 9QT
Tel 0181 313 3535 Fax 0181 468 7472 aielo

Sep. 5 - 8 HI — Housewares International V 6391 St 189 Sh £136 Sp £105 — NEC — Trade Promotion Services Ltd, 6 Warren Lane, London, SE18 6BW
Tel 0181 855 9201 Fax 0181 855 3506 aielo

Sep. 5 - 8 IAF — Int Autumn Fair (Gift Trade) V 52000 St 2200 Sh £132 Sp £102 — NEC — Trade Promotion Services Ltd, 6 Warren Lane, London, SE18 6BW
Tel 0181 855 9201 Fax 0181 855 3506 aielo

Sep. 5 - 8 IHF — Int DIY Hardware & Home Improvement Trade Show V 8803 St 117 Sh £121 Sp £85 — NEC — Trade Promotion Services Ltd, 6 Warren Lane, London, SE18 6BW
Tel 0181 855 9201 Fax 0181 855 3506 aielo

Sep. 6 - 8 European Licensing Fair — NEC — Trade Promotion Services Ltd, 6 Warren Lane, London, SE18 6BW
Tel 0181 855 9201 Fax 0181 855 3506 aielo

Oct. 7 - 10 Nat Knitting & Needlecraft Exbn V 42500 St 200 Sh £105 — NEC — Nationwide Exbns (UK) Ltd, PO Box 20, Fishponds, Bristol, BS16 5QU
Tel 0117 970 1370 Fax 0117 970 1371

Oct. 18 - 21 WELDEX — Welding Exbn V 18884(A) St 237 — NEC — Nexus Media Ltd, Nexus House, Azalea Drive, Swanley, Kent, BR8 8HY
Tel 01322 660070 Fax 01322 667633 aielo

Oct. 19 - 21 IWEX — Int Water & Effluent Treatment Exbn V 12500 St 400 — NEC — Turret RAI plc, 38 Market Square, Uxbridge, Middlesex, UB8 1TG
Tel 01895 454545 Fax 01895 454588 aielo

Oct. 26 - 28 AUTOTECH — Automotive Technology Event V 7575 St 268 — NEC — Centre Exhibitions, NEC House, NEC, Birmingham, B40 1NT
Tel 0121 767 2665 Fax 0121 767 3535

Nov. 2 - 4 CONVERTEX — Paper Film & Foil V 2511 St 157 — NEC — Reed Exhibition Co Ltd, 26 The Quadrant, Richmond, Surrey, TW9 1DL
Tel 0181 910 7910 Fax 0181 940 2171 aielo

Nov. 9 - 11 PPMA — Processing & Packaging Machinery Exbn V 9848 St 270 — NEC — PPMA Ltd, 404 Brighton Road, Croydon, CR2 6AN
Tel 0181 681 8226 Fax 0181 681 1641

Nov. 21 - 26 INTERBUILD — Int Building & Construction Exbn V 90729(A) St 1097 — NEC — Montgomery Exhibitions Ltd, 11 Manchester Square, London, W1M 5AB
Tel 0171 486 1951 Fax 0171 486 8773 aielo

2000

Mar. 19 - 22 FOOD & BAKE — Bakery Food & Snacks Industry V 14448 St 468 — NEC — Turret RAI plc, 38 Market Square, Uxbridge, Middlesex, UB8 1TG
Tel 01895 454545 Fax 01895 454588 aielo

Apr. 11 - 14 IFPEX — Int Fluid Power Exbn — NEC — DMG Business Media Ltd, 2 Queensway, Redhill, RH1 1QS
Tel 01737 768611 Fax 01737 760564 aielo

BLACKPOOL 1998

Mar. 1 - 4 North West Gift Trade Exbn V 1859 St 120 Sh £92 Sp £75 — Norbreck Castle — Hale Events Ltd, Premier House, Old Church Road, Axbridge, Somerset, BS26 2BQ   Tel 01934 733433 Fax 01934 733233

Apr. 10 - 12 Nat Union of Teachers Conf & Exbn V 1200 St 21 — Winter Gardens — Educational Exbns, 14 Gainsborough Road, London, N12 8AG
Tel 0181 445 5777 Fax 0181 446 8214

Apr. 22 - 23 ALEX — Amusement Leisure Exbn — Winter Gardens — Worlds Fair Ltd, 2 Daltry Street, Oldham, OL1 4BB
Tel 0161 624 3687 Fax 0161 665 1260

Jun. 10 - 12 CALOR SHOW — LP Gas & Appliance Exbn V 1000 St 50 — Stakis Hotel — Centrepiece Exhibitions, 91 Woodward Close, Wokingham, Berks, RG41 5UU   Tel 0118 978 6315 Fax 0118 989 4202

UNITED KINGDOM—continued over

35

Figure 2.4 Information obtainable from *Exhibition Bulletin*

groups keep a regular check on what each is doing: they send a junior to list prices.

I'm afraid you have to be a little cunning, like the *Which?* inspector. Do it anonymously. If you're setting up as something simple like a window cleaner, ask the local lad to call or check out who your neighbour or relation uses. You will be in a good position to judge not only his efficiency, but his costs, politeness and whether he wipes his boots.

Let's look at joinery or building. Pick a typical job – porch or kitchen extension. Go through the local paper and *Yellow Pages* and ask your competitors to give an estimate.

Your first impression will be how they answer the phone, a simple enough exercise but very revealing. I can almost guarantee that 5 out of 10 firms will never bother to quote, especially if they are small. It has to be said that many small firms will remain so because they are too apathetic and unprofessional. When you come across one that cares it's a revelation. Depending on who comes to quote, you will gain another impression. Do they really know what they're talking about? Are the right questions being asked? Are they trying to lead you to something they want to sell or what you want to buy? Time will pass and the quotes will arrive. The manner of presentation, amount of detail, conditions of sale and acceptance, quite apart from the price, will affect the proposition.

At the end of the exercise you should be in a better position to know:

1. The eager competitors, anxious for work.
2. The professionals.
3. Their strengths and weaknesses.
4. Any gaps that you can exploit.
5. Costs.
6. Delivery dates and thus a fair idea of the state of their order book.
7. Methods of selling.
8. Quality of staff.
9. Credit terms offered or deposits requested.
10. Inducements to order (sales promotion techniques).
11. Guarantees.
12. Sales literature.
13. Promptness of follow-up.

If you don't follow the exercise through you won't, of course, know how they actually perform – a vital part – but this you can find out by scouting out past customers.

Some will say, 'That's an underhand way of doing things.' You have the choice: to blunder on and commit funds, or learn about what you will inevitably come up against when you have started. Don't forget that the major car companies all buy the rival products and strip them down to learn of new techniques.

Published company accounts

Moving on to bigger fish, if you are aiming higher and for a more national and sophisticated market, you may like to study company accounts. Information on major (quoted) companies is easy to come by and prodigious. The smaller brethren are more difficult to find and analyse.

Companies House is where, by law, companies have to notify formation and directors' names, and file copies of their accounts. Unfortunately, many companies are dilatory in this respect and you may find the information sparse or out of date. You can see photo-copies or microfiches of what is available either by calling personally at 55 City Road, London EC1Y 1BB or, taking advantage of the postal service, from the Cardiff office for a modest free. The address is Crown Way, Maindy, Cardiff CF4 3UZ; 01222 388588. You can also search online but there is a £50 first-time registration fee.

ICC Regional Surveys produces abstracts of the previous three years' accounts for companies trading in each country. Small compa-nies do not have to reveal much information, but they make interesting reading nevertheless. There may be a copy for your country in the library.

Who Owns Whom will reveal the subsidiaries of major companies in all their varied disguises.

If you want more depth you can ask a credit agencyfor a detailed report on quoted or unquoted companies. A financial profile and assessment of their credit risk will be given. Two firms offering the service are: Jordan & Sons Ltd, 21 St Thomas Street, Bristol BS1 6JS; 0117 923 0600; Dun & Bradstreet, Holmers Farm Way, High Wycombe HP12 4UL; 01494 422000.

Your own bank, if you ask nicely, may carry out a 'bad debt' search using one of the national credit agencies like Infolink, 2–4 South End,

Croydon CR0 1DL; 020 8686 7777, which has millions of names on file. County court judgements will be revealed and whether firms are slow payers.

Market research calls for a large dose of common sense. Many facts and statistics will be unobtainable, or can only be collated by much time and expense. All the research in the world is no substitute for action. There comes a time when you simply have to get stuck in and *do* something.

Testing product acceptability

Having evaluated what is the existing market and formed an idea of where your product should fit in, the step before full production should be limited test sampling. The need for this should be transparent. Intuition has its place but production involving investment in plant, packaging and print must have a more solid basis than 'Aunt Agatha would buy one.'

A pre-production run, produced if necessary by hand, or a small batch run, can be shown to potential wholesalers, agents and consumers. Most box makers will produce a sample range on condition they receive a proper order in due course. Dummy boxes can be coloured up.

Surveys can be made, either by the time-honoured method of stopping people in the street or loaning for 'wear tests'. Be wary of small samples. Statistically, they are suspect. Try and get a genuine cross-section of your target audience or pick up every tenth person to work the law of averages. Questionnaires needs to be carefully framed. Award points that can be taken off the forms and totalled.

- If your product is a knock-down kit, give it to the 'village idiot' and see how well he assembles it from your printed instructions. You're too close to the job to see the pitfalls.
- Post the item back to yourself and see what the carrier does to it.
- Try a variety of packaging.
- Try a number of product names and see which is the most acceptable.

Almost everything about the product can be tested before it is launched on the market. The Internet is good for testing the market as the spec and offer can be varied immediately, once you have a loyal customer base. Response to different formulae can be measured swiftly. Items that change frequently can be listed on a Web site order form (eg organic food suppliers) and the likely take-up gauged at once.

The same applies to advertising. Try it in a small way first with one paper or journal before booking space in six and running a campaign. The major companies do it by ITV region – one step at a time. A big advantage of direct mail is the in-built ability to test different head-lines, offers and names with a quick response before doing a major posting.

It is far cheaper to change a pilot production than a full warehouse.

Market research should be continuous. Never forget that customs and uses change, so keep in touch with your customer.

Spotting new markets

The Internet has of course generated an explosion of new ventures and will change our shopping habits dramatically. Theoretically the world is your market, provided the goods or expertise can be shipped economically. More serious marketeers believe that the Internet works best when combined with others forms of promotion – you still have to promote the site – so should not be used in isolation. More of this in the next chapter.

Part of the continuous research must be to look out for new markets as they appear. Don't rely on all your customers staying with you for ever. The last 20 years have been noteworthy for a large shift in the structure of our society. In the engineered boom days of the 1980s the south-east notably became the byword for gross commissions, yuppie culture, inflated house prices and a credit-based society.

Now that the day of reckoning has come, it is generally recognised that we have increasingly become a divided society with the rich richer and a growing underclass. From a marketing, not social, point of view suppliers have to chase and adapt to meet different needs. In some parts of the country crime has rocketed, which is bad for the robbed, but does offer selling opportunities to the security industry, ranging from locks to rape alarms. Increasing worries about food purity and allergies have given a boost to small specialist food producers that runs from the growers to restaurants, while increasing disenchantment with conventional medicine has likewise been beneficial to alternative practitioners, herbalists, vitamin suppliers and therapists of every description.

Anything to do with computers has to be good news for small specialists. For every box that is sold mail-order or from the high street, there is a need from someone local with hands-on expertise who can sort out the real world. No business, school or government department can operate without ready access to skilled software maintenance. But the greatest long-term shift in consumer demand has to be the rapidly ageing population. Not all will have to survive on benefits and charity, and with several million enjoying index-linked pensions and good health, the marketing opportunities are increasing. According to the Official Census there were 300 centenarians in 1951, 4,400 in 1991 and will be around 30,000 in 2011. I'll save you a bit of cake.

This segment is explored above.

The marketing message needs to be tailored more to the older age group's experience and expectations. Quality is important. Few seem to have succeeded as well as B&Q with its 'Over-60s' discount card to encourage midweek store traffic. They claim to have 1 million cardholders and to have increased sales to this target group by 80 per cent.

Direct marketing lends itself to close targeting of this group. Sales letters must not remind them of their age in a depressing way. Simple things like the size of typeface and ease of reading must be taken into account.

Moving up to the over-65s, many find that using credit cards over the telephone (how many use plastic?) causes anxiety. They are also intolerant of waste and duplicate mailings. Saga was probably the first to pick up on this market by offering comfortable holidays. Its direct mailed magazine has a circulation of 500,000.

There are several distinct segments to this market culminating in the housebound geriatric. As I have already said, I know one successful business whose average age of client must be over 70. It sells comfort footwear by post to those who cannot get to a shoe shop.

Market research checklist

While there are many hundreds of areas that could be investigated, the following list should alert you to the significant points.

Size of the market

1. What is the total market – industrial, consumer, home and overseas?
2. Is it growing or shrinking?
3. Are there any regional biases or preferences?
4. What are the seasonal influences?
5. Where are the big users?
6. Proportion met by imports?
7. Is it a well-developed, sophisticated market or are new competitive products entering?
8. Is it prone to fashions, short runs, cyclical changes?
9. Is new technology likely to alter the market?
10. What changes may affect demand?
    a) Government legislation, taxation, trading standards, credit restrictions?
    b) Obsolescence?
    c) Innovation by competition?
    d) Your firm's variation in policy?

The competition

1. Who are the main competitors and what share do they enjoy?
2. What is their product range and where lies their appeal?
3. What are their strengths and weaknesses?
4. Where do you have a competitive edge?
5. What are the trends?

Your own performance

1. How do you measure up in the market?
2. Where do you make most profit and where is the growth?
3. What extra lines or services are needed?
4. Are you positioning yourself correctly?
5. How do you promote yourself and compare with your competition?
6. What is the cost of marketing, broken down into product lines, channels of distribution, enquiry or order value, market segment, etc?
7. What changes have been made or are intended?

The product

1. Who uses the product?
2. Frequency of purchase?
3. Who else could use the product?
4. Are there related lines or extra services that could be sold?
5. How can it be improved?
6. What do customers think of it?
7. Is it branded?
8. Is the price right?
9. Where does it lie on the product life cycle?
10. Are specials produced? Can it be personalized?
11. What are the returns?
12. What is the life?
13. What new products are envisaged and how will they tie in with existing lines?

The customer

1. What else can you sell them?
2. Where are the decision makers?
3. How can you reach them?
4. Is the buyer the user?
5. What is the customer profile?
6. What are their needs?

3

The Internet

Anything, anywhere, anytime. If 'dotcom' is not embedded in the marketing strategy then your company has not realized the world has changed.

Sun Microsystems

At present probably the only people making real money from the Internet are Web site designers and BT. It is important to understand that your Web site may not double your turnover; it merely provides another way of reaching customers.

The arrival of the Internet has been described as the Second Industrial Revolution and, as with the first one, there will be successes and casualties. From the small firm's point of view the technology has in theory provided a mechanism to reach buyers all over the world without the disadvantage of expensive premises or staff overheads – and for 24 hours a day. While the Internet is just the global interlinking (network of networks) of computers, and the World Wide Web is the multimedia part of it, over time the terms have come to be interchangeable. Net, Web or going online – I'm not going to be fussy. This is not the place to learn how to use it, for there are many basic guides: first buy Jim McClellan's excellent *Guide to the Internet*, published by the *Guardian*, then the *Rough Guide* for lists of sites. Also, read the monthly magazines.

The difficulty of course is that the Web has also been described as the world's biggest library but is one without a catalogue or index. No one knows how big the Web is: some way it has over 2 billion sites, and 7,500 new ones being added very day. One simple example. A small Somerset firm that I help markets an anti-radiation mobile phone

Figure 3.1   Even rural shops are getting on the Internet

case but a search on 'health scares linked to mobile phones' recently revealed well over a million references to that topic, much of it garbage. Just because it is on the Web, that doesn't guarantee authenticity.

Broadly speaking, the Web is used for two reasons: for free information and then purchasing, and from the small firm's viewpoint it therefore makes sense to combine the two to ensure that surfers are attracted, retained and *buy*. (A recent survey claimed that only 9 per cent of Internet users had ever bought anything.) While much of the Web is run on a not-for-profit basis, let's assume you want a return on all your time and input. Companies with busy Web sites have learnt to develop a strong brand image with community feel: visitors feel at home and wanted. The site is constantly changed with up-to-date news, comment and offers.

Niche products and services work best on the Internet. With millions of sales messages being blandished, the more tightly you can focus your offering the better, otherwise you will never be found. Specialisation is the key that will draw and retain a community of Web buyers. While the Net is still in the process of rapid evolution, it seems that business to business (B2B) is likely to be more remunerative than business to consumer (B2C). Till the technology improves, the Net is poor for home shopping (catalogue browsing) – the printed page is superior. Hard-to-find products rather than mass market items will succeed better.

To the beginner, going online poses five main problems:

- Your objectives.
- The cost of setting up Web page design.
- The time involved.
- Attracting and retaining quality visitors to the site.
- Handling enquiries and fulfilling orders (e-commerce).

Objectives

One of the first things I do when clicking on a new site is to look for a date. All too many have been compiled in a rush of enthusiasm – 'we need a Web site' – and then left to languish. More than with any other form of promotion, a customer is only a click away from a rival, and surveys have found that the average punter spends only 15 seconds on a site. If you do decide to go online, then resources must be found to make your site interesting and up to date to keep people coming back. Busy and profitable Web sites are topical, lively, provide information and encourage interactivity. Unless you have the skills and time to devote to this medium then you are unlikely to succeed.

Web sites for small firms can meet a number of objectives:

- Provide information (technical support).
- Sell produce (e-commerce).
- Solicit new names (e-mail enquiry form).
- Solve problems ('frequently asked questions' – FAQs).
- Provide a forum for debate (user groups).
- Encourage requests for catalogues and quotations.
- Show what's in stock.
- Reach new customers around the world and communicate better with a firm's existing customer base.
- Send direct e-mail offers out to a mailing list (much cheaper than by post, and instant).

Costs of setting up

To get online you need to pick an Internet service provider, either one of the established names – BT, Demon, Virgin – or perhaps a smaller local one, of which there are more than 200). It is difficult to choose in this frighteningly changing sphere as league tables of performance may attract floods of new business that weaken the best performers' edge. Broadly speaking, the large providers will have more expertise, have quicker servers and provide more facilities but will be more expensive. Smaller, newer and cheaper ISPs may be able to offer more personal service. Ring a few and see how long it takes to get through – in office hours and in the evenings. Check out what software is provided (it should be free, and may include filters for pornography and junk mail) and how the charges are worked out. Ask how many e-mail addresses are provided, the cost of a domain name (jimsmith-cars.co.uk) and which Usenet newsgroups are available.

The costs of going online can be as low at £150 for Web design and £30 a month (eg with virginbiz.net), but it would be more realistic to budget for more. As with adverts, the design is crucial for getting your message across and to build brand loyalty. While there are many cheap DIY packages around, employing a skilled designer could cost £1,500 to produce 10 pages of revenue-earning material, though an ambitious company would spend vastly more. As one of the main attractions of having a Web site is the ability to update at will, I suggest you find a designer who can train *you* how to keep it relevant. Stock lists, news items, feedback, special offers all add to interest and traffic flow, and will be cheaper if you can keep on top of the site yourself.

If you are going into e-commerce – taking credit card orders online – then you will need a secure server that uses encryption technology. More expense. And the ISP will take around 4.5 per cent of your turnover. Adding a second phone line will be an essential, and perhaps ISDN (marketed as BT Highway) will both speed up connection and provide a cleaner line for file transfers. ADSL is coming, and promises both to be faster than ISDN and to enable phone calls to be made while you are online. Unfortunately it is expected to cost around £600 pa.

Domain names

What you trade as is important, both so that customers find you and so that you get high up on search engine results. You must register your domain name (also known as a URL: uniform resource locator) – the site address that comes after 'www' – ('lloydstsb', for example) – with the registration authority internic.net or name specialists like netnames.com. Your ISP may well handle this for you. The cost is about £20 a year. Most of the best have been taken already, including, it seems, every town or village in the UK. Surveys claim that we tend to try only three times to find the correct URL before giving up, so a memorable name close to your trading style is most important.

Web page design

Everybody is an expert in advertising – till we have to design our own ads – but Web page design is still a developing art. It seems to me that the designers currently available fall into two distinct camps: those with the software skills (currently to the fore) and those with marketing ability. In essence we are talking about *direct marketing*, a rather different skill. Remember that site visitors are only a click away from losing you; the site will only generate profit if:

- There's an obvious benefit – what's here to catch the eye?
- The site is quick to download and looks easy to navigate.
- All the details of the company are on the home page.
- Clear product information is easily indexed.
- Selling online is by secure server.
- Visitors are encouraged to register to receive updates by e-mail.
- The site is regularly updated.
- You can measure traffic and work out the conversion rate.

What to include in your Web site

The Web is just another medium of marketing, so small firms should concentrate on niches. As the Web gets more crowded, the more you must isolate your particular offerings and benefits and increase the chance you have of moving up the search engine categories – still the

Figure 3.2 A basic Web site devoid of arty effects, but it has a clear home page and contains all the relevant contact information, with the banner headline at the top of the page emphasising the main benefits of using this company. The 'Go' buttons leave no room for doubt about what to do

main way new punters find your site. Niche marketing will ensure that availability, know-how and specification are more important than mere price, the overriding concern of most Web surfers. All your design and content must reflect what is *different* about your firm.

Web traffic will be slow at first, but many online businesses say that three to four months' trading should see a pick-up. Apart from offline promotion (probably expensive), the secret is to develop a community or club feel, a closer relationship than is possible with cold off-the-page advertising. Because the Web is instant and available, customers expect swift response. If e-mails or deliveries are not made within a day or two the whole benefit of online trading will be lost.

Good design guidelines

1. Less is more. Avoid great slabs of text, they'll not be read. People view the monitor screen for different reasons than they do books or magazines; if it were not so, the printed page would have died years ago. Leave plenty of white space around text and pictures. Use a white or pale background to aid legibility. Text should not fill more than twice the width of the screen: look at guardianunlimited for the brilliant way they handle text and pictures.

2. The home page is the first impression the visitor gets, so 'click here to enter' is best avoided. Design throughout should be simple and look easy and intuitive to navigate. You should place full address and telephone numbers on the home page, as visitors can waste time clicking through to find them.

3. Many sites I see do not make it obvious what you do next: add a 'go', or 'log-on' or 'submit'. A 'search the site' facility is also useful to track information as the site gets bigger.

4. Avoid long questionnaires asking for masses of detail that will only irritate. You want only the basic contact information so you can e-mail later with special offers. Remember you are now into *direct marketing*, so think of simple forms that encourage response.

5. In the early days, banner ads were all the rage but some now find them irritating. Unless you have a very big site, the response will be minute.

6. Avoid large graphic files and animations that take ages to download: customers won't wait. A menu index on each page is helpful so that users can navigate through the site.

7. Build in an interactive forum or notice board where visitors can comment on their problems and ask for advice. Letters pages in newspapers are often the most read part, so imitate the concept.

8. Order and enquiry forms need as much thought as the rest of the site. A heading to the page saying 'We never release names to third parties' helps overcome resistance.

9. Put an 'add me to your newsletter' box on the page to which you most want visitors to respond (ie if you're after trade rather than private customers, put it on the trade Web page). Use an opt-in e-mail request and use it frequently.

10. Apart from examining what makes good sites, try www.webpagesthatsuck.com.

11. Links are important both to and from your site. Look for compatible but non-competitive sites and e-mail with a request. Make it obvious that it is a link. Possible sites could be your local tourist board or council, trade association, buying group, club or special interest lobby.

12. Like the rest of your printed material, the brand image must be carried through to your Web site. With ever vaster numbers of Web sites appearing, it is more important than ever to try to get yours to stand out. Yahoo! and Amazon are not making any profits – it's the brand image that people want and are seemingly prepared to pay for.

13. Install a visitor counter (server log software at www.analog.ex, or try www.webtrends.com) so you can measure not just how many hits you get but which pages are most popular. It will also show where the hits came from. Personally I favour hidden counters rather than the rather naff 'you are the 21,342nd visitor since January'. Counters will tell you which pages to drop, releasing time for other tasks.

DIY design

It's the old problem of doing it yourself with help from a friend or paying a professional Web designer. There are several software packages around costing less than £100 – inevitably Microsoft's *Front Page* leads the pack (www.microsoft.com/frontpage) but Adobe products are always worth examining (www.adobe.com). Basically you have to learn your way round HTML code – that is the way the Web interprets text. If like me you've been brought up on dear old reliable WordPerfect for DOS with reveal codes, you'll understand it better. To see what HTML looks like, click on 'view source' in your browser. Some Web designers lift whole chunks of code from other sites to save time: I call that theft.

The time involved

Web sites make money only when visitors return, again and again. The secret to that is keeping the site topical and relevant, which can take considerable time. Some claim to spend an hour a day revising and tweaking, but few small firms will have that amount of time. The best sites are truly interactive with pages that have stock lists, new items, Usenet groups and mailing lists, hints and tips, and a stop press section.

If your main update is a 'stock available' page, get the site designer to show you how to update the information yourself to save on costs.

Attracting visitors

The frightening thing about the Web is its galloping expansion. Bill Gates believes that only 1 per cent of the potential has yet been realised.

Setting up your Web site is just the start: you have to promote it to attract visitors. This can be broken down to four main areas:

- Offline promotion.
- Links to other sites.
- Search engines.
- Newsgroups and mailing lists.

Offline activities embrace advertising and conventional PR, plus placing your Web address on every piece of printed literature you produce – even using it as the shop title (see Figure 3.1 on page 62). At the moment just setting up a Web site is news to some journalists, so make sure you send a press release. As having a site becomes the norm, you will have to find something more newsworthy to say.

Links to other sites should be a free and collaborative way of generating extra traffic from an identifiable target audience. Contact what look like suitable sites and see if they add a link. Don't offer a return link unless pressed. Online magazines (e-zines) and newsletters often include links, as do online versions of news-stand magazines. You will have to do a regular check to see if they are still working, as this is a fluid area. There is always the danger that your visitor will be drawn away down an ever more confusing trail and never find his or her way back.

Search engines

Surveys claim that 80 per cent of new visitors find your site via a search engine, and much of cyberspace is filled with discussions on how to improve your league-table rating.

As most Web watchers acknowledge that the biggest fault of the World Wide Web is the sheer scale of its uncatalogued resource, the hunt is always on to find quicker and more exhaustive methods of retrieving information. Venture capitalists seem willing to back new search engine methodology so that there are thousands of engines out there, though the top 10 are thought to attract more than 90 per cent of all searches. These include Alta Vista, Scoot, Google, Lycos, MSN, etc. Yahoo! is regarded as a true directory, as your Web site is listed only after written permission and evaluation by the compilers. Try searchenginewatch.com if you're into this degree of sophistication, but here is a quick run-through either to whet your appetite or to deter you.

Apart from Yahoo! search engines work in different ways. Some use robot crawlers to automatically gather information. Ask Jeeves and Copernic search the results of other search engines while Google analyses the number of sites that are linked to them.

It is self-evident that the higher up the league table your site appears, the more chance you have of getting traffic. While the Web crawlers basically have to work on text content, there are ways of improving your chances of getting listed. The crawler, or spider, visits your site, reads it and follows the other page links. It returns every month or so and updates the information. An index is compiled and is ranked in order of importance; this the key factor, in more ways than one.

The index works on key word frequency and position and assumes that a word in the title is more important than body text. In the same way that sales letters and direct marketing skills teach you to come to the point quickly, so Web crawlers abide by the same discipline. If your home page is more art than information – 'click here to enter' – then both the search engine and the punter have little to go on. Frames are also avoided by search engines, so leave your key words out of them.

Some search more frequently than others, some crawl through more pages. Having extra links to other sites implies that a site is popular and well regarded, while attempts to fool the engine by repeating (spamming) key words often ends in rejection. The technology is getting wise.

In summary, to improve your search engine results:

- Decide on the key words or phrases that best sum up what you are selling and summarise these in the HTML page title.
- Bring the same words in as title pages, and without overdoing it, ensure that the same words are used throughout your site.
- If location is important (you're only looking for local buyers) include your town in the description.
- Check that the contents section that describes your site spells out the benefits.
- Put them in meta tags (a way of marking them so the engine picks them up, though some engines ignore them).
- Keep adding to and updating your links.
- Submit the results to sites like www.websitegarage. netscape.com that will check the dead links, and to www. webpositiongold.com or www.topwebsite.co.uk for hints on improving your position.

That said, the sheer volume of new Web sites seems to be overwhelming some engines, with reports of entries taking several months to appear. Don't waste too much time on this activity: some observers believe that it won't be long before the only way of getting a mention is to pay.

Newsgroups and mailing lists

With some caution let me suggest that you try Usenet newgroups. Yes, it's anarchic and reminiscent of Speaker's Corner on a bad day, but as others have said, 'All human life is there'. With around 25,000 newsgroups your ISP will be selective about what it carries. Download via your news server to see what they hold and in addition click on news.announce.newusers and uk.net.news.announce. It can be difficult picking out the groups that are relevant to your sector. Read what else is posted to get a flavour and look at the FAQ section *before* contributing, to avoid getting 'flamed' (abused, insulted, destroyed). Commercial plugs must be subtle: just putting your URL in the signature address will generate some traffic.

A potentially valuable archive source to Usenet is www. dejanews.com, which holds several years of back postings from all the newsgroups. Jim McLellan's book is worth reading on this subject.

Beware porn and viruses, not necessarily at the same time.

Mailing lists operate online much as does the Royal Mail, but of course it is far cheaper and quicker. Make use of the names you gather from the site but keep the messages short, use a strong headline and give people the opportunity to 'unsubscribe', as Net jargon has it. Replies must be handled promptly. Back to the tried and proven marketing message that old customers are more likely to buy than new. Remembering that *Member get a Member* can work so well for direct mail (see page 159), use the same technique by inserting a link box: 'Like this site? Click here to tell a friend'. I have met a firm that set up a bogus Web site, compiled 20,000 names and e-mailed everyone. The response was a heart-warming 7,500 – but the ISP shut the firm down as it decided it was spamming.

With some caution look at www.liszt.com for lists of e-mailing lists of prospects.

Branding

With so much choice and confusion on the Web, it has become apparent that visitors do tend to stick with sites that they have found useful and easy to understand. Keep your Web site active and topical and you'll build considerable brand loyalty. Amazon.com is one of the world's best known and valuable brands but it has yet to make a penny profit. I can't work that out either.

Successful online branding is much like offline branding: image and design must be consistent; speedy and friendly customer service is paramount; while no opportunity should be lost in spreading the brand name onto other sites by means of links and newsy items.

Monitoring visitors

Yes, you can do this on the Web as well as by using coupons in off-the-page advertising. After you've built up a number of links it would be helpful to know where they arrived from – search engines, trade associations, news sites, whatever. The way to do this is to install a Web trends log analyser; one can be downloaded from www.webtrends.com (try it free for two weeks). It may help to establish the links you want if you offer a commission (5 per cent) for every sale generated that came via the webtrends site. Such sites are called affiliates, and, as when you use agents, you pay out only if you achieve sales.

Trading online: e-commerce

Most of the Web is run as a free information service, but I presume small firms will want a return from all that time and effort. E-commerce will revolutionise the way they operate once public confidence is gained in giving credit card details over the Net and inexpensive secure software defeats the hacker (some hope). But e-commerce has just as much potential savings and benefits for business-to-business relationships. At present, with such an evolving culture some sectors are better equipped to go for online trading. The graphics and print industry, for example, was among the first to demand fast file transfer (ISDN).

At present most *information* is gathered from Web-site visiting, but payment is done by post or phone. This will change.

To sell online you will need to operate through a secure server run by your ISP. Few prospects will tap in their credit card details without it. The best-selling products are those that can be posted and are already well known – CDs, books, etc – but food, spare parts and clothing are all now readily available on the Web.

It helps to adopt the shopping basket approach, where customers scroll through items, adding as they go, then enter the order page. Make the two parts quite distinct: information and buying. Highlight spaces for altering and cancellation before submitting the final order as mistakes and returns will kill the profit and repeat business.

Make the ordering form blindingly simple, as many consumers will be Net newcomers. Drop-down menus aid simplicity. Asterisk the fields that are obligatory, but make sure that if the form is rejected, what has been missed is highlighted. A common fault is to send off the form by hitting the 'Enter' key rather than 'submit', when incomplete details are sent off. Order acknowledgements must be generated automatically by e-mail by way of a detailed letter giving reference numbers, full cost and delivery dates. 'Thank you' would not go amiss either.

Make sure that terms and conditions are clear. It doesn't come cheap but your software should be linked to stock control so that the customer can be advised when it is likely to arrive. Remember that anyone in the world with access to the Internet can order, so you need to be aware of shipping costs – more complications if you are hoping to export anything that requires special packing. Best to start small and build up experience.

Business customers might prefer to raise invoices in the conventional way to diminish both fraud and credit risks.

A privacy policy is important and should be stated on any request for names. I believe that confidence is enhanced by stating loud and clear, 'No names are ever released to third parties.'

Testing the site

As with all new ventures, it is sensible to test the site before going live. Sites that crash are all too common and do nothing for client credibility. Sites crash because they can't cope with the load, but predicting the likely traffic is problematical. Business-to-business trading is easier, for you no doubt know where a lot of trade is likely to come from. The type and size of order – low-value spare parts or just enquiries for capital items – will be easier to gauge.

Conversion sales from hit rates will be significantly less than 1 per cent. Peak ordering time is usually reckoned to be from 4 pm to 6 pm. With so many unknown variables, save your big marketing promotion till you are entirely happy that your site can cope. Any bespoke software must be capable of quick expansion. Test that the ordering, stock control, distribution and response e-mail seamlessly integrate with little if any rekeying by a human required. That's when mistakes happen.

Keeping customers coming back

Apart from offering value for money and providing good service, the key to luring customers back to your Web site is to ring the changes and keep it up to date. The Web is very much like a newspaper, and nobody wants to read old news. The Web was built on freebies and, regrettably, many visitors expect to see some free or at least bargain offers. Highlight these on the home page. If you take the Web seriously then you'll find time to add features, articles, FAQs, prices and stock availability.

The Web's potential

Some of the excitement of the Web derives from the way it has fired small firms' imaginations to innovate. There can't be many more conservative backwaters than book publishing – yet one site, xlibris.com, offers unpublished (and maybe unpublishable) authors the chance of putting sample text on the web. Readers can order a single book, which is printed and bound as a one-off: vanity publishing taken to the ultimate. Best-selling author Stephen King has also put a single chapter on the Web, which 150,000 people have downloaded (and most have promised to send $1). The book will be written in instalments, doing away with boring old printers and publishers. Gutenberg did live 600 years ago, after all.

A small brewery in Scotland called Lugton Gold offers beer with your own name on – that's personalisation. Call up the Web site www.drinkebeer.com, type in your name and you will get your very own labelled beer. A German company ordered 80 crates of the stuff, so e-commerce does work.

Look up www.glennhinton.co.uk and you'll see a bespoke furniture maker who sells to upmarket customers all over the world. Every piece is individual and most clients he never meets. Using a digitising tablet, he can send sketch designs to a prospect who can make instant comments back by e-mail. The site costs as much as a good colour brochure, around £3,000, but it can be instantly updated. The furniture maker is reported as saying that a video camera will be added next so he can view the client's interior and talk face to face.

The Web is not only of benefit to manufacturers, as a number of blossoming recruitment agencies have shown. Resourceconnection. co.uk, for instance, is an ad site for marketing management posts and usually has around 50 such ads at any one time. Those looking for jobs also submit their CVs, and there are over 2,000 hopefuls registered. It is estimated that small ads and job vacancies will be one of the major growth areas for the Web because of its instant ability to update. Estate agents and the motor trade too have readily taken to this form of promotion.

E-commerce could dramatically change the role of sales personnel as no longer will they need to carry brochures and price lists. A laptop will carry all the up-to-the-minute information needed while the customer can tap in orders and even help design a project and specification to suit his or her own needs. Communications should improve and time be saved. The customer should become a more much integrated part of the business. That is the challenge and opportunity.

To keep up to date, look at 'Web watch' on guardianunlimited.

Summary

- Decide what you want to achieve with a Web site.
- Keep it simple and easy to navigate, with all the contact details appearing on the home page.
- Avoid large chunks of text; it should never occupy more than half the screen.
- Encourage feedback: gather names.
- Make offers.
- Provide information, generate plenty of links.
- Revise often, experiment.
- Respond promptly to e-mails and orders.
- Generate a community feel to the site.
- The Web may not be the golden opportunity that some portray – for your type of business. The time and money you devote to this may achieve better results by other means. Don't be deluded.

Further reading

Catalogue and E-business Magazine: catalog-biz.com
Profiting from the Internet (free from virginbiz.net)
Marketing Your Business on the Internet: Sara Edlington (internet-handbooks.co.uk)

4 *Advertising*

imp not to Overlook
simple methods
streamline the booking
process - order forms?

Advertising which promises no benefit to the consumer does not sell, yet
the majority of campaigns contain no promise whatever.

David Ogilvy

Probably the most contentious area of marketing is advertising.
Everyone is an expert. We are all bombarded with ads on the television, on hoardings, papers, the radio and now on the Internet. What
few of us understand are nonsenses like double-page spreads to
promote gas or electricity – or even BT's 'It's good to talk', when few
of us have any option but to use the product. The wastage is enormous,
but then in those situations it is not their personal money.

My role in this chapter is to focus your mind on the principles,
explain why some ads work and others don't, and convince you that
advertising should only be undertaken where the results can realistically be measured. Everything else is self-indulgent. I want you to be
able to analyse ads better, break them down and avoid the all-too-
common mistakes that are made every day.

Advertising is the link between the supplier and the consumer,
communication and information, the medium and the message.

The need for some form of advertising must be obvious. Without it
you must rely on word-of-mouth recommendation (not to be despised
but slow nevertheless) or press editorial. The main force of your sales
effort will probably be through advertising of one sort or another. It can
be as simple as writing your name on a van, pushing a handbill through
the door or buying space in the parish magazine.

Advertising *by itself* does not sell. It will not shift a bad product
(more than once) or create new markets. It must be backed up by sales
literature, order forms, a sales force, stocks, distributors and a strategy.

Figure 4.1 While you can place ads anywhere, I have my doubts what image the NatWest is trying to portray here

Let's get some of the principles out of the way first. The skill of advertising lies in reducing the global population to your target audience and reaching as many of them as you can at an economic cost. First you analyse the benefits or virtues of your product – isolate the features and translate those into customer benefits. Who has a need for your product? Discover who your potential customers are. Question all the time.

Finally, design the message and pick the medium to reach your target audience.

2 target audiences

Think of a customer

The most important principle to grasp in advertising is placing the advertisement where most of your target audience is likely to see it. That sounds a terribly obvious statement, but I have lost track of the number of times that I have seen small firms forget that basic principle. Advertising is expensive and you cannot afford the luxury of the blanket coverage indulged in by cigarette or beer manufacturers. Every

element of danger/experse
needs to be
professon

Advertising   **79**

Rates & Data   2001

Where to buy

Standard lineage 1-3 headings per heading per month	£28
Bold entry lineage 1-3 headings per heading per month	£38
Display box* 1-3 headings per single column centimetre	£15
e.g. 3cm x 1column per month	£4

*This price includes one free colour. Each extra colour £5.00. Discounts are available for bookings of four or more headings per month. Six months minimum booking.

Classified

Single insertion per single column centimetre	£17
Discounts are available for series bookings	
Spot colour	£30

Appointments

Appointments per single column centimetre	£25
Spot colour	£30
Box no. facility	£25

10% agency discount (UK) 15% agency discount (overseas) All prices exclusive of VAT

Margins

Top	10mm
Bottom	14mm
Outer	10mm
Between ads	5mm

For bleed advertisements there is an additional charge of 10%

10% extra charge for special position

Half page junior vertical
Type   260 x 89mm

Half page junior horizontal
Type   130 x 183mm

	mono	Spot col	Full col
1-5	£880	£1030	£1520
6-11	£800	£950	£1416
12	£726	£876	£1320

Third A3 vertical
Type   361 x 89mm

	mono	Spot col	Full col
1-5	£968	£1133	£1672
6-11	£880	£1045	£1558
12	£799	£964	£1460

Quarter page vertical
Type   177 x 136mm

Quarter page horizontal
Type   96 x 277mm

	mono	Spot col	Full col
1-5	£880	£1030	£1520
6-11	£800	£950	£1416
12	£726	£876	£1320

Eighth A3 vertical
Type   130 x 89mm

Eighth A3 horizontal
Type   96 x 183mm

	mono	Spot col	Full col
1-5	£475	£625	£860
6-11	£425	£575	£790
12	£390	£540	£700

Front page solus
Type   89 x 89mm

			Full col only
1-5	-	-	£1500
6-11	-	-	£1320
12	-	-	£1106

Figure 4.2   A typical rate card supplied by the magazine   *move away from newspapers 2 specialist ads*

pound must earn its keep. Forget about large-circulation papers and concentrate on where the most people of your segment can be reached. The *Radio Times* has about 4 million readers, but if your product is of interest to DIY houseowners you would probably be better off running an ad in *Practical Householder*. Its circulation is around 50,000 and possibly 50 per cent of them take the *Radio Times* as well. Target your ad to those publications that have most of your prospects as readers. There is too much wastage and the cost is prodigious. The simplest ad need be no more than pushing a handbill through the doors of houses with *dirty* windows. That simple exercise pinpoints those with a need and cuts out wastage on those who already clean their own windows. Advertising can be as simple as that.

Setting objectives

Never advertise without having an objective. You must have a goal. Effective advertising means always having a clear idea of what you are aiming to do. Advertising is used for a wide variety of reasons. Some are:

1. New product launch.
2. Changing price structure.
3. Exhibition attendance.
4. Recruitment of staff.
5. Sales.
6. Change of premises, enlarging facilities.
7. Charitable, linking your firm with a local good cause.
8. Direct response, to invite enquiries.
9. Trade ads to wholesalers.
10. Appealing for agents.
11. To iron out seasonal fluctuations in demand.
12. Reminder ads – repetitious, constantly there.
13. To announce record results or celebrate an anniversary.
14. To promote a Web site.

I have listed these to emphasise the many different roles that advertising can play. Don't advertise just because Charlie down the road does or when the local newspaper is doing a feature. There have to be some good solid reasons for investing in a promotional exercise.

Positioning

Your perceived position in the marketplace will determine where your message appears. This is a very important point to grasp. If you've an

Figure 4.3 Positioning conveys the right tone of voice to your target audience and relates to them in language they understand. The handmade sign for eggs is entirely appropriate in a country lane, but would you trust your life with the joyflight?

Figure 4.4 Arresting street sign outside a bakery

up-market product then not only must you promote in the right glossy magazines but the style of typeface, layout and presentation must convey an air of grandeur and graciousness.

Newsagents' windows are fine for handymen and French lessons, but an ad selling your daughter's pony is probably better placed in *Horse and Hound* or some such specialised magazine. If you are targeting directors for a champagne day at the races, that deserves a personalised letter on quality paper with stamped return envelopes. Any ad you design must reflect the right tone to appeal to your target audience.

Charity adverts mustn't be too slick, otherwise people may think the money is going on Mayfair agencies rather than needy orphans. In fact, charity fund raising demands a very professional approach and is one of the more difficult tasks for an advertiser.

Where to advertise

At this stage it may be illuminating to think of all the places where you can pay to display your message:

Newspapers, national and local
Magazines, general and specialist
TV
Exchange & Mart and other pure advertising magazines
Radio
Cinema
Directories and yearbooks
Yellow Pages (and *Talking Pages*)
House magazines (eg bank staff magazines)
Posters, hoardings, transport undertakings
Signs of every imaginable variety, from site building boards to your own van
Handbills, leaflets, brochures
Litter bins, parking meters, lollipop ladies
Painted buses
Balloons and streamers
Direct mail
Exhibitions
Sports team sponsorship
Packaging
Sales promotion
Point-of-sale material
Giveaways – calendars, wall charts, etc
Parish magazines, show programmes
Banner ads on Web sites
Newsagents' windows
And even in the lids of Chinese or Indian takeaways

The choice is vast. The problem is deciding how best to reach your prospect. The criteria for selection in newsprint are frequency, size of circulation, coverage, readership profile and cost.

The printed word – newspapers and magazines – will probably take most of your budget. It is the accepted medium to reach the bulk of your audience as there are magazines to cater for every imaginable interest from the lowly but not to be despised parish magazine to the Sunday supplements. Your first decision is to decide what journal to go for.

Readership

Before making your decision you need to get a *media pack* from the advertising department of the magazines. This will try to impress you with readership, circulation and profiles of its readers. Local papers tend not to go into much detail. When comparing costs, beware of falling into the trap of confusing readership with circulation. The former is always claimed to be much greater, but impossible to verify. Professional magazines with small circulations tend to be retained as a point of reference for years afterwards and can still produce results.

You must advertise where your buyers and consumers are likely to see the message. Market research should have told you where your likely prospects lie. Consulting the various publications mentioned in Chapter 2 will enable you to pinpoint which newspapers or journals to aim for. The media data form compiled by the publishers will give a *readership profile*. This is a breakdown of a publication's readers and subscribers by job title if it is a trade journal (managers, buyers, consultants, etc) and often by age, sex, interests and other relevant information.

Of major interest to consumer product advertisers is the socio-economic classification: AB – upper and middle classes, managerial, administrative and professional people; C1, C2 – lower middles, skilled working class; D – working class (semi- and unskilled manual workers); and the poor Es – those at the lowest level of subsistence. This seems to reflect class prejudices but it is important to understand the jargon and reasoning behind it. For example, *Good Housekeeping* claims to have more ABC1 readers than any other women's journal. 'Women's interest' magazines have topped the mass circulation league table, after the TV listings magazines, but towards the end of 1997 for the first time a men's magazine, *Loaded*, raced up the charts. Says something about our society.

The forms are useful but should be treated with common sense and caution. The media reps are in the business of taking your money, after all.

The simplest way of discovering what industrial buyers read is to ring up a few and ask. *BRAD* (page 50) will highlight the probables, but your real readership may well disclose that what they actually *read* is somewhat different. All the professional bodies produce journals for their own learned membership that go to all the right people. Unfortunately, some are written in a less than uplifting vein and you may learn that a more snappy, but less authoritative, paper is the one your prospects turn to. Some industries have a welter of competing papers each claiming to offer the best penetration into your market, but the acid test is your *own* research.

Frequency

The copy dates of some glossy monthlies are two months before publication. The Christmas editions of the more popular consumer titles are frequently booked up months before. This poses problems if you are waiting on a shipment or uncertain about a product change. Dailies or weeklies allow much prompter changes. The ultimate is probably radio where messages can be slotted in on the same day. Yearbooks, diaries and *Yellow Pages* require long forward notice. Your Web site has an advantage here.

How many copies?

Having targeted your audience you will want to know the individual circulations of your advertising media. This is easy when you control the output (handbills, direct mail, brochures, etc).

ABC (*Audit Bureau of Circulation*)-certified journals are reliable for cost comparisons and the figures should be beyond reproach. Knowing the circulation does not mean, of course, that all the readers will see your ad, but it is a start. Smaller circulation or new publications will have 'Uncertified' beside their *BRAD* entry. Be wary of 'Publisher's statement: 50,000 print run ordered'.

The journal's advertising department will be able to tell you of many special features planned that may be appropriate. Some UK journals have a surprisingly high overseas circulation, particularly in the medical and scientific field.

Erosion – the numbers game

A popular area for small firms is the 'Postal Bargains' slot in many papers, but research on response is hard to come by. I have carried out my own research on the pulling power of this slot. A dozen advertisers were canvassed. I picked out what looked like newish small firms, asking for the response to their ads. Few claimed more than 30 replies. Though a paper's circulation may exceed half a million, half of the readership may only buy it for the pictures, a quarter for the sport, some the crossword, and a surprisingly high number never buy by post on principle. The moral is clear: don't be deceived by massive circulations. That's erosion.

Coverage

There could be a lot of duplication when you use different advertising media. You want to establish how well you reach the audience – the penetration or coverage. A DIY product could be advertised in *Practical Householder*, mailshoted to power-drill owners, taken to a trade show to tempt stockists, pushed on TV or any combination of all those. The women's magazine market is a lively and populous one. How many women buy two or more? Which magazine gives the best penetration for your age group? Is *TV Times* a better buy anyway?

The eternal problem with most advertising is measuring the effectiveness. National corporations can afford to have poster displays, bus panels and whole-page ads in the *Radio Times*, but even they have great difficulty in isolating which medium has pulled in the most response. By definition, small firms tend to be frugal with their advertising budgets, and should avoid any promotions where the results cannot be measured. Their advertising has to be more specific, measurable and *sell*. The favoured routes therefore tend to be ads that use a reply coupon to invite a response or offer a very specific message.

Opportunities to see (OTS)

The popularity of breakfast TV (at least with the advertisers) is that they can get the message over before the shops open. Trade buyers are deluged with calendars, diaries, pen sets and message pads in the hope that they will remain in the office at the point of action when a buying decision is made. The more opportunities to see that are given, the greater chance that the company name or product will stick. This is why direct mail letters increasingly involve more pieces of literature. The theory (and practice) is that each piece of mailing is looked at before being discarded. It may only be a brief scan but it gives the seller another chance to hook a punter.

Bus advertising on the rear panels should be aimed at the motoring public, with ads for brake parts and accessories being the most popular.

Which media to choose?

Many small firms are convinced that advertising is a waste of money. They have parted with a limited amount (but large to them), relying on an ill-considered design, with no objectives or strategy, that has produced no measurable results. Let me quote from John Caples in his *Tested Advertising Methods*:

> I have seen one advertisement actually sell not twice as much, not three times as much, but 19½ times as much as another. Both advertisements occupied the same space. Both were run in the same publication. Both had photographic illustrations. Both had carefully written copy. The difference was that one used the right appeal and the other used the wrong appeal.

Advertising *does* work if you adopt some basic rules and simple techniques that can be easily grasped. I am not talking about designing your own TV campaign but just improving your own awareness either to advise an agency or generate your own ads to a reasonable standard.

The main *media* at your disposal are press and local radio, direct mail, door leaflets and the telephone. Mass media publications can deliver the largest audience at the cheapest cost per head – but many will be of no interest to you; you will also be competing with both editorial and other ads. This main use is in capturing large numbers of people from which your segment can be isolated. If you must go in a large circulation paper make sure there is an appropriate heading under which you can slot to isolate your prospects.

Develop a *direct response* strategy that can be more cost effective. Tactics are discussed in the next chapter.

And the costs

The bible of the advertising industry, *BRAD*, lists all the basic rate-card costs, though you should be able to get at least 10 per cent off those, often far more if you leave it to the last minute. If you have a reasonable budget it often pays to establish a working relationship with a magazine whereby you always pick up the last quarter page, or whatever, when available. You can pick up some real bargains.

Ignoring page rates – £31,000 for a page in the *Daily Mail* for example – if we compare a mono quarter page for the following publications, taken at random, it will give you some idea:

Computer Shopper: £791 (circulation 173,000)
Land Rover International: £435 (circulation 60,000)
Birds: £1,500 (circulation 593,000)
Model Engineer: £235 (circulation 18,000).

But this is only the start of the story.

Newspaper and magazine advertising

The two main types are *classified* and *display*. Classifieds are usually grouped together under a variety of headings. They require typesetting only and can often be rung in quite close to press date. If you run an unusual specialisation some trade papers may put in a fresh heading just for you. If often works and helps to make your ad stand out. The publisher hopes it will attract more advertisers.

Display ads are *designed* and need artwork, headlines, text, etc. These will be dotted throughout the publication and generate most of the paper's income. When deciding which paper to go for, pick the one with more advertising; many journals are bought, and read, more for the ads than the editorials. This particularly applies if you have a small budget and can only run to classified. Papers that have a very small classified section should generally be avoided. The ultimate is, of course, *Exchange & Mart*. Remarkably good responses are pulled for quite expensive items. I've even known factories to be let from these pages.

Between the two are *semi-display* used by some magazines. They tend to be small pictorial ads grouped near the classified section.

Trade setting

Pretty well every publication will lay out an ad for you from your rough. If you're desperate to meet a deadline, simple ads can be faxed or phoned through: there are no doubt some excellent in-house admen who will do a competent job. In my experience the local press are poor at designing ads, probably because they are deluged with handwritten copy at short notice. You will probably do better by following my simple advice that follows and getting the basic concept down yourself. Production costs can be charged as an extra but, in my experience, simple layouts are treated as part of the service. Colour is always extra. But by and large, for imaginative designs you should go to an outside agency or freelance graphic designer.

Some advertising jargon

Buying space. Ads are measured either by fractions of a page   half page, quarter page – or by single column centimetres. Each publication will have its own layout and a number of column widths.

Space is sold by a standard centimetre depth. Be very careful you understand what you are ordering: a '10 × 2' is probably 10 column centimetres of depth by 2 columns wide. When buying 'half a page' make sure you are getting a horizontal half when you want it, and not the vertical variety. Specify height by width in that order: remember the phrase 'hot water'.

Colour separations. Most magazines are printed by a four-colour process and you will need to pay for these separations; price varies from £50 to £120. Black-and-white ads are best printed from laser-set copy. It is usually simpler if you send copy on disk or by ISDN or e-mail. Always send hard copy (printed up) as reference with all the fonts marked. Check what format they can read: most of the quality publications are produced on Mac computers. I find it easiest to use a pre-press bureau that will translate my PC designs, drum scan any photos and ISDN the result direct to the paper. Cost is around £40.

Controlled circulation magazines are common in the technical field. They are issued free (the ads pay for them) but circulation should be restricted to those in certain specified positions of influence. There is usually an application form in the back of every copy.

Copy date is the vital date when the publisher must have camera-ready artwork in his hand to be sent off for printing. It is *not* the date when a rough layout can be shoved in the post. You will miss that issue.

Cost per thousand (CPT). One of the holy grails of advertising, cost comparisons are made to reach a given 1,000 readers of each medium. As usual, statistics can mean anything and here the picture is clouded by the intrusion of quality. The cost of reaching 1,000 *Financial Times* readers is 134 times as high as for the *Sun* (the page rate is roughly the same). The argument is that your average *Financial Times* reader has more influence in specifying products and contacts than the *Sun* reader.

Never lose sight of your *target* reader: no good reaching a million readers if only 1 per cent is your *audience*.

Editorial. The informative text written by the journalists that separates the adverts. Freesheets tend to have very little editorial and are probably discarded quickly.

Facing matter is when an ad is placed opposite some editorial – as against being submerged in a page of other ads. The space commands a premium price. The opposite is *run of paper* (ROP), where it will be placed anywhere at the discretion of the advertising manager.

Inserts can be very useful. Some magazines will accept your printed leaflet for loose insertion in every copy (or occasionally selected copies to a segment of the circulation in your target area). They'll want prior sight of it and often there is a waiting list. It's cheaper than advertising in the mag (you've paid for the production). If the magazine is in black and white only, this is a way of getting your colour leaflets left over from the trade fair out to the readers.

A media schedule (Table 4.1) is helpful to plan the preparation of your advertising material and get it off in time. It's really a glorified diary that's stuck on the wall, which tells you when your mags and ads are coming out, enabling a continuous programme to be maintained (if that's what you want).

Reader's enquiry service is widely used to generate enquiries. A pre-paid card is bound in, usually at the back of the mag, keyed in with numbered ads that can produce a prolific number of prospects. There can be a delay before they are sent on from the publisher.

Some *printing* terms are explained on pages 122–24.

Table 4.1 Typical media schedule (here used for the agricultural sector)

Title	Publisher	Contact	Copy deadline	Publication date	Size	Cost	Claimed circ	Booked to appear	Response!!!
Farmers Weekly	Reeds	Editorial: Andy Collings, Andy Moore. fax 020 8652 4005 Tim Hackett (Display) 01203 696502 fax 696573 Selina (Classifieds)	18 days before publication Alan Blagrove, 020 8652 4851 Reed Farmers Publishing Group, 6th Floor, Quadrant House, Sutton SM2 5AS Small ads: Tuesdays 4 pm	Fridays	Qtr page 132 × 96	£760 less 10% com. for 3 rate card £1,129 colour Small ad: £4.80 per line	89K ABC	See below 4 insertions	
Dairy Farmer	Miller Freeman	Editor: Rachel Potter, fax 01473 232822 Adverts: John Welford, tel/fax 01359 244659	6 April 15 May 6 June 11 July	1st Tues: 2 May 6 June 1 July 1 Aug	qtr page 124 × 89	£799 for 3 less 10% com. (rate card £1,204) colour	27K ABC	2 months from May	
Farm Contractor	ACP Publishers Iron Down House Deddington, Banbury OX15 0PJ	Editor: Jane Tarte, fax 01869 338578 Malcolm Benjamin		1st week	qtr page		10K	4 months from March	
Northern Farming	Gazette House King Street, Thorne Doncaster DN8 5BA	Adv: Marion 01485 740700 fax 740776	24th monthly	1st week of each month	qtr page 125 × 93	£300 for 3 insertions colour		3 months from April	

Media schedules are essential to keep track of what ads are run and whether they are worth continuing with.

Using an advertising agency

It stands to reason that those who are designing ads every day of the week should be able to come up with better ideas and layouts than raw small firms. Advertising can run away with your money, often to little effect. To understand the nature of the industry, thumb through *Advertiser's Annual* or *Campaign*, the trade gossip magazine. Accredited agencies earn commission on their 'billings', the space they buy, which varies depending on the medium used. It averages 10 to 15 per cent. Local papers pay less than nationals. The commission should part offset the cost of using an agency but nevertheless, don't be upset at the costs of employing the professionals.

... and how to choose the right one

Steer away from the big boys. They'll have no interest in small budgets. Find a small partnership, perhaps freshly set up, that is as hungry as you are: not *too* new or you may know more than they do. Ask for samples of their past work. Look at their roughs and try to get them to explain *why* they chose that particular theme. You want to tap into their creative abilities. The advertising jargon and printing termi-nology can be learnt, given time – it's creative talent that you need and should be willing to pay for.

A good agency will be able to advise you on:

1. An objective campaign balancing your various products and resources.
2. Market research: if not within their own partnership, where to find it.
3. Producing the material, booking the space in the most cost-effec-tive manner and evaluating the results.

Some agencies will also do PR work and exhibitions here and abroad. An agency should know a string of reliable printers for brochures and your packaging needs, and also arrange professional photography.

Go to see three or four agencies. Take along your product, if you can, with samples of any literature or ads you may have run. Let them do most of the talking. Gauge from their questions how interested they

Help save a life this Winter...

...with this FREE birdtable!

Winter can be cruel on small birds. But when you join the RSPB, we'll help by giving you this free wooden birdtable, so that your garden friends can survive these difficult months.

RSPB membership also gives you much more...like unlimited FREE entry to over 100 RSPB nature reserves... plus the award-winning quarterly magazine **BIRDS** – 96 pages of fascinating articles and stunning colour photography.

And by joining the RSPB you're helping wild birds to thrive, free in their natural environment. Just fill in and send this form today, to: RSPB, FREEPOST, Sandy, Beds SG19 2BR.

Join the RSPB today!

Yes – I want to join the RSPB

☐ Please send me my FREE birdtable.

I enclose a cheque/PO (payable to RSPB) for:

☐ £20 (A year's single membership)
☐ £25 (A year's membership for two adults at one address)
☐ Concessionary membership rates available upon request.

OR please deduct this sum from my Access/Visa card no:

Expiry date   Cardholder's Signature

(Please attach address of cardholder if different from below)

Mr/Mrs/Miss/Ms _____

Address _____

Postcode _____
Joint Member's Surname: Mr/Mrs/Miss/Ms

RSPB

Send to: The Royal Society for the Protection of Birds, FREEPOST, Sandy, Beds SG19 2BR.

Registered charity no 207076

Figure 4.5 A nice emotive appeal, combined with an attractive free gift plus a large coupon made this one of the most successful ads the RSPB have ever run

are in you. You're looking for empathy and an understanding of your product and market. A technical product does really demand some knowledge of the habits of engineering specifiers. While it is asking a lot for ad-men to have a complete grasp of the technicalities of your product, there must be some meeting of minds.

Increasingly agencies are specialising. The glamour end has always been fast-moving consumer goods (FMCG), with industrial accounts looked down on. Be very wary of agencies that have not handled direct mail if that is your direction. That really is one field for the experts. Give them time to think and ask them to produce some *roughs* on ads they would run. Don't expect finished artwork unless you're prepared to pay well for the service. At this stage you are simply looking at how well they have grasped your company and what ideas they can come up with. And then talk about budgets. In my experience very few small firms can afford to use agencies. For those with limited budgets it can still be useful to use them just to buy space. They can frequently get a better deal.

Designing your own ads

Despite the obvious advantages in going to an agency, many of you will design your own copy, particularly when just starting in business. I can't turn you into an expert wordsmith in a few pages but the ground rules can be spelled out fairly succinctly. There are many ways of getting the message over and fortunately there is no one sure-fire route to success. It would be a dull world if there were.

Advertising is a transient medium; no one is paid to read adverts. They compete for your vision and comprehension along with all the other ephemera of the modern world. Good advertisements follow the formula AIDA – Attention, Interest, Desire and Action. The first requirement, therefore, is to attract *attention*. This can be done either with a headline, a picture, colour (spot or full), special position or novelty. Some researcher has worked out that Mr or Mrs Average 'sees' over 1,000 ads each week – newspaper, posters, TV, etc. Your job when designing an ad is to get the reader to stop and digest what you have to say.

Research has shown that you get at most two seconds to catch the eye – and putting in a large illustration increases the chances. Making the picture take up half the space doubles the audience of ads with text alone. The brain remembers the visual image better. Words and pictures in combination can be powerful as long as the story merits it. All too often any old photo is dredged up to fill a space.

Interest. Unless the text appears of interest to the reader, then no matter how beautifully it is put together or how clever the pun, it will be passed over. Long text should be used with care, as again, modern research has shown that more text means fewer readers. The subject must be made to look attractive and compulsive reading. The best ads arouse an emotional reaction. You should strive to create *desire* in the reader. 'Yes, that sounds good – I'd like one of those.' It must relate to the reader's circumstances. You must always talk about user benefits, not features. And they must be readily apparent.

The ad will have achieved very little if there is no encouragement for the reader to do anything about it. This is the hard part. You need *action.* Coupons inviting enquiries for brochures or money off the next order are well-tried formulae. At the least, clear instructions must be printed to direct the reader to more information. The old buzz words come in here – 'Limited stocks, Sale, Limited edition to first 1,000 callers, Club members' preference, Free trial, Money back guarantee', etc. The best of all is 'New'. Don't fall into the trap of designing ads that are 'all image and no information'.

Some common mistakes

The firms that claim advertising doesn't pay probably make some of the following mistakes:

- They don't think hard enough who their audience is and advertise in the wrong paper.
- The put their name first instead of a benefit as a headline.
- As Davil Ogilvy says in *Ogilvy on Advertising*: 'Advertising which promises no benefit to the consumer does not sell, yet the majority of campaigns contain no promise whatever.'
- They make the advertisement hard to read.
- Misunderstanding of the need for an eye-catching headline.
- Not enough product information.
- There is no encouragement to do anything. So what?

Remember the basics

All marketing resolves around those eternal questions: Who, What, Why, Where and When?

Who is your target audience? What are they interested in and what are their needs? I've read a Fleet Street editor who kept a blow-up of a section of the Cup Final crowd on the wall. When a bright sub presented him with some high-falutin' copy, he would swing round to the wall: 'There's your audience – never forget it!'

What are the benefits? Don't try to trot out all 33 but cut them down to 3 at most and headline *1 – your unique selling proposition* (USP). Why should they buy it? What is your offer? The big world is a competitive market and in your ads you must try to put a convincing reason for immediate action or response. Use those buzz words. Alastair Crompton in his excellent book *The Craft of Copywriting* draws a distinction between two sorts of product. Some you can really say quite a lot about (DIY products or household gadgets and many technical products, for example) but what can you say that's new about springs or screws?

If your product is in the same category I think you almost have to forget about looking for distinctive features and go for the razzmatazz. Dreary products can produce tired ads so why not recognise it from the start? Nudes to sell oil filters is lazy: use a bit more imagination. Limited budgets compel you to make your advertising a little different so stand out from the herd. As a small firm make your product different and your ads distinctive.

The central idea

The core of any ad must be the product or service itself. If you can, sit the product on your desk or get a photo and study it. List all the features. How it is made, the material, colour, function, weight and fitness for purpose. Look at taste, texture, packaging, expected life, durability, originality, replacement value and spare parts, not forgetting the price. If a service, list all the attributes that should appeal to a customer.

But don't worry about some award-winning pun. Most ads state a fairly basic truth and offer permutations on known and tried reasons for buying. Turn back to page 5 to remind youself of some of the basic reasons why people buy. The most successful ads are those that can engender *emotion*.

Figure 4.6   National newspaper ad that appeals to the emotions.
A child is unlikely to buy such a protective case, so the message is
aimed at the parents

Drayton Bird in *Commonsense Direct Marketing* quotes his own idea for an encyclopedia ad. He shows a child running up a path shouting, 'Mummy, I've passed.' What parent wouldn't be touched by the *emotion* generated in that picture and caption?

How to start

You must research your market, customer and the competition quite thoroughly before you are ready to start designing your own ads. Cut your rivals' ads out and analyse the individual appeals. Find out what your prospects read and get a feel for the tone of editorial and ads in what they read. You must strike the right position for your product. Working with a good graphics package, draw the right-size space to prescribe the boundaries you have to work in. Detailed research has shown that:

- Five times as many people read the headline as read the rest of the ad; 80 per cent of your money could be wasted.
- Ads with a headline that promise a benefit are read by four times as many people.
- The reader's eye follows from illustration to headline to copy – so lay out your ad in that order.
- Photographs are more believable than drawings, and the bigger the illustration the more the ad is likely to be noticed.
- Ads with news are recalled by 20 per cent more people – so put that in your headline.
- Long headlines (more than 10 words) are read more than short headlines.
- Specifics are more memorable than generalities. ('72 per cent of housewives preferred Stork to butter' – rather than 'More house-wives prefer', etc.)
- Putting in the price is more memorable.
- Long copy sells more – if it is interesting. If you have a story – why not tell it?
- Putting large chunks of text in CAPITALS and reversed type (white on black) is discouraging to read.
- Whole pages pull in not twice as much but only 70 per cent greater response, which is a comfort to smaller ads where the same principle holds good in proportion. Strangely, one-third page ads pull more than a half.

● Colour is more important than size.
● Only 5 per cent of the readership actually reads your ad.

Start with the headline

Headlines are the most arresting part of any paper. We all tend to scan the paper for a headline that is interesting, then read into the article for more facts. Surely you should adopt the same procedure for advertising. The headline must capture your specific audience, so build that interest into the words. 'How to stop smoking' or 'How to cure baldness' will immediately filter out all those people who don't smoke or have a full head of hair and who are of no interest to you. You are like a butterfly hunter swooping to entrap a rare specimen in your net.

Interrogative or explanatory headlines are useful techniques to ensnare readers:

How to save on fuel bills
How to beat the bookies
How to keep warm in bed
Why is the Whitecliffs Hotel the most popular honeymoon stopover?
Where can you see the latest model?
Can you live on your pension?
What paint do professionals use?
Five reasons why Clegg's Garage won a top award.

You must remember that ads are read for *information*, rarely to pass the time. Make them interesting, give information and *facts*. Avoid headlines that are too clever, obscure or capable of different interpretations. The best ads are not those that necessarily win awards for creative artistry but those that *sell*. This is after all the main, most would say the sole, function of advertising, certainly for small firms. The best headline offers a benefit to answer my perpetual question, 'What's in it for me?'

Don't be misled by quirky headlines like 'Heineken reaches parts that other beers cannot reach.' That message has been repeated in thousands of TV commercials and posters over the years and bears no relation to the budgets or purpose of advertising as small firms understand it. Your ads have to state a simple benefit to an identifiable audience with a strong sales message. Headlines with a topical flavour (news) are read and recalled by a fifth of readers, so if you are announcing a new model, improved performance or can tie it in with a local event – spell it out.

If you put your headline in quotes '–' more readers will notice it. The obvious way to capitalise on this gem of research is to use an endorsement. 'Since I have changed to Archers Compounds my calves have never looked fitter,' says top breeder Joe Smith.

Make no mistake, the headline needs most attention as, without an arresting, relevant eye-grabber, you have wasted your money. If you are able to make a good offer (free trial, two for the price of one) put that in your headline.

Illustrations

Remember that most newspapers use indifferent quality paper so expect that any photo will reproduce significantly worse. The better magazines use a good art paper that delivers excellent pictures. Choose pictures with care, allowing for reduction if you have limited space. Whatever you choose should increase the story interest of your ad and must work with the headline. A golden rule is to show the product in action, if that is appropriate.

'Before' and 'after' illustrations are often telling and this is a technique capable of many variations. Drawings are less believable than photos except when an engineering or complex part needs highlighting, when a good technical drawing comes into its own.

Captions are also widely read but don't repeat what is obvious from the picture. If the picture needs a caption to explain it you are using the wrong picture. Don't neglect the picture agencies, which can supply photos (for a fee) much as libraries supply books. It may avoid commissioning a professional photographer to take that special shot.

Text

If you adopt a telegraphic approach to all your writing you won't stray into unintelligibility. Use short concise words rather than the journalese so beloved by politicians and trade union officials. Say what you mean in direct, simple language.

Remember that 1 million British citizens are illiterate and many of the rest receive their view of the world via the *Sun*.

Make every word mean something. Most of your first efforts are capable of being condensed, I am sure. Don't forget you are paying for that space – wasted words cost money and squeeze out those that *do* count.

The offer

If you can make a good offer this should be your headline. Offers can be anything you like, such as 'Two for the price of one', 'Free trial', 'Free credit', 'Install now, pay later', 'Beat the budget', 'Prize draw' and so on. In inflationary times a powerful argument is 'Buy now at the old price...'.

Remember the benefits

You and I buy things because of what they'll do for *us*. With the sole exception of charity offerings, and in that I include Scout sales of work and PTA Christmas card drives, we part with money because we can see a use for the product. A particular shampoo is not bought because it contains malathion. That's a feature. The benefit is that it kills nits! The benefits of a tungsten-tipped saw blade are that it lasts longer, saves downtime on changing over, and reduces sharpening costs.

It is very easy to fall into the trap of always talking about the features of your product and particularly of a service. It is of little interest that your service vans may all have mobile phones to save van mileage: the benefit to your customer is prompt round-the-clock attention.

By and large, your customers are not interested that you have ISO 9001 for your dry-cleaning business – just that you never lose clothes and give a quick turnround.

Price can be a benefit. If you are selling a product that is going to save someone money, then multiply the savings up. Fifty pence a week is neither here nor there, but £26 over a full year is a headline! Few would go out and buy an encyclopedia on French cooking, but if it is sold every week as a partwork – 'only' £2 every Friday – you've captured an audience. Petrol-saving devices are pushed on the same lines. No one notices 5 per cent off a gallon of petrol, but projected over a year's motoring of 12,000 miles, the savings (in theory) are memorable.

All your advertising should be looked at in terms of customer needs.

Some advertisement techniques

Copywriters use a variety of techniques to get the message over in an effective and memorable manner. A straight headline and text would be confused with the editorial, so papers now insert 'Advertisement' over layouts of this type. Convention has defeated imitation.

USP

First favourite among many advertisers is to find and isolate a *unique selling proposition*, ie a benefit that you alone possess. Enhance and create that so it contains your main message and appeal. Many products are composed of a mix of different benefits, most of which are embodied in the competition. It could become tedious to analyse and compare them all so why not concentrate on just one and highlight that? When I meet a firm for the first time I invariably ask, 'Why do people buy from you?' and not always do they know. It may be because of the range of products, the hours they keep, the in-depth knowledge they possess or a host of attributes. It's often a useful exercise to mount a simple market research exercise and ask customers. Once you know, you can major on that in your advertising. Most adverts are glanced at for about 1½ seconds, so there is little time to present a comprehensive argument!

Before and after

Illustrations that show improved performance before and after treatment can be persuasively telling. This technique can be used for double glazing, paint treatments, lawn fertilisers, hair shampoos, chair covers and many other face-lifts. It can be invaluable for services as distinct from products.

Sell the extreme

Often the best way of selling the benefits of a product is to show it in action. And don't stop at the natural use. Go to the extreme. A

Growth Appeal

Herb/Flower Welly

A superb incentive for kitchen and home related products

Touchline's brightly coloured PVC wellies make fabulous containers for growing herb and flower seeds, giving a new dimension of interest and decoration in the kitchen and home.
Apart from the fun of watching their almost daily growth, the fresh herbs have a genuine practicality in the kitchen. The Herb Welly has a superb visual appeal when printed on pack, making them ideal for redemption offers, etc. A promotional pack includes a Pair of Wellies, 2 packets of seeds and a bag of peat.
The Herb Welly can, of course, be branded with your logo, etc.

TOUCHLINE PROMOTIONS LIMITED, 17 RAYLEAS CLOSE, SHOOTERS HILL, LONDON SE18 3JN. TEL 081-856 1115. FAX 081-319 3035

The use of the unusual. An eye-catching ad in a promotional trade magazine

"Ten reasons to buy a Tanyard quality phone case"

Prices from £12.49

Real leather, including the full lining

Leather bindings

Leather covered steel belt clip

Velcro fastening

Smart & stylish

Crease resistant window

Elastic gusset for different size batteries

Designed to be used in the case

Corners protect against dropping

Range of models that cover 91% of the market

"That's nine. What's the tenth?"
"Money back guarantee if not delighted"

Buy direct from the manufacturers
Satchel, 2 The Tanyard, Street, Somerset
BA10 0HD Tel 01458 42371 Fax 01458 841245
Quality trade enquiries welcomed

VISA   All prices subject to VAT   Access

One way to promote everyday items. Line drawings can often work better than photos – and picking out the details serves to differentiate your product.

STEP THIS WAY FOR A COMPLETE FINISHING SERVICE RIGHT THROUGH TO IN-HOUSE NATIONAL AND INTERNATIONAL MAILING

- Fully automatic cutting, creasing, perforating and embossing up to 920 x 1260mm
- Hand finishing, glueing and assembly
- Programmatic guillotine cutting
- Electronic counting and padding
- Multiheaded drilling, eyeletting and hand stringing
- Shrinkwrapping, folding, collating, enclosing, labelling and addressing for mailing and distribution
- Database Services
- Laser Printing
- Fulfilment
- Hand Packing
- Polythene enveloping

Spama
PRINT FINISHERS

BS5750 Applied for
260 Abbeydale Road
Wembley
Middlesex HA0 1QA
Tel. 081-998 0018 Fax 081-991 5681

A trade mazagine ad – but set in reversed type that is too small to be easily read: most won't bother.

Independent Traveller's World

Seriously Exciting Travel Ideas

Bristol
Watershed Media Centre
10 – 22 Jan 95

●

London
Business Design Centre, Islington
9 – 11 Feb 95

Full Details 0117 930 4440

BARCLAYCARD   *Kiss* 100fm

The newsprint on which this is printed won't take such small type. the same applies to some *Yellow Pages* ads.

Figure 4.7   Examples of the impact of different ad designs

manufacturer selling outdoor tables to pubs could use a rugby team climbing all over them. The publican would hope that this would never occur, but it would ram home the point of strength. If your paint is weather-proof, illustrate it in severe situations. Dulux used it on a lighthouse. I can remember a new type of toughened glass coming out years ago. It was pictured supporting an elephant. No one would use it for that, but the absurd combination made the point very effectively. People will think, 'If it's good enough for that, it must be OK for what I want.'

Endorsements

We can't all afford television personalities to push our turkey joints but there are homelier ways. Extracts from letters from satisfied customers, 'Mrs S of Worthing has told all her friends to rush out and buy Bloggit since this cured her aches', can work wonders. Endorsements are probably more easily used in direct mail because you have more room to quote long extracts. ('The original letters are on our files and open to inspection.') The pools promoters use endorsements widely. A picture of Mr Y from Burnley clutching his cheque for half a million and grinning from ear to ear tends to personalise the message: 'That could be me.' Technical products lend themselves to endorsements as well. 'As used by Rolls-Royce' or even by a defence contractor implies some standing and credence. Obviously, ask the firm's permission first.

The endorsement you use should be easily related to your customer profile. A professional person should be used for selling to technocrats while housewives must be used for washing-up liquid. (Oh dear, how sexist.) The stereotype still rules the world of advertising.

Most firms will have a ready file of endorsements to hand but if none is exactly suitable send out a questionnaire to customers inviting comments and you are certain to get something appropriate. Apart from its being quite unethical, you should never have to invent them.

Comparisons

The selection of products is all a matter of comparison. The consumer does it when deciding which product to buy. He looks at the features and benefits. However, until recently it was considered unethical to indulge in comparative advertising – 'knocking' copy. The motor trade seems to have adopted this method completely, with adverts continually running down the opposition. Manufacturers should surely be able to find enough reasons for buying on their own merits.

Comparison advertising can be successful and ethical if carefully handled. I wouldn't mention competitors by name, as the motor trade does, but by implication. A local double glazing firm competing with the nationals could stress that 'The money you pay goes into the goods, not to pay for TV advertising, commission salesmen or celebrities.'

Newsworthiness

Newsworthiness is very difficult to achieve with long copy dates but the weekly or daily papers will allow your ads to have a topical flavour. You could hit the bull's-eye with this if you look ahead and plan. Changes in legislation, budget tax changes, royal events, are all fairly predictable. A carefully worded ad placed on the same day will attract attention. It all needs flair, imagination and sometimes a bit of luck.

Novelty

An ad can stand out by being out of context. Some unexpected feature pictured in the layout can highlight your message. We're not necessarily back with the nudes but anything you can legitimately pull into your advert that would not normally be expected to be there can be successful. It's our first rule of advertising – attraction. Smirnoff do it with skydivers, White Horse Whisky with white horses. You don't have to go to such extremes. A man knitting or even cooking is worth a second glance. Perfectly reasonable pursuits but not within the normally accepted way of portraying domestic chores.

People matter

Try to portray the product in action, in a real environment. Kitchen designers tend to show yards of gleaming cupboards and shelves and not a soul in sight. Put a bright young housewife preparing food in the picture and it comes to life. You lose a bit of the product but you gain in appeal.

People identify with the subject portrayed. Figures in ads tend to be younger, more handsome and virile than in real life. That's poetic licence. The women's equality organisations are always complaining that you never see a tired, harassed housewife with buttons missing selling products. The reason is that people believe scruffy people sell scruffy goods. Perhaps we see what we want to believe. It's all a fairy-tale world.

Your characters should be believable, with a touch of dressing up. The person using the product should be closely associated with your type of audience. If it's a DIY gadget, pick a man who looks like a time-served tradesman as the model. Capable, gnarled, expressive hands do a lot for a photograph. The way he handles a tool will say a lot too.

If you're involved in handling food, make sure no hygiene regulations are being broken.

Babies are a good attraction especially if you're selling to mothers. There can't be many household products for which you can't work in a good baby shot somewhere in the life of the campaign. Animals are worth the same treatment. How many products can you think of that have had a backcloth of rustic simplicity – a nice clean field of Jerseys or Friesians?

Humour

Anyone who has struggled this far with the narrative will realise I'm a firm convert to a touch of humour: perhaps not in ads for undertakers but that still leaves plenty of scope. As not everyone laughs at the same things it does demand a light touch.

Cartoons

Picture stories can be very successful. I don't know whether that is a reflection on the low standard of education of the readership or whether cartoons stand out on a page of grey text. You don't have to go the whole hog of commissioning a cartoonist to draw up a full strip. A cartoon character, ie one single figure or caricature, can act as the lead in introducing the text. That can become your logo, your instantly identifiable feature. Such logos tend to be animals of the lovable sort – bears, dogs and other household pets. Basset hounds have become indistinguishable from Hush Puppies shoes, so much so that one small boy, observing our two hounds, was heard to remark thoughtfully to his father, 'Do they really make shoes from their ears?'

Illustrators tend to be a freelance breed and most towns have one or more. Your better local printer should be able to suggest one or two. Naturally, there is a concentration around London where most work is.

Figure 4.8 A trade flyer aimed at fan ventilation stockists. The industry is dominated by one major company – the reader will know exactly what the message is. It doesn't have to be spelt out

Inserts can be the most effective of all

As the ubiquitous *Innovations* catalogue has shown, an increasingly popular way of reaching your target audience is by means of a magazine insert. This is a separate card or brochure supplied by you to a carrier journal or customer mailing. Technically, an insert is a loose copy – an inset is one which is bound in. The advantages are obvious:

1. No envelope addressing or list compiling.
2. You have great freedom to design your promotional message.
3. A reply card can be easily incorporated.
4. It is generally the first thing people see when they open the magazine.
5. A decision must be made. Is it read or discarded? A very high proportion are read, unlike ads buried in a back page that may never be seen.

As against the *drawbacks*, which are:

1. Only the first reader tends to see the insert. Inserts are rarely retained. Base your costings on circulation not readership.
2. You are sunk if the reader opens the magazine over the wastepaper basket.
3. The reply mechanism needs some thought. If you're printing on card make sure it is substantial enough to come back through the post. The business reply card must conform to post office preferred sizes. Perforating the card improves response. This is much more expensive than printing on paper, which requires a fold-up return and from which response is much poorer.

Compared with direct mail, inserts enjoy a much better response. The same rules for design still apply: use a good headline, eye-catching illustrations and colour.

The costs vary between magazines, of course, but tend to be based around the page-cost mark. There are, however, bargains to be had among the specialist journals of restricted circulation that often carry little or no advertising anyway. The return rate for these can be very high. For business-to-business promotions-designing, the insert as a fax-back form can generate more response. In my experience most businesses will now use the phone or fax rather than use any reply-paid mechanism. It saves time.

You may have to book up some issues ahead. Periodicals have to ration the number of inserts they will take because of the postal steps. *British Rate and Data* (page 50) will tell you which magazines take an insert.

Position

The page position of your ad is very important. The best and most expensive places are the covers. These are usually booked up for some time ahead and are probably beyond the reach of most small firms.

Local papers love to run features on everything from spring weddings to changing your car. The editorial matter is sometimes painfully thin. The sprat is to hook advertisers to buy space round the article. Be wary. It's your money they're after.

Recent research has shown that it matters little whether you pick a right- or left-hand magazine page, though there is a slight advantage in being nearer the front.

A good spot is next to the *reader's enquiry service* if the paper runs one. Cheapest position is 'run of paper' (ROP), which is anywhere the make-up person can fit it in.

Figure 4.9 Sunday paper ad. Simple but very effective, in that it segments a distinct part of the market and makes it feel wanted. Hill House tell me that this has been one of their most effective ads, better than full colour splashes in more up-market papers

Trade directories and yearbooks need careful thought. Many have modest circulations and few sales are made beyond libraries, and they are cutting back. You will have to do some research among your buyers to find what directories they regularly use – if at all. Some well-produced colour illustrated directories are undoubtedly worth advertising in, as long as there is an appropriate heading. The best place is the spine or the bookmark, but inevitably these are expensive and tend to be booked up.

Use white space

There is always the temptation to fill every bit of usable space on your dearly bought ad with persuasive text. The vast majority of newspapers and journals are printed in black on white paper and therefore carry advertising matter in the same restrictive medium.

By leaving a generous margin around the actual copy you can make *your* ad stand out: simple and very effective in a mass of otherwise anonymous grey text. Test it for yourself. Reach for your local paper and open it at the classified section or any other that carries a lot of advertising. When you open a paper you tend to do so at arm's length and scan before homing in on what looks like an interesting item. Those that are more likely to catch the eye, I would suggest, are the few that stand our clearly from their neighbours.

The concept has, of course, been carried through with whole-page ads and even posters. Large areas of blank or single-colour paper surrounding a short message act as a focus.

Coupons

There are two sorts of coupons beloved in ad-land – *money off* redemption (soap coupons) and *address* coupons. Soap coupons have become a term of derision, perhaps surprisingly, because they undoubtedly work in creating brand allegiance. No, they have little place for small firms. A better variation is to print a discount coupon in your ad to encourage prospects to attend your shop. It has two effects. First, it attracts people, but second, it acts as a test of your advertising. A direct measurement can be made if you place the ads (and key them, see page 139) in different media. Price-off coupons, to manipulate slack periods in restaurants, travel trades, dry cleaning, stately homes and garages, can be very effective. Address coupons, ie requests for literature or sales visits, undoubtedly increase response. We are now straying into *direct response advertising*, which deserves a chapter all of its own (see Chapter 5).

Freephone

Adding a freephone telephone number does increase response when you're competing against other advertisers who want you to pay for the call. In fact the whole tenor of encouraging response has shifted from reply-paid coupons to telephone sales. Many businesses that sell off the page or operate from catalogues run evening or night-time services either themselves or through one of the burgeoning call-answering agencies. This is not a cheap service and at present few small firms are likely to take advantage of it. The monthly charge is probably going to be a minimum of £300 with an individual call charge of £1 or so extra.

Freephone costs are at present £25 connection and £50 quarterly. Daytime phone rates are charged at 12p a minute, 9p in the evening. If you want a distinctive number then there is a one-off fee of £300.

How do you say it?

Having covered some of the techniques I must come back to the language you use. Advertising is salesmanship in print. The most successful adverts have been those in the language we speak and use every day. It's the natural way. Just because you go into print doesn't change the manner of presentation. You're not a scriptwriter for the six o'clock news. Forget about that classical pun or double entendre. You must think about the *product*, your *audience* and what the customer needs. Those are the three vital elements. Avoid words that have become distorted or played out through over-use: fantastic offer, unre-peatable bargain, exceptional opportunity, and unique. Would you use those words in speech? Try to find something *new* to say in your copy. Make it interesting and lead the reader on – inform. Nobody reads dull ads. Always be truthful and don't make claims you can't substantiate. Wild and extravagant claims will be seen to be just that. People must believe in the product.

Write in the present tense and assume the consumer already has the product. Not: 'This hedge trimmer will save you hours of arm-aching work.' Better is: 'This hedge trimmer saves you…'

Remember value

Don't talk in terms of price – talk about *value* and worth. The price of a pressure cooker may be £50 (or rather £49.95), but its value is a saving in time to the busy housewife, a reduction in fuel bills and a versatile extra pot for the imaginative chef. A visit to a health farm is the way of relaxation for stressed executives, to purify the bloodstream and recharge the batteries. Air conditioning in cars stops you getting hot and bothered before important meetings.

David St John Thomas (of David & Charles) tells of the care needed in designing a book. The pages must be carefully weighted to give the right feel, and to be seen to be worth the price asked. Books can be dramatically thick or thin depending on the paper and binding chosen yet still have the same content.

It is often in this critical area of how you present value that sales are made or lost.

Cooperative advertising

Newcomers to marketing quickly realise that more than half the cost of promotion often lies in the idea and origination. It is not much more expensive to order 5,000 leaflets than 1,000. How much better then to club together and form cooperative groups and attack the market under one heading or brand name. The motor trade have done this for years. When a new model is launched the manufacturer buys a large amount of space and gets the dealers to buy a portion of the ad for their own location. Collectively, perhaps 30 dealers in the franchise can make more impact than any one individually.

It works particularly well in the tourist trade. Farm holiday operators can form a group in a region and product a joint leaflet, but only one reference point is given for bookings. It is a simple matter for one person to allocate parties to separate farmhouses and it makes booking more attractive for the clients.

English vineyards have never had an easy time, contending with our climate, snobbery and increasing cheap imports. Those that have survived rely on a large element of retail – or farmgate sales. The best way is to join together in association, form wine trails and produce attractive leaflets aimed at the educated tourist.

There are lots of opportunities in cooperative advertising that have been barely touched. Garages that rent out part of their forecourt to allied activities like valeting, van hire, trailer manufacturer, etc, could combine to draw more prospects to their doors. Non-competing industrial products could be combined in mailings and part of the packaging sold to other producers to advertise their products. Cooperative mailings are a valuable, cost-effective way for small firms to reach identifiable markets.

The Internet is ideal for working cooperatively as you must continuously look for links to other sites. Depending on your activity you could link with your trade association, tourist board, local council or even village group. For an extreme example click on LondonTown.com and you will see links off to all manner of sites, from tourist buses to city farms, restaurants to airports.

The *Yellow Pages* problem

Despite the best efforts of Thomson, *Yellow Pages* must be the most commonly used advertising medium for any business. Almost every phone in the country must have a yellow book nearby. If you want a quick lesson in advertising technique pick up any edition and be amazed. If you happen to be engaged in double glazing, kitchen installation or motor insurance, how are you going to get your ad to stand out? For example, the Bristol edition has 15 pages of double glazing and 41 pages devoted to insurance. Many firms will tell you that *Yellow Pages* tends to attract a certain type of caller: those who want it as cheap as possible, and who are prepared to spend an hour on the phone – preferably using your 0800 number – to save a few bob. Well-established companies I know believe that worthwhile business is obtained by being more pro-active – targeting by their own sales force or by direct mail, rather than by hoping for casual contact.

I would entirely accept that *YP* is invaluable for the distress purchase and occasional capital items for which we have no regular supplier. Once you are competing with many other almost identical suppliers it becomes vital to make your ad stand out. You may need to stress your location and convenience (all things being equal consumers will pick the nearest), your USP, and avoid crowding too many messages into a tight space. Leave room for the ad to breathe in what is a crowded page.

Talking Pages is an enigma to me. Though they claim a million calls a month I could not quote the phone number to you and I doubt whether many can. It is very selective and arbitrary (at least every business phone subscriber gets a free *YP* entry). For my own discipline of marketing there is just a single agency listed for the whole of Somerset – and that has received no business from it. I will accept there is a use if you are needing a service outside your area.

Project a corporate image

You may be a brand-new small firm but you can still have a corporate image. This grand term describes the face you present to the world, usually in terms of printed material – posters, letterheads, sales tickets, brochures and signs – all of which conform to a master plan. There is a single style of lettering and logos and use of colours. Some extend the term to describe the company philosophy – the *corporate identity* – which covers staff selection, training and attitudes. Clean overalls, perhaps with the firm's name on the pocket, are effective if they are regularly laundered. Small firms are usually content to stop at the printed matter.

Most firms grow haphazardly. The first item of print is often a business card, sometimes produced in a rush, perhaps by a friend. Little thought is given to style. Letterheads and invoices follow, perhaps from another printer, which will produce its own version, and so it goes on.

How much more professional if it were all planned from the start. Strangely enough, it hardly costs any more, but your image is greatly enhanced. There is a feeling of hanging together, belonging in one family. People recognise your literature without actually reading it. Try it yourself. We all recognise the Ford or Boots sign long before we can actually read the word, the shape and outline are so familiar.

Presentation is very important. For mail order, where the customers never see the proprietor, the sales letter, design and weight of paper are vital. It always depresses me to see good products undersold. For small runs – 5,000 or so – the cost differential between a good paper and a poor one is slight but the advantages enormous.

It hardly needs stressing that your Web site should look as professional as your budget allows. With most business transacted at a distance, it is important to add an address and telephone number (not a box number) to improve credibility.

What's in a name?

Corporate image starts with the *trading name*. Many proprietors simply trade under their own name. Fine. If you are well known locally, why throw away that advantage? Otherwise try to convey in the title what you are doing. Somerset Wholesale is not very illuminating but Somerset Electrics is better. 'Crafts' is becoming a bit of an overworked word. If you are only dealing in your own locality, build a local feature into your title.

A memorable title without being too obscure is worth aiming for.

Business cards should be brief and encapsulate your activities. There are several firms which will print your picture (if you are vain) on the card as well as your name to help recall. Better perhaps to portray your product. Flashy cards can be supplied on metal, photo-etched or on gold and silver foil. Take your time and look around.

Colours

Colour is important. Browns, greens and yellow generally denote rural simplicity not to say folksiness. The deep purples, reds and black imply wealth and opulence. If you are an exporter check that the theme colour you are using means the same thing abroad. White in Japan means death. Packages for display in supermarkets should be compatible with the lighting.

Don't hide your light

Few firms have no form of transport but there are a lot of anonymous grey vans running about: trade vehicles with all that lovely bare space demand imaginative signwriting. People pay good money to have their name on a bus. The arrival of large-format inkjet printers now means that superb full-colour graphics can be produced on vinyl to cover everything from vans to curtain-sided artics. Colour fastness should be better than five years.

Once you've paid for the display – keep it clean.

A painter and decorator asked me to help, once. I asked about his board and he ruefully produced a filthy battered object with one side hanging off. Not the best advertisement for his trade.

Put your visitors at their ease. Display some product samples or pictures of completed work in the reception so they can learn about you. If you don't manage to sell them anything first time at least they'll go away with a pleasant image of harmony, competence and professionalism.

Keep the outside of the building swept and free from rubbish. Tidy the front office and don't let mechanics sit on the front office chairs in their greasy overalls. That visitor may 'only' be a rep – but he'll carry away an image of the firm that could make or mar your business. He could even be that buyer you've been trying to hook.

Premises signs – what you're allowed to do

Signs outside the premises are also important for your image but are often neglected. It is important that your premises are clearly signed. The planning authorities control what you are allowed to display through the Advertisement Regulations (part of the Town and Country Planning Acts). Some signs are deemed exempt from control. These are:

1. An advertisement sign on your own premises giving the name and description of what you do. To avoid putting in an application, the highest part of the sign must be below the first floor window sill. In certain Areas of Special Control – conservation areas, for example – the area of the sign must not exceed 10 per cent of the wall surface up to 12 feet above the ground.
2. You are allowed two signs if there are two frontages to your premises.
3. Do not use letters or figures more than 0.75 m high (or 0.3 m in an Area of Special Control).
4. A single flagpole (why not?).

Figure 4.10 Signs that work. An AIDS shop in Soho, fish restaurant and nostalgic bike

Any illumination of a sign requires permission.

Highway signs are something else. Tourist enterprises in particular rely on clear advance warning and directional signs to pull in passing trade. There is invariably conflict between the highways department (at County Hall), the owner of the business, local planning officers and the inevitable do-gooders in the village. Apart from certain permitted signs for stately homes, youth hostels, licensed caravan sites and the like, all other directional signs need planning permission. Practice seems to vary between counties, and even districts, on how blind an eye they turn to rogue signs. You stand more chance of success if you produce a well-designed sign, not too flamboyant or large, placed in a friendly farmer's field rather than on the highway itself. Never tack it to a telegraph pole or highway signpost. Signs on the highway, as distinct from the other side of a hedge or ditch, are controlled by the highways department, which tends to take a much stricter view than the local planning authorities.

Your county tourist officer may have worked out an official policy on paying for authorized signs. In consultation with the highway men (I don't mean it like that) they may allow you to pay for a proper brown and white sign. You have to convince them that there is a reasonable throughput of visitors and that people would have difficulty finding you otherwise. As ever, road safety is paramount.

I should add that every planning officer dreads questions on the Regulations. They are terribly involved and arguments often centre around the minutiae.

Read the free booklet 'Outdoor Advertisements & Signs' provided by your planning office.

Buying print

Your corporate image depends largely on the quality of your printed matter. Printers are a fortunate breed. Every business needs them. If it's only a humble business card and a letterhead then a printer has a job. Unfortunately, a mystique has grown up around printing, which the industry has no interest in dispelling. Despite the arrival of the Web, the printed word is likely to remain the main method of communication for sales and marketing techniques for some time to come.

Printers come in all shapes and sizes. Top of the list are the book printers who can turn a roll of paper into a paperback on one machine.

At the other end of the scale are backroom part-timers turning out the parish magazine or raffle tickets. It is important to understand that 'horses for courses' was rarely more true than for print.

The jobbing printer

Always ask to see samples of a printer's work. You will only get a feel of his technical ability, flair and level in the market by studying completed jobs. You may not be aware yourself what good print looks like or how a simple leaflet can be turned into an attractive, arresting piece of propaganda.

Unfortunately, many small jobbing printers have been crushed to boredom by years of churning out jumble-sale leaflets and school programmes. They've forgotten how to dress up a mundane product with a bit of sharp artwork. Everything has the same ruled border. And don't talk about colours other than black! Perhaps it is unfair to blame printers too much. The margins are very slim at that end of the game and the client is usually only interested in one thing – the cost.

Figure 4.11 These upside down ads go in cycles: normally I would say people don't bother to turn the page. However, the advertiser assures me he has a good response. Maybe the message helps

The key to good print

If you don't know what good printing is, go and see some *graphic designers*, the freelance variety.

They have to live by their skills and most are way ahead of any back-street printer. The cost of printing lies largely in the origination – the artwork, design and film preparation. Graphic designers now have their beloved Apple Macs, where everything is done on screen and can be transferred without a trace of Cow Gum or getting near a scalpel. The actual machine time is of less importance unless you are into long runs. Once you have the artwork this forms the basis for all your printing. The letterheading design can be carried through to your business card, invoices, compliment slips, delivery notes, packaging, etc. You may get years of use out of some original designs. It is sensible to leave the designer to choose his or her own printer and oversee the job – but don't abdicate the responsibility of proofreading.

Discuss the purpose

Printers will usually tailor the job to your price providing a sensible job can be done. Let your printer know your budget. He will ask the purpose of the job: no point in running expensive handbills if they are to be given away at a children's funfair.

Paper sizes will be discussed, and weight and surface. You have the choice of one ink colour (usually black) or several. Sometimes the addition of just one 'spot' colour will highlight part of a brochure very effectively.

You could well use several printers for different items. The printing industry is in a transitional phase at present with advances in digital printing set to take over from offset litho. There are now many dot.com print-buying sites where you can do simple things like design your own business card and get it next day, or even complete brochures. Most printers now never see artwork; it is all done on screen and disk. Files are zipped and sent by ISDN all over the country. Increasingly print plants go direct from screen to platemaking (ctp:computer to plate), doing away with the film making up: the buzz word is 'digital'. Turnround times are shorter and costs should be more competitive.

Don't be mean with printing costs. Most of this book is geared to harbouring your money but I don't believe that skimping pounds on print is ever worthwhile. It shows. This is not to say that every job needs the full colour treatment – far from it. Try to use the most appropriate image. Full-colour brochures will be expected for an upmarket kitchen designer but a handbill giving notice of an opening sale can be treated more economically. Think hard about the number of leaflets that you will need. The first 1,000 will be the most expensive because they must bear all the costs of artwork, colour separation, plate making, etc. The 'run on' will be considerably cheaper, perhaps two-thirds of the first cost. There is no point in running back to the printer each time you want a further batch. You will be paying for setting-up time, cleaning down the machine, folding and guillotining on each occasion. Work out a sensible requirement for at least the next two years.

Proofreading

Half the mistakes occur with poorly prepared copy. The temptation is to get it away to the printer and feel it is 'under way'. You will only be compounding your errors if you do that. Always give *typewritten* copy to your printer. Keep corrections to the absolute minimum.

Corrections before platemaking are usually simple. Never *proof-read* on the printer's premises unless it is a very simple job. Take the proof home to a quiet room. Check and recheck. There is nothing worse than having a misspelling staring at you after the job has run. Double-check phone numbers. And don't just check from your typing – check with your source. You may have transposed a number. The printer should provide a slip to say that you have proofread so there can be no dispute later.

Desktop publishing

The great revolution in printing has been the swift arrival and cost-effective solutions of DTP. A quite modest PC can use advanced software that a few years ago would have been the preserve of major print houses. Everyone can now – theoretically – design and print their own brochures and in colour. You have to recognise that having the facility to do your own printing has not brought with it the in-built design and creative ability to match the output of a professional graphic designer. I am going to rebut the many DTP advertisers' claims that gaining cheap access to thousands of clip-art symbols and £50 scanners has enabled any small business to produce its own professional print. Invariably, all too many of the results are disappointing. If it takes three years' college training to turn out an inexperienced graphic designer than how can a busy small business owner hope to compete? Digital cameras are also being marketed into this sector with ever decreasing costs but somewhat extravagant claims. Yes, they certainly have their place in terms of speed and convenience, but if you need quality, contrast and pinpoint sharpness then the conventional film camera is still some way ahead unless your digital camera cost more than £2,000. My own modest software gives me a choice of several hundred fonts, but I have painfully learnt that I am some way from mastering the art. DTP is wonderful for in-house price lists and newsletters, but where you need to reach out to a critical audience, then still please be prepared to pay for a professional.

Some printing terms

While accepting that a little knowledge can be a dangerous thing, the following common terms may help you to communicate better with your printer.

Artwork. Almost extinct, but the general term for the output of a studio – graphics, illustrations, etc. *Camera-ready artwork* means everything laid out and pasted up ready for the camera. Invariably now it is all on disk.

Bleed. Not a nursing term but an extension of the print area to the edge of the page, in fact beyond, as the excess will be trimmed off: hence 'bleed off'. Usually used with a solid colour or photo.

Colour separation. Photographic copying through colour filters to provide (usually) four negatives from which colour blocks or plates will be made. The quality of colour work depends largely on the skill with which the separations are matched and balanced. Digital printing – ctp or computer to plate – is quickly making this intermediate process redundant among the more innovative printers.

Copy. Textual matter provided for typesetting; the 'body'.

Four-page cover. A baffling term – refers to the cover of a brochure which wraps around front and back. It comprises four pages referred to as cover 1 (the front), cover 2 (inside front cover), cover 3 (inside back cover), and cover 4 (outside back cover).

Half-tones. Black-and-white illustrations that have been photographed through a screen, and a block or plate made. The size of the screen will determine the quality of the finished article, depending on the paper used.

ISDN. The rapid and clean method of transferring graphic files through telephone lines.

Justified type. Type that is spaced to leave straight edges on both margins. Formerly used for all printed matter but it is now quite common to see much of today's material (except books) unjustified on the right, ie ranged left. Occasionally the left-hand margin only will be left unjustified – called 'justified right' or 'ranged right': regarded as 'arty'.

Landscape. Illustration in which the width exceeds the height; 'portrait' is the opposite.

Lower case. Small letters, not CAPITALS (or caps), which are called upper case.

Offset litho. The most widely used method of printing today among small printers. A thin metal (or occasionally paper) plate is photo-chemically prepared from your artwork or text via a process camera. Once the plate is made there can be no alterations to it, so corrections must be made early on if great expense is not to be incurred.

Page. In printers' terms one surface of a sheet, thus one sheet of paper equals two pages. Be careful when numbering. Technically, every page will be counted even if not printed, so the front cover of a paper-covered brochure will be page 1 and the first right-hand interior page will be number 3. Bad numbering causes mistakes!

Perfect binding. The final process after printing that glues the pages into the cover. Often carried out by specialist trade finishers.

Plate. Thin aluminium or polyester-coated sheet that carries the image used in litho printing.

Print size. The measure of type size. 72 points make 1 inch, so 6 point type is $\frac{1}{12}$ inch high. Different measures may be used overseas.

Proof. The first sheet of the finished set job, to be read through for mistakes.

Ream. 500 sheets.

Reverse types. Type that is reversed out, ie, white lettering on a black background. Harder to read, especially in small letters.

Saddle stitched. The common form of stapling a leaflet on the centre fold, unlike stab-stitch where pages are stapled near the left-hand edge.

Screen. A glass screen inserted between the process camera and the photo to produce the negative for plate or block making. This breaks up the picture into dots or lines. The higher the screen number the finer the screen.

Serif type is the most legible type-style to use. Long copy set in sans serif repels readership. I have yet to see a newspaper or book set in this type, so why break convention?

Typeface. The style or design of the type. Times Roman, Helvetica, Univers, etc. Type also comes in different *weights* or thickness.

Photography

Closely allied to printing is photography. At the time of writing, the price of digital cameras is dropping rapidly. The cheap ones are fine for record shots and home snaps. In a marketing context, where the printer cannot improve, only reduce, the quality of a photograph, the finished printed brochure is largely dependent on the original. The press photographers have taken to digital photography by storm, but their main criterion is deadlines. The result is instantly available and can be wired from anywhere. Unless, like the press boys, you are prepared to spend over £2,000 on a digital camera, then I would – at present – stick to film.

You will need photographs of your product for your leaflets and when you come to exploit the media, but photography is a specialist field and not for the Instamatic user. Black-and-white prints are best for newsprint and perhaps your own brochures if you cannot run to colour. Many people will tell you that you can take a black and white off a colour picture – but only if it is of good contrast. When in doubt, stick to black and white. I like to use Ilford XP2 rated at 400ASA, which is developed in the C41 process. It gives excellent latitude in poor light. *Outside* shots can be taken by most practised amateurs. The normal rules of photography need to be followed. Get close in, avoid fussy backgrounds, show some human interest, beware reflections and shadows. Most important are prints of good contrast (muddy prints don't reproduce) and needle sharpness.

Above all, make photos interesting and tell a story. I can recall a major company sending in a photo of its latest export order. It showed a pile of crates on the dockside. Goodness knows what was inside.

Interiors are much more tricky. Lighting needs to be professionally managed. Some objects such as jewellery, glassware and architectural models are extremely difficult to bring to life. Anything involving machine processes requires a lot of experience to make interesting.

Black-and-white prints need to be no larger than half-plate size (or 5 by 7 inches) and glossy. Quality colour magazines prefer transparencies. Keep staples and pins well away from prints. Use a self-adhesive label on the back of the photo with the details to identify it: never write directly on the resin back as it may show through or transfer to the next print.

Photographers tend to work alone. Go for a commercial or industrial specialist rather than the home town weddings photographer. As usual, ask to see samples of his or her work. Try to retain the negatives otherwise you'll have to go back continually for reprints. Some tend to charge a fairly high fee for this, whereas if you have kept the negatives you can go direct to a local photo laboratory. If you are really impoverished, go along to the local amateur photographic club. There are bound to be some keen lads and lasses looking for some revenue to offset an expensive hobby. But, as in life, you get what you pay for.

Finally, if you are in the field of producing one-offs, be it furniture or specialist joinery, pictures or pots, build up a portfolio of record shots that you can show future customers. A digital camera here is ideal for use on your Web site. Build up a photo album that you can carry around with you. It will be invaluable as the years go by.

Product liability

The advertiser must always be aware of the implications of product liability. It has not reached the litigious levels of the United States, but cannot be ignored. I must also draw your attention to the stringent hygiene regulations that now encompass all food manufacture, preparation and handling. The defence of due diligence will only hold water if thorough examination and identification of all the hazard points have taken place. Trading Standards and Environmental Health Officers are there to help and advise in a free consultative capacity. Importers will be sued for defects – they cannot disclaim liability simply because they had not been involved in the manufacture.

The main points are:

- Don't make claims like 'So simple a child could understand'. You are laying yourself wide open to rebuttal.
- Instructions should be crystal clear both on the packet and on the article if possible.
- Textiles must carry fibre content, labelling and washing instructions.
- Because the Acts cover the European Union, if you are exporting to another country in it you must double-check translations. It is now possible, for example, for a Frenchman to sue you as manufacturer in a French court for goods exported to France that have a product defect.
- The CE mark must be shown, certifying compliance with European Standards.

Aside from advertising, it is worth mentioning that you must keep records for 10 years and be ready to institute a product recall operation if necessary. On the plus side, insurance companies are as yet taking a fairly relaxed attitude and many conventional policies already cover product liability. The premiums seem modest – unless you want to export to the United States.

Packaging and point of sale

For the small firm packaging can be an expensive nightmare. Despite the best efforts of environmentalists, packaging is still a vital part of getting stockists to list your product and attract the consumer. It must be attractive, informative, protective, functional, convenient and help sell the goods. Labelling is getting ever more complicated in terms of type size, ingredients, care instructions, CE marks, bar codes, nutritional information and place of origin. And don't forget the influence of colour under different display lighting, and connotations in different countries if you are exporting.

You may need two sorts of packaging: a tough outer to protect in transit, and that which is seen on the shelf. Packaging suppliers, like printers, specialise in different types. For small runs you will probably have to use a wholesaler, but for specially designed and printed boxes go direct. Like printing, the unit cost will only come down if you order long runs. For example, full-colour labels of a reasonable size will cost about a penny, but only if you order 100,000. Before embarking on any packaging it is best to see your stockist and ask what they are looking for. Look at how the competition is displaying its wares. For example, some products are designed for specific racks, and if yours does not fit, it won't reach the shelves. Box makers tend to stick to either corrugated or solid board; some do complex colour printing, others stick to basics. There are now few willing to produce short, hand-made runs.

Part of the cost is making the cutter, so for simple boxes a good tip is to ask the box maker what standard runs he is doing and ask that the machine be left running for another five minutes for your order.

There is a good theory that delicate goods – jam in jars, for example – should be just shrink-wrapped on a tray base, so that the many handlers can see that CARE: GLASS! means what it says. Transit packs need 'This way up' and any other instructions – no hooks, or do not stack more than three high. Most goods are now shrink-wrapped and palletised for ease of handling.

Care leaflets

If instructions for assembly are involved, get the 'village idiot' to check one through without reference to you. It is often quite surprising how the simplest instruction is overlooked – because you know what is coming next. Where possible, screen print instructions on the product as well as a separate leaflet. Pictograms are also helpful.

Trading standards officers can advise (free) on what legislation demands of leaflet information, though interpretation seems to differ between authorities.

Point of sale

POS display material is provided by the manufacturer to the stockist to highlight the goods at the critical moment of decision: the point of sale. A trip round any grocer's stockroom will highlight that there is more waste here than in almost any other sphere of marketing activity. You will see leaflet dispensers, posters, racks, price lists, coasters, show-cards, catalogues – down to Open/Closed door signs. Some POS material will be very helpful and appreciated, but please talk to your stockist before rushing into print. The POS Centre at 73 Weir Road, London SW19 8UG (020 8879 3070) stocks a wide range. *Shop Equipment News* (publishers EMAP) is a good place to look for additional suppliers.

Franchising

Franchising is a term with many meanings, but in this context is a method of expanding a business using other people's energy and capital. J Lyons' Wimpy Bars was the first British company to exploit the concept, but there have been many other high-street names following in their wake. Companies such as Dyno-Rod, Body Shop, Prontaprint and most of the fast food chains are all franchise operations. Most of them are service orientated and anything near the high street demands a lot of capital.

The banks like them because, unless you are one of the first franchisees (the person who takes the franchise), there should be a proven track record. Failures should be fewer. The British Franchise Association is the regulating body (Thames View, Newtown Road, Henley-on-Thames, Oxfordshire RG9 1HG: 01491 578049), though its authority is periodically challenged. Not everyone belongs. Potential entrants should go in with both eyes open as there are still franchise adverts that make it seem all very simple. Ask to see audited accounts and lists of existing franchise holders. Go and interview some of them.

Franchisors should likewise not see franchising as a quick route to expanding a business idea. It needs patient and skilled management to iron out all the bugs before attracting innocents to part with their money. You should run several pilot operations for at least a year to prove the concept. A thorough operations manual and audited accounts will be needed. It helps to get the franchise department of your bank involved so that it can endorse the operation.

All too many franchises are close copies of existing operations. A few years ago print shops followed by fast food outlets were all the rage. Too many similar schemes can make a nonsense of profit projections. Most important, of course, is the marketing support and training provided from the centre. Many franchisees have not been in business before, let alone have a nose for marketing.

There are several magazines devoted to franchising (but they never seem to print bad news) and two trade shows. Research first.

Further sources

Incentive Today, 2–6 Fulham Broadway, 3rd floor Broadway House, London W6 1AA; 020 7610 3001.

Packaging Today, Angel Business Communications, Kingsland House, 361 City Road, London EC1V 1PQ; 020 7417 7400.

Franchise Magazine (consumer publication) Franchise House, 56 Surrey Street, Norwich NR1 3FD; tel: 01603 620301; fax: 01603 630174; E-mail: fds@norwich.com.

Franchise exhibitions are organised by the Venture Marketing Group, Carlton Plaza, 111 Upper Richmond Road, London SW15 2TJ; 020 8394 5100; Web site: www.franinfo.co.uk.

All the major banks have franchise departments.

The British Promotional Association Web site: www.bpma.co.uk (to find those elusive and imaginative gifts).

The Institute of Sales Promotion Web site: www.isp.org.uk (for industry views on this sector).

Summary

- Who and where is your target audience?
- How can you reach them, what do they read?
- What segment of the market are you talking to?
- What do they need?
- What are the benefits?
- Position the product in the right market slot.
- Research the competition, customers and rival ads.
- As a small firm, make your products different and your ads distinctive.
- Remember AIDA (Attention, Interest, Desire, Action; see page 94).
- Put your promise in the headline. Ads that promise no benefit don't sell.
- Write factually, honestly and simply, using short words rather than long. Give plenty of product information.

- Avoid too many capitals, reversed type and cluttered layout; make your ad easy to read.
- Use specifics rather than generalities.
- Test, test, test but don't change more than one thing at a time. Once you've settled on a formula leave it alone till response falls. Repetition is reputation.
- Don't make your ads all image and no information.

5

Direct response marketing

When a little girl asked me what two and two make I'm supposed to have answered, 'It depends if you're buying or selling'.

Lew Grade

It is dawning on many small firms that the Internet may not be the easy way to market that it has been held out to be. If a fraction of the venture capital thrown at many of these dot.coms in the last few years had been spent simply on mailing brochures, the returns would have been dramatically different. 'A fool and his money are soon parted' has never been more true than for these overnight entrepreneurs. The glamour and excitement of easy riches have clouded the judgement of many who should have known better. This chapter examines more tried and proven methods that fall under the heading of direct response: maybe not so glamorously, but less prone to disaster.

The main object for most of us running a business is to make increased profits with less hassle. As communications have become more sophisticated and generally lower in price, the route for many small firms has been to develop closer relationships with their end customer. This has come to be known as *direct response marketing* where you make the offer direct, rather than through intermediaries.

It therefore covers the exacting and exciting areas of direct mail, selling off the page, mail order, telesales and party plan among others. It is not only of interest to manufacturers, as much of the huge growth in direct mail over the last 10 years has been in the previously staid areas of insurance, financial planning, holidays and health care. The service sector is fully aware of the benefits of developing a personal approach.

Two major areas of consumer spending – the grocery and DIY/hardware/houseware trades – have become alarmingly contracted to multiple chains: groceries in the hands of Sainsbury's, Tesco, Safeway, etc and DIY in the hands of B&Q, Texas, Great Mills, etc. Both these consumer-led sectors are now effectively closed to the small firm. In addition, the food wholesale chain is dominated by giants like Booker, finding it difficult to accommodate smaller operations.

These developments since the 1980s have forced those who wish to survive to look at fresh ways of marketing their wares. In the case of specialist foods, for example, Organic 2000 has set up a boxed delivery service based on regional distribution points to take vegetables direct from the farmer to the customer, bypassing the multiples. The customer gets a fresher, better product and the grower gets not just a more realistic price, but the satisfaction of seeing his or her produce appreciated.

For the manufacturer, Britain is a well-developed country with road and rail networks to reach most parts (unless you live in the Western Isles). Traditional methods are to move goods from the manufacturer to a wholesaler who sells on to a retail stockist. But there is a conflict here built into the system. The wholesalers may carry thousands of lines and can rarely do justice to all. Naturally, they will tend to stock brand leaders and those that give most profit. Retailers do not want to be caught out with out-of-date or unfashionable stock so tend to under, rather than over, order. Both tend to be unadventurous and stick to what they know. Unfortunately, manufacturers usually require long lead times to place raw materials, design and produce, and cannot deliver at the turn of the tap. The small firm caught in this dilemma is rarely able to influence stock levels by offering sufficiently juicy discounts or long payment terms.

Conventional distribution works well with an established, calculated market where demand is evenly spread. It tends to break down to the detriment of the small firm where product costs are high (nobody want to buy them in) and the demand is scattered or highly seasonal or fluctuating.

Direct response and conventional marketing are not mutually exclusive as one frequently can help propel the other. A mail-out to retailers can encourage more orders through the wholesale chain – *pull through*. A telephone sales campaign to selected department store buyers can achieve the same thing.

This chapter will look at the varieties of direct marketing that can be profitably executed by small firms:

- Mail order.
- Direct mail.
- Telephone sales.
- Door to door.
- Party plan.

For the small firm direct marketing has obvious advantages: flexible hours can be worked; part-time staff can be brought in for rush jobs; cash flow can be improved and, potentially, sales can be made more immediately profitable. Direct mail and mail order do not need lavish premises in the high street. Sometimes it is a positive advantage not to be there. More people, I suspect, will happily send for Fair Isle jumpers to the remoteness of Scotland than to an address in Slough.

The biggest advantage of promotion by direct mail over other methods is surely the ability to *test*. So much of advertising is hard to quantify that this feature should come as a godsend to small firms. Any aspect of the mailing can be changed (offer, brochure, sales letter) and the response directly measured. Not only can the effect of changes be accurately recorded but the result is quickly known. There are no long waits for agents or distributors to react.

Don't neglect your old customers

The most profitable way of expanding sales is by selling more products to your existing customers, not by continually hunting for fresh clients. We are all creatures of habit. Provided we've had good service we tend to go back to the same supplier. All the volume motor manufacturers, for example, like to cover the range, from cheap small car to luxury saloon, in the hope that the purchase of one model will lead to another.

It takes money to keep hunting for more names to influence through promotion and advertising. How much simpler to mail out fresh opportunities to contented known customers who will come back and buy more of the same or some of a similar product.

The openings are there but how many take them? Think of all those firms sending out monthly invoices and never using the same stamp to push more products. All it takes is a handbill and an order form. I have a monthly account with an oil company and its statement arrives every six months. I happen to know that it also owns a hardware store, garage and gift shop but the company is very shy about letting me know what bargains are on offer.

There are a number of areas where businesses could exploit their existing direct links and make more money:

1. Technical reps doing service or repair work. Are they trained to sell? Frequently they are in the best position of all to generate further business. I am often amazed to see businesses firmly divided between sales and service staff. Is there not common ground here?

2. Always look for add-on products to sell. The electric drill ushered in a range of labour-saving devices from sanders to polishers, lathes and circular saws: it's the attachments that make the money. Make the first purchase – the drill – and you will be hooked on all the accessories till you have a complete home workshop. Try to get people to buy a set. Franklin Mint does this with china plates, spoons and thimbles. Collectables.

3. Anything related to return coupons or guarantee cards gives a ready-made bank of names. Mail out something that will harmonise with the original product.

4. Any business that regularly mails out statements or newsletters. If you are really stumped for offers sell the facility to others.

Where the profit lies

The only reason for adopting a direct approach is to make more profit. The response to direct mail is often quoted as between 1 and 2 per cent, although even my puny efforts have helped to generate 17 per cent to DIY outlets. A return of ½ per cent can be perfectly profitable if the unit cost is highly priced. The response rates are therefore basic to the whole operation. One of the major attractions of direct mail is that your costs are easily calculated. You can get quotes from printers, designers, list owners and packers. Postage costs are known. The only variable is the response rate: but you can test a representative sample and predict the eventual profitability. Everything can be varied and tested: your offer, the goods, the audience and the price. You are in control, dealing direct with your prospect.

A comparison can be made with selling through distributors with their margins and promoting direct. Whichever method is adopted, and it may well be a part combination of both, aim for a long-term strategy. No one expects you to make a profit from your first mailing as you are initially looking for customers you can sell something else to. Your first response costs will be high as you are looking for customers with the right needs. Successive mailings that have been honed to converts will be considerably more responsive. This is where the profit lies.

Off-the-page advertising

The mail order industry is dominated by the catalogue companies, GUS, Littlewoods, Freemans, etc. Around 90 per cent of the market is cornered by these lavish producers of home catalogues and something over 80 per cent of the sales are on credit.

As the cost of colour printing has reduced and computerisation has made life simpler, the mail order catalogue market has become much more specialised. I have before me catalogues covering kites, cooking accessories, quality paper, educational software and inevitably *Innovations*. There are now many opportunities to exploit specialist areas and develop profitable businesses. If every customer's order is broken down into a multitude of data – age, sex, size, colour, fashion, use, etc – you can buy in or make an item that you can mail out specifically to that niche of the market. Wastage is cut to a minimum and you develop a very close and profitable relationship.

Let's look at where many small firms start off – selling 'off the page' from small space ads placed in special interest magazines or the more general *Exchange & Mart*. The national newspapers have their own truncated version in their 'Postal Bargains' slot. They all present the chance to reach millions of readers at a moderate cost. But whether they pull or not is up to you. To summarise the drawbacks first:

1. Black-and-while newsprint gives limited scope for creative ability.
2. The space allowed in many of the slots is not sufficient for products that require a lengthy explanation.
3. Space is often booked well in advance, particularly near Christmas.

4. Quite rightly, you have to abide by the codes of practice that cover mail order advertising, but practices seem to differ between papers.

The Mail Order Protection Scheme

All adverts that ask for *money in advance of the goods*, with the exception of classified ads, must conform to the Mail Order Protection Scheme. It is there to protect the customers' money in the event of the advertiser's failure. The details to be submitted are:

1. Latest accounts.
2. Bank reference.
3. Stock levels – to convince them you will not forward sell.
4. Advertising agents.
5. Details of the advert and product.

It should take no longer than a month to gain clearance. You will then have to pay a fee to the common fund based on the advertising costs.

Full details of the scheme are available by sending a stamped addressed envelope to Mail Order Protection Scheme, 16 Tooks Court, London EC4A 1LB; tel: 020 7269 0520; Web site: www.mops.org.uk.

How to increase your sales from small ads

Small ads are a popular medium for new small firms but so many expect too much from a modest expenditure. A national paper will charge around £100 for a space not much bigger than a large postage stamp. Strangely enough I haven't yet found a paper that has researched the response to its own columns. My own small sample suggests that you can expect at best 30 enquiries for each insertion, and this is from a Sunday paper with a circulation of over 1 million copies. It is therefore vital that your sales forecast is realistic. As you are required to deliver the goods within 28 days of receiving the order it is obviously important that supplies are to hand. Some golden rules for successful small ads are:

1. Don't cram too much into your copy. Go for one *headline* that proclaims your main selling benefit.

2. Use a good illustration. Because of the cramped space in this instance a line drawing is probably better than a photo.
3. Give clear *instructions* on how to order.
4. Always give a cast-iron *guarantee* – 'Money back if not delighted.'
5. *Timing* is very important. Most small ad sales are impulse purchases, so take account of seasonal influences, weather, holidays, etc.
6. Always state the *price* and keep postage as a separate item.
7. Quote the *delivery time*.
8. *Avoid box numbers* – response is poor.
9. Key your ads so you know where the response is coming from (see page 139).
10. *Avoid fragile items* and ones that require elaborate packing.
11. Make a good *offer* – 'Buy three, get one free.'
12. Sell one of a series. *Avoid isolated products* that do not lead to further desirable items.
13. Refund the cost of a *catalogue* by knocking it off the price of the first order.
14. Don't be too ambitious in going for high-priced items. Keep your promotion in the lower range. Once you've got your prospects hooked tempt them with your de luxe items.
15. Advertise in papers and magazines that carry a lot of small ads with, of course, similar products to your own. Don't be a trail-blazer.
16. Allow for the use of *plastic money* – Barclaycard, Access, etc; 60 per cent of the eligible UK population now hold a credit card.
17. Handle all *returns and complaints* promptly. Dissatisfied customers can quickly get you into bad odour with the journals, apart from being bad business ethically and commercially.
18. If space permits, always use a *coupon*.

You'll get your fair share of loonies – 'Mickey Mouse', 'Madonna' – of course. The harder ones to spot are educated children filling in for things they *would* like.

When you've been at this lark for some time you will develop a nose for the spurious enquirer. The postcode will be wrong or the franking on the envelope does not marry up with the reader's address. Keeps you on your toes.

Monitor for results

Log all your returned and keyed coupons plus all your telephone enquiries in a *sales enquiry book* or on computer. Columns should be ruled for every method of promotion you undertake so that a check can be kept on advertising expenditure. Make sure you include 'personal recommendations'.

You can check response in a number of ways:

1. You ask. On the phone after taking details say, 'Oh, by the way, how did you come to hear of us?' Most people are only too pleased to let you know.
2. Keying in all your ads (see below).
3. Printing a line of boxes on your order form, one for each medium.

It will be very helpful if you would please indicate where you saw the advertisement:

Exchange & Mart ☐
Radio Times ☐
Practical Householder ☐
The Observer ☐
I am an existing customer ☐

Watch the conversion rate. One ad may pull a lot of enquiries but few orders. Prune accordingly.

There is always the problem of 'Do I ask them to write for a brochure or do I ask for cash with order?' The decision will depend on the nature of the goods, their price and the space you have booked. Many people are reluctant to send cash to new, unknown firms.

Only small ads are exempt from the Mail Order Protection Scheme. Display ads that ask for money direct with the order are subject to contributions to the fund. All but cheap, simple items will have to be fully described by means of an illustrated brochure. Colour can then add impact.

Learn where your response comes from

Before you start you rarely know the perfect place to advertise. All successful mail order operators *key* their ads. Place a code in your coupon or ad and monitor the replies. The address can be slightly varied, even misspelt to indicate the source, as long as the post office can deliver. People tend to copy exactly what is printed. For example, if your address is 14 Castleton Street, use Castletown instead. Invent a mythical person. Miss North for *Guardian* readers or Miss Moon for readers of the *Sun*. The clumsy way of doing it is to use 'Dept ST1' for *Sunday Times* or 'RT' for *Radio Times*, etc.

Once you can afford a large ad include space for a reply coupon. Research has shown that it undoubtedly increases response by at least 20 per cent, and the larger the coupon (within reason) the better the response. Many people just cannot write with small letters and I despair sometimes at the tiny space some advertisers allow for a lot of information. Use a coupon to invite prospects to send for your leaflet (with no obligation); that gives you more chances to spell out the appeal and benefits. If you make the coupon attractive there is more chance of it being filled in, then and there. It saves hunting for paper and envelopes and encourages action (back to AIDA – see page 194). The position of the coupon is important. Print it in the 'gutter' or fold and it is more difficult to cut out. Ask for it on a bottom corner. Make sure that your address is printed on the coupon *and* the ad, as once it has been cut out there is no record for the buyer.

Test your packaging

Packaging can be an expensive item in mail order. Ask your packaging wholesaler to call and try out various materials, posting them back to yourself. Experiment with corrugated, tri-wall, bubble pack, polystyrene, polyurethane foam and all the other materials now available. For small packs and fairly low volumes you may find a trip to your local box maker fruitful. You can probably pick up 'offcuts' and make up wraparounds yourself. You can waste a lot of time on inefficient packing, so gear up properly for it. Set aside a separate packing area with plenty of clear flat space. Suspend your rolls of paper and card in position over the bench and use dispensers for parcel tape and string. It's still hard to beat rolled newspaper to fill up corners in packs. See also page 126.

Dream up an enticement

Mail order definitely works better if you put in a good offer. In the adman's phrase, always work for 'perceived value'. Your offers can come in many forms:

'Buy the set and get a free travelling case.'
'Buy two sheets and we will include a pillowcase – free.'
'Bring your film to us and get your next one free.'

The attraction for the supplier is to encourage loyalty, a higher value per sale, probably no extra packaging and paperwork, and continuity.

The real secret

Don't expect to make money from your first promotion. The hard part is landing your first fish, finding customers from all those prospects. Once you have isolated what may well be under 1 per cent of the readership go on and sell them something else. Your conversion rate to this second mailing has to be significantly higher. If it isn't then you haven't chosen your sequence of products carefully enough.

Aim at least to break even on the first sale: profits will follow on.

How to choose the right product

The national mail order catalogue companies can sell virtually anything, from coats to cookers. Without having the name, credit terms or advertising muscle, small firms are necessarily restricted. The most successful items for those with limited resources tend to have the following attributes:

1. *Uniqueness* or at least rarity; an item that is not generally available in the high street. This attribute could be either because it is a minority interest (cigarette cards) and sold only through a few specialist shops, or it is custom made to order. Its scarcity makes it desirable.
2. The price asked could be more attractive than the high street offering. Usually it is not a wise move to rely on low margins to shift mail order items.
3. Easily packaged and transportable.

4. Does not need to be *demonstrated*.
5. The attraction can be described within the limitations of a small space ad.
6. Fulfils a genuine consumer *need*. There is a ready-made market for the product. The reader should be saying, 'Yes, I could do with one of those.'
7. It is a *proven* product. You won't be troubled with unreliability and consequent returns, replacements and refunds.
8. A large demand (if you're lucky) can be met quickly. Fashionable and trendy items seem particularly vulnerable on this score. Computer games software, kids' toys and whatever pop group is flavour of the moment can generate huge unforeseen demands, to the discomfiture of the supplier.

Beware of components that have to be imported. When does the next boat load get in? Some are also subject to import restrictions.

The acid test

Garnering requests for leaflets is one thing, converting them to orders is more difficult. Many small firms find it relatively easy to get a respectable response but fail to secure profitable orders – closing the sale. It is the *conversion* rate that is vital. Perhaps your leaflet is not attractive enough, the order form is confusing or inhibiting, or the product offer does not live up to your original claims.

Whatever you feel may be the reason, you *must* find out. Ring a selective sample and politely ask when you can expect an order. The replies should put you on the right track.

Alternatively, your original ad may be too imprecise and appeal to too wide an audience. By drawing the appeal to a more select segment perhaps you can cut out some wastage. Charging for the catalogue, to be refunded on first order, often does the trick.

Why direct mail can be so cost-effective

Yes, I am talking about junk mail, yet handled sensibly and with some imagination it can be the most cost-effective tool with which to expand your business. So why has it got such a bad name, where does it go wrong? Maybe because it is:

1. Impersonal.
2. Puerile letter.
3. Wrong subject matter.
4. No benefit.

1. The essence of direct mail is that one person – the seller – is making a *personal* approach to one identified recipient. Anything that dilutes that mystique lessens the impact. So letters addressed to 'Dear Sir/Madam' or even 'The Occupier' get scant attention. Even letters addressed to 'Mr Stationery Buyer' or 'The Managing Director', though they may have identified the position, are one step down from a unique individual.

   Time and money spent on identifying that named individual with his or her job title are never wasted. A list of 500 named individuals, personally addressed and individually signed, is better than a 5,000-name bought-in list of job titles. Quality not quantity.

2. Most sales letters I get treat me like a moron. 'Your numbers have already passed the first stage and you could win a new yacht.'

3. Invite me to sales seminars at exotic London hotels at *only* £350 a day.

4. Offer me a free pen rather than say why I should tie up £100 a month for the next 20 years.

Direct mail's major and unique advantage is the ability to pinpoint your prospect exactly. It's the rifle rather than the shotgun approach. If you can draw up a list of all the people who might be users of your product and send them a *letter* explaining what it is, you have eliminated much of the waste of space advertising.

However, life or selling is not that simple. I once asked an architect friend to save all his post that fell into the direct mail category over a three-week period. (I reckon that architects and doctors probably get as much as anybody.) It came to about 10 pounds in weight (it is only a small practice). Around 70 per cent was of no relevance at all as it was directed at surveyors, structural engineers and other professions. The senders had not even tried to understand what architects were responsible for. There were several instances of duplication and, in one case, triplication of the same promotional material.

Success springs from your list

The first rule of marketing is to identify the target audience. Spend as much time on compiling your *list* of prospects as thinking about what you want to say to them. It is *that* important because the right message to the wrong people is money wasted. That list, once you have struck the right profile, is your most valuable commodity.

Lists are by definition collections of names, of real *people*, with a common interest, be they stamp collectors, vintage car enthusiasts, chemists or timber importers. If you always think of them as people and not just addresses all your promotions will be human.

Direct mail is a huge and expanding industry in its own right and there is a very good chance that someone already holds the list that you want. But there are pitfalls in using existing lists. We live in a fluid world. The national average for moving house is once every eight years, with regional variations. Putting it another way, a list of house-holders will be 12 per cent *inaccurate* in a year's time. The commercial world is not much better: hundreds of businesses a month close their doors – either through liquidation, merger or because their owners have had enough.

You can build your list from a variety of sources:

1. From your own internal records.
2. Compiled from publicly available lists in yearbooks, directories, *Yellow Pages*, etc.
3. Bought-in lists from databases or list brokers. These are specialist agencies which deal solely in tracking down and renting or selling mailing lists.

The most productive list will be your *own*. You are sending out a proposition to customers who already know you and have dealt with your staff and products before. Concentrate on these first. Work through your sales ledger, exhibition visitors' book, reps' leads, enquiries to ads, guarantee cards – any scource that will yield names and contacts of relevance. Never throw away a name.

If your own list is not big enough or you want to expand, there are several directions to pursue. Look in the *Directory of British*

Associations and *Current British Directories* (see Chapter 2) for leads. Some association secretaries will rent out their list of members or you can, somewhat laboriously, copy out the list you want from a library copy. Most of the lists will probably already be held on a computer file somewhere. Your list broker will find out the details. BRAD's *Direct Marketing* is an accurate source book for what is available. A few central libraries may stock a copy.

The magazine *Direct Response* will give further clues. The *Yellow Pages* data bank for the country is available for trades and industry in 2,700 categories. You need not order names for the whole country but can split down precisely to postal code districts. Contact The Business Database 01753 583311.

Many journals will rent out their circulation listings. This is usually a reliable source as readers tend to keep the publisher advised of changes of address.

Compiled lists can cover literally everything. You can even rent a list of wealthy people. Consumer and industrial lists are built up from a variety of sources. A consumers' list could be nothing more refined than the electoral roll split up into districts. Some are often replies to adverts – enquirers rather than purchasers – though you can get access to these as well.

Another way of acquiring names is to exchange an agreed number of yours with a similar product held by another.

What to ask before ordering a list

1. Is it available for rent or to buy? *Yellow Pages* will rent you a list for one time only, not *sell* it, ie not for continual reuse. However, a reordering for up to six postings can be done at 50 per cent of the cost. There is now an increasing trend for more lists to be sold outright rather than rented – probably due to policing problems. Many list brokers will sell you lists. It is usually the original list holder – and the most up to date or in demand – that still rents. Control over rental lists is exercised by *seeding* with hidden names who will pass on sales literature.
2. *Costs.* The market seems stable at about £90 per 1,000 names to buy – but watch for the add-ons. There is often a minimum charge of £300, and extra costs for having it on disc – probably £40 – telephone numbers, delivery (£30 from one firm I would love to name). Make sure you are aware of all the extras.

Delivery times are often poor. Allow two to three weeks. It is normally extra for named individuals rather than job titles. Exceptionally, you will be asked to pay much more. One NHS-based list holder wants over £300 per 1,000 – but claims every name is authenticated regularly, and the potential sales value of selling capital equipment into NHS Trusts is large. Needless to say, haggle.

3. For what purpose was the list compiled? It will be helpful to find out the source of names, when they were last mailed and how up to date the information is. For example, a list of rose growers could be taken from the circulation list of a gardening magazine, the enquiry list to a rose advert or postal buyers from a specialist nursery. Are they lists of enquirers – box tickers – or actual purchasers?

4. You want to be reasonably happy that 'gone-aways' have been removed. One major problem is that the post office will not guarantee to return gone-aways if posted second class. If any user mails first class the subsequent returns could dramatically clean the list.

   You can try printing the return address on the envelope but this can deter people from opening it: 'It's only a circular.' Check what the terms of any refund are. Some will refund only for more than 8 per cent returns – a pretty expensive exercise.

   Duplications are sometimes rife. Apart from the waste of money many people are so irritated to receive several requests from the same source that they won't buy even if they like the offer.

5. What size *sample* can you test? There's no point in sending out thousands of your expensive mailings to a bought-in list till you know that the profile is *your* target. Test response by sampling a smaller number first. List holders will stipulate differing lower limits: under 1,000 names is statistically unreliable. Many would go for 5,000 if you are aiming for say 50,000 and above. As the national response is between 1 and 2 per cent you have little to judge on if few reply: you could easily jump to the wrong conclusions when you come to roll out the remainder. Some companies try and set a foolishly high minimum sample, but always haggle. You don't need to mail 7,000 to find whether it is going to work or not.

6. Try to find the *price bracket* that previous prospects were mailed. Response will have differed if it was a £10 or a £100 offer.
7. Is the list by firm, job title, or named individuals? Response is always better if the mailing is to a specific person, though you do want the job title as well.
8. Standard issue is sticky labels; better is availability on disk.
9. Some lists are not available to competitors. Find out the restrictions before you get too excited.
10. The world can be divided into those who buy by mail order and those who don't. You will get a better response from a list of actual *buyers* than coupon redeemers or competition entrants. It's a case of finding the most potentially responsive audience and, by extension, lists that are mailed frequently generate more response than those that are left to slumber.
11. Finally, you will want to know how long it will take to get your list after ordering so you can prepare your brochures and sales letters in readiness.

Regrettably the rapid growth in the direct mail industry has spawned some dubious list brokers who see this as the latest way to make a quick buck. As in so much of life make your own enquiries and form a common-sense judgement of the firm you are dealing with.

Lifestyle lists

Industrial databases are readily available with many accurate sources. Quite simply, the numbers are much smaller – but companies don't move around as much as individuals. The consumer market is more problematical. The dream of every direct marketeer engaged in consumer goods and services is the ability to target thousands of prospects in their homes. The combination of masses of data held on all of us and sophisticated computerisation has theoretically brought this to pass; this has come to be known as a lifestyle database. First attempts were made in identifying areas of the country by using the argument that householders in a street in Surbiton would have the same disposable income as one in say Harrogate or Pembury. Overlay that with the electoral roll and you have 20 million households to play with.

Going beyond that we have a different approach by a company like Experion Ltd (tel 020 7664 1000) which has built up millions of names by extracting data from either guarantee cards returned when we purchase goods or filling in consumer questionnaires. It claims many millions of names and the ability to pinpoint, for example, 547,000 golfers, 101,000 motorcyclists or 507,000 home computer owners. Overlay that with an income bracket and/or number of children and you should have a closely defined target list. All with names and addresses.

You can also give Experion a selection of your own customer profile and it will marry up to thousands of its own to produce at one swoop whole libraries of new prospects.

This all sounds very wonderful. My own admittedly limited experience has been disappointing. I suspect that these firms have generated millions of box tickers, rather than potential purchasers. The difficulty is that there are so many variables – including your own offer and timing – that it is hard to evaluate scientifically. There were also a higher proportion of post office returns than I would have liked.

What do you send?

You should sent a prospect *at least* four items:

1. Your sales letter.
2. An illustrated brochure or specification sheet (may be fax-back if to business).
3. Order form.
4. Return envelope; reply paid if you are mailing the home.

Depending on your product and purse this list can grow to include a sample, catalogue, testimonials, competition or giveaway. If you have a fertile mind direct mail is where you come into your own.

I have come across plenty of firms which go to some trouble to design a nice brochure and believe all they need do is to mail it out, the 'If they want to buy they'll contact me' approach. It doesn't work like that. People need persuading and to get results you have to make it convenient for them to order.

The most important of the four essential items is your *letter*. It is perhaps no more than convention that we communicate by writing a letter but if it works, why pioneer? Each part of your mailing package requires careful thought and planning as every piece can contribute to the response. But in turn it can also provide traps for the unwary.

Presentation

It is essential that your readers form a good impression of you. Photocopied letters are therefore *out*.

Poorly printed letterheadings, indifferent paper and bad spelling are really unforgivable: most important is to spell the prospect's name, firm and address correctly. We all get a little irritated when we receive letters incorrectly addressed: it's that old word 'courtesy'. Forget that you may be sending out 5,000 letters. A mailing house will laser print and match in the letter and envelope. The more personal your communication looks, the more chance you have that it will be acted upon.

I have heard of one very successful firm that actually hand writes all its direct mail envelopes – all 20,000 of them. It has had complimentary letters back: 'How nice to get a personal letter.' But that is for the consumer market.

Avoid brown manilla envelopes, at least for the outer pack. They look cheap and nasty. Self-seal envelopes, although dearer, save time if you are sticking by hand. Window envelopes save typing the address twice and are finding favour: everything from phone bills to invoices are now sent out in one of these. The envelope can be a creative weapon as well. It should look exciting and inviting. Some part of the offer – a teaser – can be printed on the outside and you may find it worthwhile experimenting with different colours. With all direct mail promotions I try to put myself in the recipient's position, with perhaps a host of other mailings to be opened. You have to make yours stand out and receive that extra bit of busy people's time and attention.

How to write effective sales letters

The major drawback to using direct mail is that many others use it too. It has lost its novelty. Although it is true to say that most mail is opened (over 95 per cent, research suggests), you have only a few seconds to make an impact. That is the decision time. It is that *first glance* which will determine whether the reader is hooked enough to carry on and absorb your proposition or it finds the wastepaper basket.

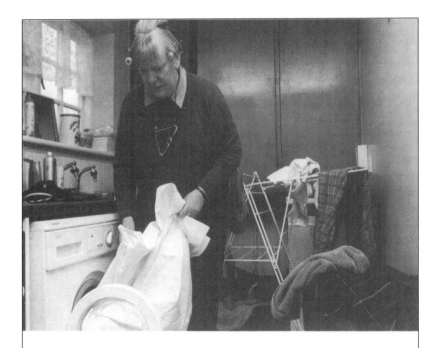

Let's talk about
mould treatment

ENVIRONMENTAL SYSTEMS

Figure 5.1   Cover of a mailing leaflet aimed at local authorities with condensation mould problems. Most firms in this field just show pictures of mould. This is a different approach that would at least attract the reader to open up the leaflet

Your headline or opening sentence must spell out a major benefit and answer the reader's question, *'What's in it for me?'* This really is the key to successful direct mail and is why the national average for response remains obstinately, at best, 2 per cent.

Make sure the user benefits are spelt out early in the letter.

Think out the objective

You must be clear in your mind what you are trying to do. Are you trying to get direct orders or simply elicit enquiries for personal visits? Are you announcing the opening of a new shop, inviting competition entries or magazine subscriptions? The style of your letter must reflect the task in hand. Don't ask too much of one letter: you may need to do it in two parts.

Long letter or short?

Two factors determine this question: your audience and the product. On the assumption that few businessmen have time to read a two-page letter it seems folly to deter them with 1,000 words of type. It is far better to use the letter as a prelude to a personal visit or to back up an illustrated brochure or sample. Let pictures tell the story.

Mailings to the household tend to be longer as your audience has more time to digest your pearls of wisdom. Never write more than you need to, however. Padding is a turn-off and people will read only as long as their interest is held.

What do you say?

Think of your audience and write as if you were speaking face to face. This must be the essence of all good communication. Leave your high-blown phrases and contrived jargon behind and use simple, direct English. The letter must flow and lead the reader along. The techniques to use are not particularly subtle or devious. Avoid long sentences and keep to one theme per paragraph. To keep the reader hooked, carry on one idea to the next paragraph by using open-ended questions or statements, for example, 'Why do you think Rolls-Royce used Connolly leather?' and then answer it in the next sentence.

Be *factual*. Opinions are always suspect. State what the product will do in terms of performance and translate this into user benefits. Always write looking through the user's eyes, as though he or she already has possession. If you stick to the facts you must carry *conviction*, which is the most important quality that can shine through.

As with all advertising, the misuse of overworked words like 'unique', 'fabulous' and 'extraordinary' will produce the opposite reaction in the reader's mind. Legitimate buzz words like 'new', 'free trial', 'money back' should certainly be employed in their proper context.

Always be *sincere*. I have never believed that the American style of salesmanship – 'Have a nice day' – can cross the Atlantic, with all its overblown bonhomie.

We all believe the BBC news because of the simple, direct way of broadcasting. There is no arm waving or histrionics. Contrast that with some of the tabloids' methods of presentation.

Give a reason to act

Having aroused interest and desire you must then give a *reason* for action. The hardest thing to achieve is an immediate response. Unless it is done *then* it won't be done at all. The most telling way to open your letter is to make the reason your offer: 'limited stocks', 'pre-budget', 'end of range', etc. Remind the readers again at the close and give them a strong reason for making contact.

Don't forget the PS

I don't pretend to understand why, but everyone reads the PS. Maybe because it stands alone. Surely no one really believes that you rushed back to the printer and asked him to squeeze an extra vital point before he went to tea? No, but the PS can work for you as well as the opening benefit.

Drayton Bird in his excellent book *Commonsense Direct Marketing* quotes a lovely example of the value of the PS. On his first mailshot to Bullworker prospects he received a 10 per cent response. An American, Bernie Silver, showed him how to pull more: *'How many units have you got in the warehouse?' 'About 300' was Bird's estimate. 'Great. Write a PS and tell them that's all you've got, so they should reply now.'* He did and the response doubled.

What else can you send?

The more pieces of literature you can send the more chances you will

Dear Cosyfeet Enquirer,

Have you given up all hope of finding comfortable, stylish footwear that will fit your feet with ease?

Do you find it impossible to buy footwear ROOMY enough to cope with the problems and discomfort caused by:

- swellings
- bunions
- arthritis
- diabetes
- oedema
- enlarged joints
- exceptionally wide feet?

Now that you've discovered Cosyfeet there's no need to despair ...

When you slip your feet into the blissful comfort of Cosyfeet, you'll be amazed at just how ROOMY they really are.

And how LIGHTWEIGHT and SOFT they feel too.

Order any of the styles of Cosyfeet footwear and we're positive you'll find they're ROOMIER than anything you may have struggled with in the shops.

And luxuriously comfortable too.

Take a look through our 1994 catalogue. It's packed with EXTRA WIDE, DEEP and ROOMY slippers, sandals and shoes all of which are widely recommended by chiropodists, physiotherapists, occupational therapists and nurses.

They know how much damage ill-fitting footwear can cause and appreciate the way Cosyfeet have been carefully designed to cope with problem feet.

So go ahead and place your order, safe in the knowledge that Cosyfeet footwear has been approved by professionals.

What are the Benefits of Buying Cosyfeet Slippers?

Cosyfeet EXTRA WIDE, DEEP and ROOMY slippers have been designed with a long opening so they're incredibly easy to get on and off.

Their wrap around velcro fastenings adjust to fit individual widths and swellings, bringing soothing comfort to painful feet and ankles.

Available in brushed nylons and soft cottons, these softly lined fabrics are washable so you can keep them bright and clean. The ultra soft leather and aquatex styles are showerproof and cope well in outdoor conditions.

If outdoor shoes are too painful to wear, then the collection of slippers with harder wearing outdoor soles could be the solution to this problem.

What are the Benefits of Buying Cosyfeet Sandals and Shoes?

Cosyfeet EXTRA WIDE, DEEP and ROOMY sandals and shoes are made from soft leathers and have carefully placed seams and stitching so they're kind to problem feet.

Made on a ladies EEEEE+ last and a mens H+ last they really are the WIDEST, DEEPEST and ROOMIEST sandals and shoes you can buy.

As heavy, rigid footwear is the last thing that problem feet need, the soles are incredibly lightweight and flexible.

And because the soft leather uppers are durable and longlasting, the blissful Cosyfeet comfort goes on and on.

If you want to join the tens of thousands of customers whose feet are already benefiting from the soothing comfort of Cosyfeet, then place your order now.

Ordering is Effortless and Worry-free

Simply fill in the order form, deciding which method of payment is most convenient. If you have a credit card, you may find it easier to order over the phone.

Remember – every order you place is protected by

THE COSYFEET NO QUIBBLE MONEY BACK GUARANTEE

We promise to refund what you paid in full (less p&p) if you're not entirely satisfied with any of our footwear.

There's no need to worry about ordering the wrong style or size. If you make a mistake or change your mind we'll exchange your order promptly.

AND IF YOU ORDER TWO PAIRS OR MORE OF ANY COSYFEET STYLES, POST AND PACKAGING IS ABSOLUTELY FREE.

Please don't hesitate to phone or write if there's anything concerning Cosyfeet that you're unhappy or unsure about. Our aim is to provide you with the best service possible and a range of footwear that's unbeatable in terms of quality, style and value.

I hope you enjoy choosing your footwear from the Cosyfeet collection.

Of course, the sooner you place your order the sooner we can start helping you to foot comfort.

Yours sincerely

David Price.

David Price
Proprietor

***P.S. We try to dispatch all orders within 48 hours. Order
now and soothing comfort could be yours within days.***

5 The Tanyard, Leigh Road, STREET, Somerset, BA16 0HR   Telephone: 01458 447275

Figure 5.2   There is no attempt to personalise this sales letter, but the target audience – elderly housebound people – like the simple direct style. This letter, here reduced from an A4 sheet, uses a larger typeface than normal

have to make a sale. But watch the postal steps. Most people will pick each piece up and scan it, no matter how briefly, which gives a further 'opportunity to see'.

Unless you are launching a brand-new product you should be able to include some testimonials from satisfied customers. Reprint their actual letters exactly as received – spelling and all. It carries more conviction. (You must get their permission first, of course.) An endorsement from someone else means much more than if *you* are saying it.

Direct mail lends itself to imaginative treatment. An American fire insurance firm mails letters looking as though they've been scorched.

A stain-proof contract carpet has been sold to architects by sending a 4-inch square sample with a sachet of tomato sauce. They are invited to spread it (spatula provided) on the carpet and then wash it off under a tap.

Two-part mailings can be done in the same way. I'm hoping a local sedimentation expert I know will be mailing consulting engineers with a small plastic bag of sea sand, asking them to identify it. The second posting will bring the answer and offer his services for pollution and scour prediction.

One of the more imaginative uses of direct mail has gone down in history as the Ida Clackett letter. The letter was written in a childish hand and said:

> Dear Mr Manager,
>   I am writing to you because I'm your cleaner. I was in your office and saw a lot of papers on your desk and they meant nothing to me but when I was in the pub last night a man said to me I'll give you £500 to borrow your keys and go in. I don't want to do that, I don't think that's right but five hundred pounds is a lot of money.
> (Signed) *Ida Clackett*

A few days later a rep called from Ofrex, a shredding machine company.

You can use direct mail to send out keys, only one of which will open a safe on your premises at an open day, or start a new car, etc.

Other techniques

1. Provide emphasis by printing in two or three colours and underlining to bring out the main points.

2. Start saying 'I', move to 'we', finish with 'you'. Build a partnership. Change from the general to the particular.

3. Handwritten marginal notes, used sparingly, bring personalisation a bit closer. By handwritten I mean you should add a few words on to the original before printing.

4. Never put 'Dear Sir/Madam' or 'The Occupier'. Avoid the salutation altogether by starting off 'Good Morning'.

5. If you are writing to a female audience try a tinted paper. Pink is supposed to be most effective. Or scented.

6. I don't believe it is so important to reply-pay the envelope if you are mailing business users. All mail will tend to go through the franking machine anyway, but if you are only mailing small firms then many will not have the luxury of such a machine and will be counting the cost and convenience.

7. The return envelope can be cheap manilla. There is no point in wasting money on incoming mail.

8. The outer envelope can work as well, arousing curiosity without divulging the contents. If you include a free gift or sample, say so on the outside. In effect it should be saying, 'Open me'.

9. Make it easy for prospects to respond by enclosing a pre-printed reply card with all the alternatives listed:

Please send further details

Please make an appointment

I would be interested in .... months' time

Please send .... items on trial

Name .... Address ....

Phone ....

---

10. Use a separate order form. It should be just as nicely designed as the sales letter – after all, it is asking for a commitment from the prospects. Leave them in no doubt what to do, and when to use BLOCK CAPITALS. Design the form with plenty of space so that it gives you minimum trouble in taking off quantities and checking. Print your address on this as well as on the sales

letter. The order form should be coded so that you know from which mailing it was generated. There is sometimes a considerable time lag between mailing and response.

If you are selling a relatively limited range of lines you should print them all, including price, to encourage the prospect to order more. All he or she has to do is run down the order form and decide how many to order. An order form can be attractive as well. All too often this is left to last and given little forethought, but a moment's deliberation should remind you that this is the most important part of the psychological process. Your graphic designer can make this as inviting as the leaflet. Buying should be a pleasure and you can try to contrive a relaxed atmosphere.

Restate the terms of your offer and spell out what commitments you are asking the prospect for. Enclosing a second order form can also increase response. It can be passed to another colleague or member of the family or retained for future use.

The order form is a good place to ask, 'Who else might be interested in this offer?' Recommendations to friends enjoy a much higher response than your original mailings. A fax-back order or enquiry form also makes life easier. Print the fax number large as an inducement to adopt this procedure.

11. Always keep a record of what you have sent. How can you learn and improve if you don't record your mailings? When it comes to testing different ideas you will have lost the comparison.

12. Tie up with the main credit card companies. Offering credit increases results.

Testing, testing

The great advantage of direct response advertising over other forms of promotion is the ability to measure results quickly and directly. Change your offer and, provided your mailing isn't too small, you would expect the response to vary – all things being equal. You can test more than the offer.

1. Change the layout, headline, picture, position – anything of importance – to see whether you can pull in more punters, but only change one thing at a time, otherwise you won't know which one was the attraction.
2. Split your mailings in half and vary the theme to see which is the more attractive. Repeat with a large mailing. If you're aiming for a very big posting it is safer to do a test sample again.

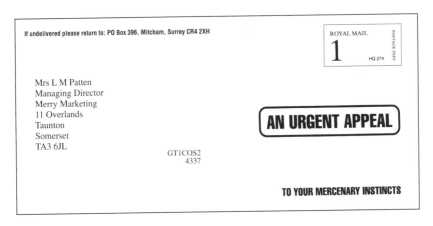

Figure 5.3   We get junk mail by the sackful. This is a delightfully honest way of getting you to open the letter, which was for grouptrade.com – an office supplies Web site

When you are working on very low response rates a few either way can upset a large number of percentage points.

Test sampling with industrial users has to be more sophisticated to produce reliable results, as one user or specifier could be responsible for bulk purchases whereas there are more private consumers but each buys less. All I suggest to a new small firm is to beware of jumping to hopeful conclusions on one small mailing. If in doubt test again. There is plenty of skilled advice now within the industry to advise you on predictions and probabilities.

Why you should test

Much of advertising is hard to quantify. Exhibitions can be very expensive and often it is impossible to say what business has resulted directly from them. Display ads, unless you put in a coupon, will not let you know what has been achieved. The same goes for all the rest – posters, programmes, giveaways, diaries and the like. Direct response advertising allows you to form a judgement on the expenditure.

Testing, with its quick response, allows scope for adjustment to give you better value for money. Testing can prove your ideas. The most skilled agency in the country does not *know* what the public will buy until the offer is made. You are committed by then.

We will be delighted to send you our 1994 brochure due in October 1993

At **High Places** we believe in:

* reducing unwanted mail

* not wasting paper

* keeping running costs low

We update our address list every two years.

If you return this card with your name and

address you will stay on our list. If you don't

you won't!

Have you a friend who would like to receive our '94 brochure?

Name _____

Address _____

_____

_____ Postcode _____

Name _____

Address _____

_____

_____ Postcode _____

High Places is a fully licensed and bonded tour operator. ATOL 2836

Figure 5.4   A mailing card that will both clean the list and encourage more prospects

Test against a bought-in list

When you are in the mood for expansion and thinking of renting a new list of prospects, test a sample against the same number of your own. Your own list should give a better response for the reasons already indicated, but it will be a good yardstick for comparison. Make sure that the identical offer is made to both listings and at the same time, of course.

How to test small ads

If the readership profile for two magazines is thought to be identical you can run two ads on the same day. Make an adjustment for circulation. There must be several fields of interest that are in direct competition, such as the present welter of computer, hi-fi and motoring magazines that are aimed at the same market segment. Probably the more trustworthy way is to alternate your ad in successive issues.

Instead of one big ad, try two smaller ones in the same issue.

The great fascination about all advertising is that there is never one answer. We all think we know what makes a good ad, but the only measure of acceptability is whether it *sells*. And the only way to find out is to *test*.

The response you can expect

I've talked glibly through this chapter about the magic national average of a 2 per cent enquiry rate as if that were immutable. Every promotion is different. Even a ½ per cent actual order rate could be quite acceptable.

Promoters are naturally very reluctant to disclose what response they get to mailings but there have been many that have achieved higher than 15 per cent. The best I ever heard of was from a post office official who claimed to have helped mail to America, using First Day Covers and achieving a 50 per cent response.

You have to cover your costs and meet your objectives. The main point to bear in mind is that the results of your first mailing to a strange list will probably be marginal. Your second effort to the converts should be very much better. If it isn't, there is something very wrong.

Member get a member

MGM campaigns can be very fruitful. We all recognise that the best advertising is by personal recommendation and it's the same with direct response. It sometimes helps to offer a premium to the introducing friend when the new member places the first order. Your order forms should have a space for 'further addresses'. When sending on these requests always do a fresh personal letter: 'Mrs Jones suggested I send you our new catalogue.' The response from this added touch has proved to be the greatest of all. First, because the friend knows the likes of the prospect, eliminating most of the wastage inherent in all direct mail. Second, perhaps the new member 'doesn't want to let her down'.

It all costs money

The costs of mail order and direct mail operations are more easily predicted and measured than other ways of drumming up business. Printing, list buying, postage and handling can all be computed in advance. By testing against a representative sample, an informed decision can be made on profitability if a large list is then rolled out. But distinctions should be made between the different areas where costs are incurred.

The *enquiry* cost is the cost of just getting a prospect to reply and ask for information. This is made up of a mailing list rental (if bought in) or what you have spent to compile your own. It is the costs of getting the names onto labels, envelopes, all your printing bills, stationery and postage, plus the cost of adverts if you've derived enquiries from that source. Divide your total expenditure by the number of replies to arrive at a unit figure.

The *reply* cost is the total amount spent to satisfy enquirers: more leaflets, stationery and postage.

The *order* cost is the grand total divided by the number of actual orders received. You are then in a position to work out your break-even position for each article. A critical figure is always your *conversion ratio*. Are you getting a lot of casual enquiries that fail to materialise into orders? Should you make the ad more explicit to deter these time wasters or make the reply mechanism harder by cutting out freepost? Or is there something wrong with your sales literature or follow-up procedure? Telephone research will probably reveal the answer in short order.

These are some of the direct costs involved. It is to be hoped that you will not be launching an unproven product. The upset could be *returns*.

Doing the sums

Because direct mail is susceptible to scientific analysis, let's now look at the mathematics. Take an example of selling a set of Victorian railway photographs to enthusiasts. There are many clubs and magazines so lists should be easy to come by. The costs of producing leaflets, letters and the list rental may be £400 per thousand (including postage). Break-even is therefore £400 divided by the response rate to arrive at the cost per order, compared with the profit per order. To improve profitability you must either improve response rates or reduce the cost of the package. Assuming a 2 per cent response, the order cost is £20 per order. What you cannot ignore is the better response rate you should get from mailing those 20 converts per thousand. You should better 10 per cent, another two sales per thousand. If the pictures show a profit of £30 differing response rates alter the picture like Table 5.1.

Table 5.1   Profit/loss of direct mailing

Response rates	1%	2%	3%	4%	5%
Orders per 1000	10	20	30	40	50
Costs per order	£40	£20	£13.33	£10	£8
Profit (loss) per order	(10)	£10	£16.66	£20	£22

This makes no allowance for breakages or returns, some of which you may be able to use again. This simplified exercise, assuming a single mailing for one product, highlights the necessity of picking only profitable lines for direct response. As a general rule you should work on at least a 3:1 ratio. One-third the cost of product, one-third promotion and one-third profit. Anything less and you will be struggling. Many of the household names in direct selling that you see in the Sunday supplements rely on 5:1, as you will find out if you try to sell anything to them.

Growth areas

Industrial, or business to business, selling has greatly increased the use and sophistication of direct mail. Few small firms can afford the costs of employing a full-time salesperson (£40,000 and upwards a year including all the costs), so 'cold' calling is out. An increasing number of large businesses have also slimmed down their sales forces, relying on direct mail and technical journal coupon replies to solicit enquiries. Work it out for yourself. Few salespeople can make more than six worthwhile calls in a day, which works out at nearly £30 a call. As the generally accepted success rate is that one in seven calls produces an order, you can see that a well-planned mail shot must be more cost-effective.

Another growth area is in selling financial services and other intangibles. Since the privatisation of many key companies, lists of shareholders have opened up huge markets to reams of promoters for everything from home banking to penny share offers and insurance plans. You don't have to send brochures any more. The cost of software duplication onto a CD ROM or disk has plummeted and they are ideal for complex messages. Monotype, the font seller, for example, puts its catalogue of 4,000 fonts onto a CD ROM and in return for a payment will release the unlocking code over the phone. The advantages are obvious. The equivalent of whole catalogues can be sent out at greatly reduced postage costs and movement, colour and sound enhance the message. They are certainly a more flexible sales medium, with consumer magazines leading the way. The cost of duping PC disks is so little that trials can be cheaply undertaken.

I particularly like the idea of video as a sales aid. Complicated plant and machinery can be videoed and copies made and sent all over the world. It can be retained to act as a maintenance manual afterwards. Still video cameras can be used for similar purposes. These digital cameras capture the image on a small disk that can be downloaded to a computer and seen immediately. The quality is some way from that of a conventional camera but it has its uses. Estate agents and the motor trade seem to be the main users at present. Digital images do eat memory though.

Catalogue design

Despite the Internet, catalogue selling by direct mail is still a growth medium and you no longer have to have the resources of a Freeman's to grasp the potential. One of my old clients deals exclusively with the elderly housebound and it is hard to see them switching over to using the Internet. In seven years their business has gown twentyfold, largely on the backs of a good home shopping catalogue. Placing a colour-printed catalogue in the right hands will still beat puzzling over an indifferent Web site.

But design sells, and it is important to get the basics right. Try to work through the following well-proven steps:

1. Work out a timed schedule to allow for product photography, proofreading, price checking, print run and delivery, and build in slippage.
2. The overall design must reflect the audience's taste (positioning).
3. Format and size: A5 seems to be popular for consumer, A4 for trade mailings. If going for unusual sizes check with your printer first – and the postal steps and envelope sizes.
4. A strong front cover, representative of the range, is crucial. It must say 'open me'.
5. Visually it must look attractive, but be easy to read. Avoid too arty a look or too many typefaces. Four-colour is essential.
6. Think benefits and headlines for each product. Keep it simple.
7. Put a best-selling line at the top right corner of the page – the eye looks there first.
8. Include an easy-to-use order form. Allow enough room for those with poor handwriting.
9. Go for the biggest run you can afford: most of the cost of producing a catalogue lies in origination. The unit cost for printing say 20,000 catalogues will be around 12 times the cost of 240,000 (inverse proportion).

Catalogue design is a complex and difficult job. Once you have got beyond a few pages I would suggest you approach a specialist in this field. Try catalog-biz.com for ideas.

Door to door

An alternative to selling off the page and direct mail is unaddressed door-to-door distribution.

There are several ways of arranging this. The post office itself can distribute your message along with the morning post. This is the most expensive yet reliable way (£38.50 a thousand). In some areas you will have to wait till 'free days' come up and there is little freedom of choice. It is of most benefit in rural areas where the time between houses is greatest. There is a minimum charge of £500 and delivery is made on postcode areas. The Royal Mail will send you details of the number of delivery points within each postcode area for you to make your choice. The average is around 2,500 for each code area. No deliveries are accepted in December for obvious reasons. I would agree with the Royal Mail's claims that your message stands more chance of getting opened and read if it comes with the post rather than cheaper alternative methods.

The Association of Household Distributors (the trade association for this field) produce a useful directory of members (*The Letterbox Marketing Handbook*) showing the areas covered by its members, largely based on freesheet newspaper distributors. Contact them at 3 Brunswick Square, Gloucester GL1 1UG, tel 01452 387070. The cost can be as low as £20 per 1,000 for shared delivery. Solus (single) deliveries are inevitably more expensive and are not popular. If your target area tends to be rural, few freesheets go outside the town or village limits, as it's just not economic for the underpaid people who deliver them. AHD members abide by the Code of Conduct, which includes spot checks on deliveries. My own regional delivery agency admits to a high staff turnover – not an industry I could like to be engaged in.

If you have big ideas beyond your known locality various direct marketing agencies will match known householder profiles (PC-based ACORN for example) across the country that could generate hundreds of thousands of potential target drops but not necessarily replies.

There is also a number of national and often regional distribution organisation subsidiaries of newspaper groups. Your local newsagent (or I have heard of the milkman doing deliveries) may include a handbill in every *Daily Mirror* or *Times* according to your audience. Lastly, the local Cub pack is always looking for ways of fund raising.

While you do have the advantage of being able to pick your precise area, traditionally the response is very low – less than 0.1 per cent – and much worse than for direct mail. This is because most door-to-door advertisers seem to expect the vast majority of their handbills to be junked, with little thought that this can still be a cost-effective and profitable venture. Few of the leaflets I see use the back. Door to door can be almost as selective as direct mail in that you can choose the area of the town you want to attract and even individual houses, depending on their apparent lifestyles. A direct mail operation could cost you £400 a thousand names delivered, a door-to-door delivery just £60. Door to door is also a tried and proven method of sampling, traditionally for toiletries. I've not come across a small firm using this method, but for small areas there's no reason why it shouldn't be used.

Form a club

Direct response marketing is all about developing a warm relationship with your customers, and one of the most cost-effective ways of doing this is to form a club.

The club has many applications.

1. Garages can offer 10 per cent off future services or accessories on all cars sold over a certain price. It keeps the customers coming back and gives the sales department further opportunities to retain their custom.
2. Tour operators can give priority booking to members who have had holidays with them before: a very valued offer with areas much in demand, eg *gîtes* in France.
3. Advance notice or special days on sale.
4. Book clubs enjoy reductions on publishers' prices provided they buy so many books a year.
5. Hold regular get-togethers and social events, invite expert speakers or organise trips related to your club's interest.
6. Produce a regular newsletter and invite contributions from the members. Highlight any new products or services that you are bringing in, making an introductory offer to members.
7. Once the membership has built up you should be able to negotiate bulk buys for commodities, discounts for patronising certain establishments and other goodies like insurance and finance, depending on what your members' interests are.
8. Run an advice service.
9. If you really want to push the boat out you can go in for club ties, T-shirts, badges and car stickers.

Party plan

This is the home sales method pioneered by Tupperware and now used by countless others. It has great appeal to small firms because you can reach the public quickly and the profit margins should be good. It is particularly suitable for items in the craft field that need to be seen and handled. I think party plan has had its day, though there may be odd areas where it still survives, selling exotic (erotic?) lingerie, Christmas gifts, jewellery, etc. For new firms I suggest that they encourage existing agencies to tack a product on to the end of an evening rather than start from cold.

Party plan organisers tend to be self-employed and arrange their own parties. They make their commission on the difference between the price at which they purchase the goods and the price at which they sell them.

The Post Office

This chapter would not be complete without a word about your friendly post office. Direct response marketing couldn't exist without it.

Go along and see your local postal services representative (the address is in the phone book under Post Office). Reduced rates for bulk postings can be obtained by prior postcode sorting but they tend to apply to relatively high volumes. The parcel service has lost ground to the many guaranteed next-day delivery carriers.

On a more mundane level, if you take more than 120 letters all the same size and weight along to your Crown PO or sorting office it will run them through its franking machine. Sort them the right way round and in bundles of 50.

Trackback is useful to help you locate slow, or missing parcels. For a fee of 10p bulk users can ring a freephone number and find out where in the system their package is.

Useful addresses

Direct Marketing Association, Haymarket House, 1 Oxendon Street, London SW1Y 4EE; 020 7321 2525.

Direct Mail Guide, free from the Royal Mail, Direct Mail Marketing, Basildon; 0800 581939.

Direct Response, Haymarket Publications Limited, 174 Hammersmith Road, London W6 7JP; 020 8267 4436.

Buying by Post, Office of Fair Trading (useful free leaflet). This is available from the distributor: OST, PO Box 366, Hayes, Middx UB3 1XB; tel: 0870 6060321; tel/fax: 020 8813 6564.

Direct Mail Data Book, Gower Publishing, Croft Road, Aldershot, Hampshire GU11 3 HR.

Catalogue & e-business, 115 High Street, Ilfracombe EX34 9EZ, or www.catalog-biz.com. Excellent monthly magazine for those producing mail order catalogues.

Telephone marketing

Telephone sales techniques are covered in Chapter 7 on selling (pages 213–16), as it follows logically from my discussion on face-to-face selling. It is, of course, a powerful direct response method of marketing in that you are making your offer direct to the prospect.

Research is often best done on the phone. A large number of people can be contacted and direct answers quickly obtained. A good telephone manner can winkle out an amazing amount of detail but you must practise and be prepared. Start by pinning up a poster above your phone that reads:

> Check that brain
> is in gear
> before engaging
> mouth.

Network marketing

Otherwise known as multi-level marketing – but in my book still a version of the outlawed pyramid selling. Readers may write in droves and say that millions have been and are likely to be made by this American method of selling/distributing, but I still don't like it.

A few months ago I was invited to a 'business presentation' by an old acquaintance. Smelling a rat but willing to try anything once I attended the local hotel, and many smart business types were there. Within five minutes I knew I'd been conned. In two hours of hard chat, not a single product was shown nor any open questions invited. It was all about 'lifestyle' and 'aspiration' and 'freedom'.

If you could have got in first then maybe you would have made money – but sorry, it's not for me.

Summary

- Do your sums and see if direct response is likely to be more profitable than going through distributors.
- Where is the market, how can you reach it?
- What your objectives? To get more appointments for face-to-face selling, to reach fresh markets, to research for market gaps or to complement your marketing efforts in other areas?
- Identify your market segment and customer needs.
- How can you make an irresistible offer?
- What customer names do you have already?
- Create the message.
- Do a pilot run and evaluate.
- How can you improve the response?
- Test variables.
- What else can you sell them and who else needs the product?
- Record all promotions with the response. Analyse and learn.
- Put the Web site address on all your literature.

6 *Public relations*

You have failed from that which causes nine-tenths of all failures in the
world, from not doing quite enough.

I K Brunel on the failure to secure the SS Britain

Once upon a time PR was a gentle profession, tailor-made for Old
Etonians, Debs' Delights and ex-Gentlemen of the Press. Then along
came pressure groups, lobbyists, quangos, MPs who could be diverted
and Big Business. That is a pity, because at its simplest public relations
can be a useful and entirely ethical trade for the small businessman.
Much of it is plain common sense, some can be learnt, occasionally
you may need to pay a professional to achieve the results.

To the purist PR is 'a conscious planned campaign of informed
communications to induce a favourable climate of opinion'. By itself it
is not a selling medium but can prepare the way for an advertising
campaign. PR and advertising often work side by side. It should
project your corporate image. In my experience it is the area that
receives least attention from small firms, yet a little thought can
achieve lasting effects.

PR objectives

All your PR activity should have a planned objective. Think of the
people whom you wish to influence: they are your target audience in
the same way that advertising defines your market. If your market is
defence equipment there is little point in cultivating the local freesheet. The public you are seeking to influence could be the local

council, factory neighbours, buyers and consumers, your banker and your employees. The information you put out should be strictly factual and not an attempt to gloss over some shortcoming in your service. Too often 'a spokesman said' is the ill-considered front for some disaster.

PR should be planned on a long-term basis: it is not something that can be generated overnight. Sometimes it involves showing social responsibility – providing heaters for flood victims or waste drawing paper for the local kindergarten. The costs involved need not be large, it is the thought that counts.

PR for the local community can take the form of modest sponsorship for the school lollipop ladies, old folks' outings, 'keep our village tidy' bins, loan of the firm's pick-up truck for the cricket team roller and all sorts of other innocent causes. The small business columns of your local papers are always ready to print good news that shows your efforts in a favourable light. Amid so much gloom a cheerful item should find ready acceptance.

Understanding the media industry

To get maximum impact from your PR activities it is important to know how the media go about their job. It is a sophisticated and highly fragmented industry with considerable expertise at your disposal if you know how to tap into it.

You should first understand that, with the exception of the national press, the local media (press, radio and television) have very small news-gathering staff. They rely on being fed stories from the community.

All operate broadly in the same way, ie they all have reporters, sub-editors, a news desk and an editor who decides the overall balance. Where they differ is how they like the news presented and in the matter of deadlines. Unless you have a major story it is rarely worth sending to the national papers, or mass circulation magazines. They all get hundreds, yes hundreds, of releases every week – most from big corporations, regular and heavy advertisers, branded goods and the shoals of lobby groups all pushing their favourites. Far better to spend your time and money on news outlets nearer home and with highly specialised journals catering for your interest. You must also distinguish between news and features. The mass circulation magazines (mainly monthly women's and home interests with circulations often over 250,000) write in-house or commission their own feature articles from free-lancers. Each magazine will tend to have a stable of freelancers who feed them topics on their speciality – food, holidays, health, finance, etc. It may help to scour through the top magazines and build up your own list of writers who are worth cultivating. They will probably be in a better position to get your angle into print as they have better connections. The smaller circulation trade and technical press – which are normally not seen on the news-stands – are generally much easier to approach. The editors are not surrounded by protective PAs and you can invariably speak directly to them. Most have been in the trade much of their lives and are keen to keep up to date. You will stand more chance of getting features in these magazines than the more competitive monthlies.

The centre of any paper is the news desk. The editor lays down the house style and the journalists write in that vein. Short punchy sentences with no long words will tend to be used in the popular tabloids. More in-depth detail and analysis are the prerogative of the heavies.

The sub-editors are the linchpins. They cut the stories and rewrite them (if they have the time) to fit the space available. That is where the pressure is. You may come across researchers (particularly for TV) who work some way ahead of the programme, digging out background material. The lowest are the cub reporters who get lumbered with attending the local council meetings, quarter sessions and MPs' fête openings. Every paper has its 'stringers'. These are freelance journalists who feed several papers, and possibly a national, with their own local news.

The best guide to named journalists in the media is *Pims Media Directory*; it gives subject categories across the country. The national press can be split between the tabloid rubbish end, where pictures are more important than words, and the quality broadsheets. Increasingly I have found that it is the total trivia that makes the nationals, while hard news stands more chance of getting printed in your local or regional press.

The local press is the most important

Everyone reads the local press because, unless we're hermits, we like to know what's going on in the area. Where's that bypass going and did

Councillor Harris really pass building tenders to his brother-in-law? Apart from the gossip news, the pull of local papers lies in its advertising. The classified small ads are a mine of information to bargain hunters. In many areas the local press can be split between paid-for papers and the freesheets. While originally the freesheets were set up to rival their more legitimate brothers, as time has gone by most of these have been brought up and absorbed by the paid-fors and are simply advertising pages cloaked by a thin veneer of news. I have always believed – having seen no hard research – that the reaction and response to freesheets is much poorer simply because they are seen as throwaways. Advertising rates are cheaper in a freesheet – sometimes included 'free' by those publishers who produce both the paid-for and the freesheet; so perhaps they agree with me.

Newspaper proprietors are in business just like you and are out to make a profit by increasing sales. They will not achieve this if the stories are stale, inept or inaccurate.

What they're looking for

What makes news? Topicality, originality, personality and sometimes humour. You must find a *topical* peg to hang the story on. It's not news that your business is making, say, coffins, but it will be if it's your tenth anniversary or you have just taken on your fiftieth employee, or sold your thousandth coffin or had an order from Russia. There's a story everywhere if you look with a journalist's eye. The School of Journalism will train you to believe that there are just five topics of news: royalty, babies, animals, crime and, yes, sex. So when I wrote a serious release for one of my commercial willow clients and, as the last line, mentioned they'd made a dog basket for the Queen, the story made most of the nationals; Radio 4 generated a live broadcast for *Radio Montreal* – in French. Crazy, and dispiriting for those of us trying to write hard news.

I once put out a story that a local cabinet-maker had made magicians' tricks as a sideline for years. That by itself was not news. The impact was that his main customer was giving a show at the local theatre. The regional TV station wanted to lock him up in one of his own trunks. The story got him half a page plus picture and many nice direct quotes. All for free.

The only space where you can get away with a less noteworthy story is the local features page. Many papers have a women's page, craft or business section where an in-depth story can be laid out, but these opportunities are rare.

The press release: telling the media

It is perhaps not generally realised how much of a paper's output comes in unsolicited. Many reports are straight reprints of stories that are fed in. These come in the form of press releases sent in by individuals, associations and firms. Because the press work to deadlines, your news stands more chance of getting printed if you observe some basic ground rules.

1. The item should be *typed* on a sheet of A4 paper headed up 'Press Release' or 'Press Information'. Address it to the 'News Editor', 'Newsdesk' or a named journalist.
2. Double spacing should be used to allow room for alterations by the sub-editors. Wide margins should also be used to allow for instructions to the printer. Write only on one side of the paper. Paragraphs should not be broken at the end of a page.
3. Date the item and use a headline to identify it. Don't worry over much about a witty gem of a headline. Invariably the sub-editors will write their own even if yours is brilliant.
4. Most stories can be told in three paragraphs. The meat should come in the first line. If space is short then the sub's blue pencil will delete from the bottom. Even if the bulk of the story is cut, at least the main facts will get printed. The first paragraph must say 'Who, what, why, when and where' and succeeding paras can expand and colour the detail.

   The papers are always looking for fillers – short items that can be dropped in at the end of a column. A brief story has a very good chance of getting published as it stands, if it is simply written in plain English. However, if the story warrants it, write at greater length but avoid padding.
5. Your story should contain at least one direct quotation or comment. Not from that dreary spokesperson but a named individual of some standing or relevance.
6. Keep it simple and write for the readership. Reserve technical jargon for the technical press who will understand, indeed require, the detail. In the popular press an announcement that an improved car jack has been produced can simply state that it

will aid the elderly. Motoring magazines will want to know whether it is hydraulic, pneumatic, what psi it will work to, if it's of chromed steel or a painted pressing.

7. Abbreviations are the bane of life today. Some, but only a few, are well enough known not to need spelling out but most will. NATO or EU are all right but NUT (National Union of Teachers) or MAA (Motor Agents' Association) should have the full spelling. Every industry has its jargon and you should remember that *what is familiar to you may be incomprehensible to your readers*. You need only spell it out the first time – successive mentions can be abbreviations.

8. The local press can be distressingly parochial. The classic story of 'local man lost at sea' instead of 'Titanic sinks' has its parallels today. They are more likely to print a story if you can tie in to a local dignitary or personality. My local paper is obsessed with everything that the mayor does. If you can rope him in somehow you're almost guaranteed coverage.

9. An *embargo* is a request to the press not to publish before a stated date. You can put an embargo on your release to prevent prior announcement of your earth-shattering speech, but at the same time alert the press to be ready for it. In practice it can be abused for trivial reasons. There is no point embargoing a church fête opening but there could be some point at a new product launch. With differing copy deadlines it is sometimes helpful to issue a release to a variety of media, safe in the knowledge that most will play the game. It is helpful to them if they are given advance notice of a major announcement or personality appearance. At the top of your release it should therefore say either 'Release immediate' or 'Embargoed till 12.00 July 31st'. Use the device sparingly.

10. Finish with a contact for more information. Give a phone number at work and out of hours. This will tend to be used if a gap appears in a radio broadcast schedule and a journalist is looking for more detail.

11. All the media work to strict *deadlines*. Be aware that if you ask television crews to appear in the middle of the afternoon you will be very unlikely to make the six o'clock news or magazine programmes. Many locals sold on a Friday are printed on a Tuesday or Wednesday morning. A release that fails to make it

by then will probably be spiked. The national dailies, of course, have more flexibility and often have several editions. At the other end of the scale many colour supplements and monthly journals have a cut-off date at least six weeks in advance. If you're planning a Christmas story think ahead.

That covers the basics, now let's look at what and how to write.

What makes a good press release?

You must steer away from *selling* your firm and product, and write *news*. Anything else is advertising and will be discarded. You're not writing an advert, you're telling a story to interest the readers. A simple attractive statement of facts is all that is needed. Cut out the waffle and come to the point in the first sentence. Nobody's going to wade through six paragraphs to find out who did what and when. Editors are busy people – they just won't bother.

The *introduction* is the most vital part. You should ask yourself, 'Will it make the reader want to read on?' Avoid detail and sidetracks. The paragraphs should have bite and flow. Keep the sentences reasonably short. State the main point of the story early on and isolate the news. For example: *not* 'Delegates from 20 countries watched as the Lord Mayor opened the first International Congress of Snuff Taking at the Wigmore Hall', *say* 'The First International Congress of Snuff Taking was opened today by the...'.

Quotations from your speaker should never open the story. The readers' impression of the *value* of the remark entirely depends on the standing of the personality. You must know *who* is speaking before any weight is put on the reported remarks. 'British coal is too dear', announced by Arthur Scargill, the miners' union leader, would have been sensational but the same remark by the head of the Electricity Board would have been more understandable. Put the speaker's name first. There is another rule to remember: statements of *opinion* should be printed in quotes " " or ' ', statements of fact should be left alone.

Watch the tenses when changing a statement into reported speech. Avoid starting the story with a present principle or 'As', eg saying, telling, announcing, etc. It's a poor way to begin. 'Announcing the start of the Round Robin Wheelbarrow Race, the Sports Minister foretold a big demand for cornplasters.'

Finally, try to keep lengthy titles, official bodies and complicated names out of the introduction. Write with a light touch and save the essential details (if any) until further on in the piece. Don't discourage your readers too soon.

Good pictures are always welcome

Every picture is worth half a page of text if it's a good bright subject. News photos are definitely best left to the professionals. Editors are always on the look-out for good examples. They must be glossy prints and of good contrast. And make sure they are sharp. Seven inches by five is quite large enough. Don't forget to label the reverse of the photo when sending it in. Resin-coated prints don't accept many inks and ballpoint pens show through. If you forget to identify the print, your release and the photo may separate in a busy newspaper office. Use a self-adhesive label on the back and never use pins or staples. Paper-clips are the only practical method of attaching the print to the press release.

Digital photos are welcomed by the press but only if they have been taken with a professional digital camera, ie one that probably cost over £2,000. Use ISDN to get it to the picture editor.

If the story is strong enough the paper will send its own photographer. Don't forget to ask for several copies – always useful.

Once in a lifetime you'll come across a scoop picture. Always keep a camera in the car. Fleet Street will readily process the film for you immediately if you tell them what you've got.

Occasionally a *press pack* is called for. This is not just the release but supporting literature on the firm, background notes on the directors, product leaflets and photographs. Wrap it up in a nice folder. There are several specialist binder firms which can do a very professional-looking job on very short runs using hot-melt glue or slide binders. Save the treatment for the big occasion. Press packs can tend to be pretentious.

You will get better results by following up afterwards with a quick phone call. It is distressing to discover how few get past the first sifting. Almost as good is to fax or e-mail it off: the media seem to know nothing else these days.

To save money on photos it is sufficient to say at the end of your release 'photo available' – with a brief description.

Merry Marketing

4 December 2000

11 Overlands · North Curry · Taunton TA3 6JL
Telephone & fax (+44) 01823 490782
email · merrymark@cwcom.net

Kate Wallace
Country Magazines
London Road
Sayers Common
Brighton BN6 9HS

PRESS RELEASE

Muck spreading without a tractor

One of the most tiresome chores of owning a horse is getting rid of the muck when you don't own a tractor. To ease this problem Devon based Hall Engineering have produced a small muck spreader that can be towed behind a large quad bike or Land Rover.

Managing Director Peter Hall says that as a smallholder himself he knows the problem well. "Massey used to sell a towed muckspreader but they stopped making them 30 years ago. We've adapted their design using off the shelf components, beefing up the bearings and making a stronger fabrication all round. I use it for my two ponies on the Blackdowns and it works a treat."

Called the Land Drive Spreader the trailer has a moving bed driven off the wheels by chains and gears that shifts the manure to the rear where it is shredded and picked up by flails. Special deep tread traction tyres ensure a good grip. Peter says that it is not only horse muck that can be shifted as smallholders with a few house cows or chickens or pigs have the same problem.

Priced at under £1500 Hall Engineering expect there to be a good take-up amongst smallholders and horse owners. They are based at Market Square, Hemyock tel 01823 680073.

ENDS: 214 words: enc leaflet and photo
More details from Peter Hall, Hall Engineering, Market Square, Hemyock, Cullompton, Devon EX15 3RQ. Tel 01823 680073, fax 01823 680544.
Website hallengineering.co.uk

Practical marketing: strategy, copy writing, advertising, leaflet design, PR, research, direct mail, exhibitions, new product launches, inventions. Principal: Dave Patten

Figure 6.1   Simple press release

Figure 6.2 Photo of the muckspreader that accompanied the press release in Figure 6.1. It includes the horse to attract the eye of the 'horsey' readership

Keeping up the momentum

Once you start getting results you'll want to keep it going. Try to find a story regularly for the local press and get to know your local journalists and editors. Perhaps there is a news agency in your town that sends stories off to the media. It can be very helpful as it earns its money by the number of lines that get published or seconds used on the air. If the agency does its job properly it will be on intimate terms with all the right people. There's no charge to you.

Always be frank and helpful and *available*. If a journalist rings you and you're at a meeting, make sure you always ring back. This applies even more so in adverse times. Don't pump papers with material in good times and expect them to print it if, when a bad story breaks, you pass a 'No comment'. The local press in particular will rarely wish to knock a local firm. They know that jobs and prestige are at stake. They are very much part of the community themselves.

Most important: always be truthful. Half-truths will always be found out.

One company near me invariably gets a piece in the paper every week. It can be something as riveting as one of their drivers being awarded a 10 years' accident-free certificate or a gold watch presentation. It's rarely of desperate news value – the company happens to have an active press officer.

You've got to *study* your media and learn what style of items get printed. If your paper habitually prints trivia make the most of it. You're simply keeping the firm's name in the public eye and for the price of a stamp that can't be bad.

The trade press

Research has shown that 40 per cent of buying decisions made in large firms are based on information gathered from the trade and technical press. It is therefore very important that you regularly send press releases to your relevant journal. Details of how to find them are given on pages 50–51.

For these journals you can spell out the technical performance in the expectation that the readership will not only understand but wish to know more, particularly if it's a new product.

But still don't fall into the trap of writing a 'puff' for the product: the *advertising* manager will be more interested in grabbing your money. You can spell out the specification without saying that it's the best since Edison. It is a difficult art to write a story about your product that is newsworthy yet does not read like an advertisement. The tone must be more flat and subtle.

Personnel changes, factory openings, mergers, trade shows, unusual jobs either by design or speed all warrant an airing in your trade journal. Study what gets published. Your stories all help to build up an image, inspire credibility and improve awareness. You will then find it's easier getting in to see the buyers.

TV and radio

With the growth of local radio and TV it is not hard to get on air. You make the approach in the usual way – by press release – but the response tends to be different. Don't expect a great deal of positive feedback, as you will get more from the written word. TV and radio are more ephemeral media and few viewers and listeners sit there with pen and paper poised to note down interesting items. TV is always more interested in visual stories, so life and action and human interest are more likely to grab their attention.

Both TV and radio tend to react quickly but with little lead times. I have been rung up at 9.00 am and expected to be willing to be recorded either immediately 'down the line' or walk into a studio. TV will rarely record after about 2.00 pm as an item won't make the evening bulletins.

While your release may be taken at face value, occasionally you may be approached first to comment on some issue.

Some simple rules:

1. Never agree to be recorded straight away. Ask what the 'angle' is – what is the purpose, what's behind the questioning, who else is being asked for comment?
2. Prepare three points that you need to get over and write them down.
3. If you have the choice, go for a live rather than recorded interview; that way you retain some initiative. I can recall the representative of one of my firms being interviewed on a live TV programme and I told him to take some leaflets along. He waved them around and they could do nothing about it. The response afterwards was marvellous.
4. For TV take some visual aids – some of your product if possible.
5. Look at the interviewer, not the cameras, and avoid loud checks and striped shirts. Dress soberly and don't drink beforehand.
6. Don't slouch, lean forward slightly. Avoid mannerisms, keep control of your hands.
7. Smile, relax, look human. No matter what you say, people won't remember. All they will recall is whether you were a 'nice guy'.
8. For tricky questions, turn it back with a question of your own. 'What you really mean is why...' Don't let the interviewer put words in your mouth: stop at once and correct.
9. Radio demands a light, varied voice. Don't sink into a monotone.

Other PR techniques

There are many subtle ways of engendering a nice warm glow about your company, and not all of them are expensive (such as that shown in Figure 6.3 below). Another, and a delightful example, comes from Hinton Poultry at Norton St Philip near Bath, a factory with social awareness. The factory has been successful and grown rather large for the village. A few years ago it sent a letter to all the local children (it is shown in Figure 6.4 on page 184).

The result was overwhelming. Probably every child in the village (125 of them) chose a tree but grandparents also wanted their grandchildren, living out of the village, included as well. The annual party with an entertainer, tea and presents must be the highlight of the year. The goodwill now generated must make it all very worthwhile.

You have received a floral gift from Sandy James Flowers at the Flower Shed in Taunton.
We would appreciate your assistance in ascertaining the condition at the time of arrival. This will enable us to monitor the quality and service to our customers. Please tick appropriate box and add any further comments you think will be helpful.

FRESH
☐ *Fresh & not damaged*
☐ *Slightly damaged*
☐ *Dying or dead*
☐ *Pleased to receive flowers this way*
☐ *Not particularly impressed*
☐ *Presentation was good*
☐ *Presentation was not good*
Comments:..
....

DRIED
☐ *Flowers were not damaged*
☐ *Some crumbling*
☐ *Crushed and broken*
☐ *You were pleased with the product*
☐ *You were not pleased*
Name of sender:
....

Figure 6.3 Postal florist. This card is sent with every postal delivery – and has not only brought a warm response from the recipients, but has increased business by recommendations

The motor trade has become adept at trying little stratagems to win appreciation. One I like is to leave a tissue in the car after a service with the printed legend, 'The steering wheel and controls have been cleaned by our mechanic but this tissue is for your added convenience.'

Still with the motor trade, I know another garage which always leaves a bouquet of flowers, attractively presented, on the rear seat of each new car sold, addressed to the female customer (or spouse of a male customer). The garage has a regular contract with the local florist which keeps the price down. Believe me, the new owner values that personal touch out of all proportion to the cost.

The garage also sends a birthday card on the anniversary of the purchase assuring the customer of its continued interest. Figures show that people tend to change their car when the HP or bank loan is nearing completion. A timely reminder at this stage can be very cost-effective, but send it three months before the loan runs out – people do plan ahead.

I've heard of a restaurant that asks when any children present have their birthdays. A note is made of their address and a card is sent on the due date. The crafty host encloses a voucher for their meal. Naturally their parents have to come too...

On a humbler note, our local butcher keeps a box of sweets under the counter to be given out to toddlers. Of course, the kids always want to drag their parents into that shop.

Charity work

Every business seems to get tapped into supporting the local cause. More often, causes in the plural. It's a fact of life and unavoidable if you set up in a small community. Try to be fair to everybody and let it be known that the same, probably small, amount goes to them all. It can very easily get out of hand. Look on it as your PR contribution. A little can go a long way. Why not present a trophy to the local Guides' sports? If you are a builder, giving away demolition materials to the Scout hall can do your image a power of good, or lending your portable heaters to old people in a power cut.

Open days

Open days are a good PR exercise for your customers, prospects, local dignitaries, suppliers, neighbours and the media, not forgetting the wives and husbands of staff. Choose something interesting to show and talk about. Provide a light buffet and some liquid refreshment. Keep someone working the machines to bring a bit of life to the place. The motor trade do this rather well when a new model is launched. Get the local beauty queen or sports star to grace the occasion. It need not cost a great deal at all but the benefits could be many.

If you supply the trade and the public, don't mix both at your open day. Traders expect more respect, time and courtesy to be devoted to them.

Sponsorship

The *Guinness Book of Records*, Michelin Guides, the FA Carling Premiership are all sponsored events right in the mainstream of PR in that they generate goodwill in a pleasing, innocuous way and keep the sponsor's name in front of the public. Small firms can cover a little bit of the same route in their locality by more modest means. Every village has its cricket or football team and no one would turn down sponsorship of the match ball in return for a little publicity. There are always apprentices grateful for help with tools. A bursary for which deserving causes were invited to apply annually would receive mileage in the local press.

There are lots of permutations on this theme. School prizes for accomplishment presented by the local store or a photographic competition on an industrial theme will reflect goodwill.

Become an authority

Never turn down a speaking engagement. There are masses of clubs and societies always on the lookout for a guest speaker, from Rotary Clubs to the WI, wine circles to bird-watchers. It's all good PR. You never know who might be in the audience and what it may lead to. Take along some slides and samples and tell them all about your speciality. Don't forget to leave a few discreet leaflets behind. These sorts of things can never be anything other than sowing the seed but can be very rewarding.

On the same lines, if you really are an expert submit learned articles to the appropriate magazine. The simple byline mentioning which company you are from will bring forth some business. One thing will lead to another – very good for service trades and professionals.

When you are one (or one hundred)

When you have survived your first year in business hold a birthday

Dear Children,

Would you like to own a tree? Hinton Poultry would like to give a tree to each of the children in Norton St Philip. Lots of trees will be planted between Churchmead and the chicken factory. They will be quite small when they are planted, and you will be able to watch your tree grow, as you grow yourself. I expect you all know Dr Peter Thompson of Oldfield Nurseries. He is going to plant all the trees and he will plant your name on the sort of tree you choose. The trees wil be quite delicate for a few years and Dr Thompson will look after your tree for you.

Factories are dangerous places and we do not want any of our children to get hurt, so I thought the best thing to do would be to have a special day each year for all the children to look at their trees.

May 2nd is a school holiday and a factory holiday, so on that day, I shall arrange a picnic for you all and you will be able to see your tree. May is blossom time, so the little trees should be very beautiful. We shall have a special day every spring when you can look at your tree.

When you have decided which kind of tree you would like to have, please fill in the form. You can take this into the Norton St Philip Post Office. Mr Peter Walker will pass it on to me.

I shall write to you again soon to tell you all about the picnic.

I am really looking forward to seeing which kind of tree you choose. Please let me know soon.

With love from

Yvonne Boore

Figure 6.4   A delightful example of how to engender a warm glow about your company for very little

party! Have a cake, ask along anyone who has helped you in any way – suppliers, builders, the landlord, clients, etc, not forgetting the bank manager. And the media: it could make a lovely story. I did the same thing with a shoe cooperative and for an expenditure of under £100 coverage was obtained on three TV channels and in half a dozen newspapers (see page 186).

Run a newsletter

The subtle way to increase product awareness is by producing your own newsletter. Subtle? If you simply fill it full of praises for the product it will never be read. The newsletter approach can be successfully used where:

1. You have a wide and increasing range of products.
2. Your product has many applications.
3. You have a wide range of clients in many different activities who have but a spasmodic use for your expertise.

I believe it is particularly suitable for a *service* trade. You can preach by illustration and example what others are doing and how they are benefiting from your particular skills.

It helps if you have a known client or prospect list that you can mail on a regular basis. The advantage that a newsletter offers over advertising is that there is more room at an economic cost to display and expand your message. Good photographs can be used with a technical explanation of why you were able to help. Above all it should be interesting and newsworthy. Put in a few jokes or cartoons borrowed from trade magazines. Most journals will gladly give permission for short extracts to be reprinted if due acknowledgement is made.

Let me relate my own experience. I used to be involved with the marketing of industrial and architectural models. Our clients ranged from consulting engineers, architects, oil companies, advertising and PR consultants, exhibition promoters both here and abroad. To reach them all by advertising would have meant taking space in a dozen journals at inordinate cost. Even the most productive client rarely ordered more than one model a year. By adopting the newsletter method, 400 specifiers were gently reminded of our talents every quarter. The latest model was shown with the name of the client and an explanation of the project was given. Very soft sell. There were usually about 10 good enquiries as a result. Total cost? About £100.

Paddy Mounter, Langport

Figure 6.5 Minehead Shoe Cooperative birthday celebration invitation

You could do the same with, say, stone restoration. Various examples of churches before and after would soon get the message across. Or outside catering – different grand houses with marquees on the croquet lawn. Or interior decorating. The list is endless.

Summary

- A planned PR campaign can be productive and influential, but don't look for an overnight success.
- Think who are the people, your 'public', you are trying to reach.
- Don't neglect internal PR – your own staff who need motivating and involving.
- Publicity. Develop a nose for a good news story. Don't neglect what may seem trivial as outside readers may find it fascinating.
- Study your customers' papers and technical journals, if appropriate. Learn what goes in and copy the format for detail, gossip, technical level. Write for the readership.
- Follow the basic ground rules for setting out a press release and try to send a good photo where possible.
- Never turn down the chance to appear on TV or local radio, but always prepare well beforehand – and you may be asked back again.
- Explore other cheap and effective PR techniques if appropriate for your trade.

7 *Selling and sales promotion*

We are not here to sell a parcel of boilers and vats, but the potentiality of growing rich, beyond the dreams of avarice.

Dr Johnson, 1781

The most hated and feared aspect of marketing among small firm owners must be selling. The fear of rejection, the prejudices of buyers and the low esteem in which salespersons in general are held defeat many small businessmen before they start. Many of the techniques can be learnt, and once you realise that salesmen can be made as well as born then some of the terrors may decline.

So who'd be a salesperson? There are two firms near me that carry the following forbidding notices in their reception:

We shoot every third SALESMAN and the second has just left

Representatives calling without an appointment will be invoiced at the rate of £15 an hour

Research will pinpoint the gaps and throw up what customer needs are, but those needs have to be met by a trained, motivated and persistent salesperson.

Selling is hard, but the skills and techniques can be learnt and reasonable proficiency obtained. You will get rejection – perhaps many times – but if you have belief in your product and *yourself* you can succeed. Many people will try a product once, but the art of selling is to generate repeat business. Both parties must be satisfied; customers that they have found a reliable source of what they need will come back again. Life becomes much simpler when you don't have continually to trawl for fresh faces. Running a small business is no picnic but selling is one skill where you really should get to know the basics.

You *can* appoint agents, but you still have to be able to pick the right ones and give them back-up in the field from time to time. There could also be important trade shows and major distributors you would wish to deal with personally. A working knowledge of selling techniques is vital to survival. You cannot abdicate all responsibility – not if you want to grow. In many respects you have to *sell* yourself to prospective lenders, your banker or investors.

Rejection is probably not rejection of *you*, but the timing, or presentation. Learn, ask and listen. And adapt and persevere. You will improve and realise that the same questions from buyers will tend to recur, giving you the opportunity to try a different approach and be ready for the obvious.

People who buy people

The first rule of selling is to sell yourself. If you don't like meeting people and learning what makes them tick, you'll never enjoy or be any good at selling.

A knowledge of psychology helps. People are different, everyone is different. The same person is different at nine o'clock and at lunch; over a drink, cold sober or talking about work or his hobby; on a Monday morning after a weekend with in-laws or on Friday thinking about that business trip to the Caribbean.

This is the fascination of selling. People buy people first. The product comes later. Watch real professional salespeople at work. All the time they are looking and listening. Looking for reactions, the eyebrows, the shrug, inflections in the voice. Looking for an opening, a buying signal, a chance to sign up an order.

Figure 7.1   Yes, an unusual sign. On the side of a garage, however

Try to *be yourself* – don't adopt a stance or affect to be more knowledgeable or polished than you are. Selling is a conversation but one where you are controlling the direction. Take care over your appearance – no one takes to a scruff – but a pin-stripe talking to farmers would be out of place. Wear clothes you feel comfortable and happy in yet which carry an air of confidence. Suit your clothes and tactics to the situation. Bank managers are fond of relating stories of farmers dressed in suits, obviously ill at ease, who have come to raise some money.

Honesty is the only policy. If you don't know the answer, say so and make sure you come back promptly with the information.

You are allowed just two lies: 'It's my fault' and 'You're right'.

Setting objectives

Many salespeople drift round firms like milkmen. They call on the same people week in, week out. 'Nice day', 'How's trade?' or more daringly 'Same as last time?'. They are order takers. They make no attempt to develop their business or show an interest in their clients. The only people they listen to are themselves. They are defeated before they start. The buyers are the enemy. Secretaries are fair game, and a warm office is definitely to be preferred to knocking on strange new doors.

But you can afford none of this. Every hour away from base must be used efficiently. The object of selling is to get orders. Each face-to-face call must have that end in view. Perhaps not on the first visit, but each call should end with a new bit of information of use along the road. Good accounts need working on. Remember, there is always a competitor in there already, possibly cheaper, invariably satisfactory but above all – known.

If you do walk out with a large order first time there is probably something wrong. The suppliers may have stopped credit or your prospect may know of a price rise on its way.

The reason for setting objectives is twofold. It gives you something to aim at and plan for as well as a fall-back position. Don't set too high an objective or you will easily get discouraged. If you aim to sell 500 items, can they take half at once with the balance over three months? Work out a trial offer: sale or return, perhaps, or a promise to tender next time. Even as low an objective as more contacts within the organisation can be worthwhile, keep your spirits up and make you feel you have achieved something. You have to find ways of keeping *your* motivation going.

Know your product

As proprietor you should be fully versed in all your products; their performance, quality, reliability, cost, delivery, after-sales service, etc. It is no good setting out your stall without all these facts at your fingertips. Is your sales literature correct with the up-to-date prices? If you are going to demonstrate the product, does the sample work?

Don't forget to check an old customer's account before pumping more into that firm. Has the last order been delivered without any hiccups? You don't want egg on your face.

Planning saves time

You need to plan several areas. Your prospects (and customers), your geographical area and, of course, what you're going to sell. Paramount is how to make the best use of your time. The small firm owner's hardest decision I have found is to accept that so many days a month *must* be allocated to selling. It is a hard discipline for many that time away from the business will not be wasteful but is essential for expanding the customer base and keeping in touch with the outside world. It is all too easy to remain locked in the day-to-day crisis fire-fighting of running your business.

Market research will have told you where the prospects lie, and advertisements and coupon replies or mailshots set out the pattern of calls to be made. As invariably your time is the most precious commodity, try to train someone else to arrange appointments by phone. (For more on telesales techniques, see pages 213–16.) Get a map and divide up the territory. It may help to run a circle around your base representing one hour's driving time, then further circles beyond that. Try to avoid dashing about haphazardly as time between prospects is dead time. In a city use public transport, if it is physically possible.

If often pays to ask the buyer when is the best time to call. You may be surprised at the odd hours that people would welcome a sales presentation. Although as a general rule the safest time for a first call is after 9.30 am, to allow post and messages to be dealt with, an increasing number of businesses are starting before 8 am or run into the evening. Selling is highly competitive and picking a time when your more lazy rivals are not astir could well pay dividends. Victor Kiam, in his book *Going For It!*, relates that calling on Saturdays or working through lunch has paid dividends for him. There are no queues of reps at those times and the buyer often welcomes a more relaxed discussion. Different trades require a different approach in your timing. Publicans, doctors, vets and head teachers have a 'best' time to call.

Don't always call in the same town on the same day of the week.

That way you may catch that buyer who is always out. It is strange also how different places look on other days of the week.

If you can afford to go out every day, then work on a rotating pattern. This will shift the week on. Friday afternoons are generally a poor time to call. Leave them for your record-keeping and paperwork.

It is best to allocate a set time each week or month when you will go out selling. This will vary if you are a brand-new business or well established. But the time never to neglect calling is when you are busy. Your spate of business may not last and trying to establish fresh customers when you are in a slump is too late. The time to establish contacts is at the crest, not the trough.

You must develop a system

Invest in a laptop PC or do it manually and get a good loose-leaf binder. There are several that take 200 sheets (400 sides) and will slip in your glove pocket. Use it to record your prospects' names. Unless you adopt a routine approach to your canvassing from day one you will get into slipshod and wasteful ways. Don't write the names alphabetically but group them in towns or convenient, logical areas. This method will give alternative choices to plan your calling time, rather than thumbing through all your records to pick out the appointments.

On each sheet record the exact name of the firm (for invoicing purposes), the address and phone number, buyers, product lines and who does the existing business. List the delivery address if that is different. Record the date of your call and any other relevant information, which can be the name of the secretary or receptionist (most important – courtesy is the great door opener) and topics discussed with the buyer. Staff come and go so jot down not just the name of the buyer but his or her exact job title. It could be 'Consumables' or 'Fasteners' or 'Plant Manager'.

There are many cheap computer-based organisers or 'task schedulers' that can remind you of follow-up calls, or just make a note in your diary or a multi-pocket file. For the last of these you will need 43 pockets – 31 days and 12 months. A reminder can be slipped in either the next month's pocket or, if you want to be more exact, the correct day file. Don't leave your binder behind. It could be invaluable to a competitor and you'll be lost without it. Write your name and address (private home) inside.

One of the secrets of selling must be to take a genuine interest in the growth and success of your customers. *Their* success, not yours. Remember, the customer comes first. Between calls keep your name subtly in front of your client by clipping and sending odd paragraphs of trade news or gossip that he or she may not have seen. You don't need to write a letter – just staple it to your compliments slip – with a note 'may be of interest to you'. It all helps to build a warm relationship. There are more ways of getting business than writing an order form.

How to get past the secretary

Cold calling (ie without an appointment) is rarely rewarding. Buyers are busy people who generally abhor door knockers. You won't always be able to make appointments and indeed, some firms are relatively easy to get into without that magic phone call, but your time is valuable and your car costs a lot to run.

The more people you can see in a day, the more chance you have of making a sale, so make an appointment where you can. Ask for the buyer and make sure you record the name. If you are stuck for the name it sometimes helps to make one up. Say: 'Mr Johnston the buyer, please' to which the receptionist may reply, 'Don't you mean Mr Whiteside?' or whatever. In some firms the buyer's secretary guards the boss like the Crown Jewels.

Offer *alternatives*, and always be positive and self-assured. 'Good morning. My name is John Richards from XYZ Company. I am in your town next Wednesday and Thursday morning. Which day is more convenient for me to see him? I have a proposition I would like to put to him which will take no more than 15 minutes.'

Try not to get involved in long discussions with secretaries. Good ones are trained to winkle out time-wasters, and you are not selling to the secretary but the boss. As with all selling, be persistent, courteous yet firm. Don't forget the secretary could well control that vital appointments diary, so you mustn't get on the wrong side of her. Sending a letter in advance, spelling out the major benefit, is often a good door opener that reduces delay from the secretary. 'He will have received my letter' seems to stop procrastination and implies an established relationship.

Make sure that you are seeing the *right* person. Many large firms split buying functions right down. Finally, when you do get an appointment make sure you understand where the prospect is situated.

If you are fobbed off, be persistent yet firm, and always be polite. A firm may genuinely have completed its buying for the season, or only work on annual contracts. Never put the phone down without having learnt something of value, some extra fact that you can come back on. You must leave yourself with a lead-in for the next time.

The presentation

At last you've arrived for your appointment in good time. In your case you will have a notebook and pen (that works), brochures, your diary, colour photos of your product range or past successes that aren't in your leaflet, samples if size permits, and your order book (why not?).

When you are shown in, introduce yourself, shake hands – and *smile*! The smile is the ice-breaker, it shows you are human, just like the buyer. A smile means warmth and understanding. It relaxes tension and removes the worry lines round your mouth. A smile is also the shortest distance between two people.

Breaking the ice

First impressions are most important. Psychological research has shown that we are conditioned and judge people in the very first moments of meeting

'Body language' or 'non-verbal communication' has also been studied. Apart from the words you use, the manner in which you respond and behave is often just as telling. Eye contact is very important. Avoiding looking at the speaker is regarded as shifty while an alert interest encourages a warm response. An open approach conveys integrity and sincerity. Nervous movements of the fingers, hands and legs, combined with shifting about, fail to give an air of confidence.

The rules of the game allow you first bite to get your presentation under way. Keep pleasantries to a minimum. Don't throw that advantage away by rambling on about the weather or admiring the buyer's rubber plant.

If the buyer is not familiar with your company, a thumbnail sketch of the setup, personnel and specialities is in order. Starting on a subject you are totally familiar with helps to break your nervousness and encourage a natural flow of words.

Your whole manner should be positive, enthusiastic without being overbearing, sensitive to responses from your audience and on a stance of equality. An attitude of craven humility or the reverse can be equally disastrous. It will be difficult at first to sound natural but strive to conduct your sales pitch as a normal conversation, for this is, after all, what salesmanship is all about. Ask questions – *open* questions. By that I mean questions that can't be answered simply by a 'Yes' or 'No'. For instance, 'Shall I send you some?' can only provoke either yes or no and if it's *no* then you've rather run out of steam.

Probing questions like 'How many do you use in the course of each shift?' or 'What do you look for when you buy this product?' will involve the other person, who has to think and give intelligent replies. You are showing an interest in his or her business, problems and needs.

By shifting the emphasis you should develop the sales patter into a discussion, not about you but about the buyer's world and how your product can help *make more money for his or her company*. Questions should be aimed at discovering whether and in what quantities the firm uses products similar to yours. The old standbys of what, where, how and when should be used.

What the buyer worries about

Look at it from the *buyer's* point of view. Someone doing the job properly must always be on the look-out for products that will do the job more efficiently at better cost from a reliable supplier. They must meet the company's quality standards and be available at the right time in the correct quantities.

Once the buyer has found a supplier that meets perhaps very exacting requirements, it is human nature to stick with that supplier rather than be chopping and changing about. Unless you can offer some very cogent reasons why the company should change, then the status quo will prevail.

What we loosely term 'the buyer' may well not be the person of influence. Some department stores now have 'controllers' above buyers, who determine initial strategy and look for new products. They decide what is sometimes called the 'range plan' that sets the trend for their image and merchandise. Once this has been settled. the more mundane decisions of quantity and delivery are handled by our friends the buyers. Every company is different, with increasingly more sophistication entering the world of the professional purchasing manager.

The more complex and expensive your product, the more likely it will be that several people, and layers of management, will want to have a say. A new computer system may involve a whole host of departments with differing needs and specifications. Such a contract may take years to negotiate and design. You must try to understand how the buying process works for each target company and perhaps the strong internal politics and pressures on the decision-making process. Your initial approach could well be fairly low down the ladder – perhaps a shopfloor supervisor who actually has to use your kit – but you must attempt to influence the key person. The user and buyer must be separated and distinguished. Each has different motives. The user, who may not be paying for it, probably wants the best, the most expensive. The buyer, who may be on a profit scheme (or it may be his or her own company), will look harder at cost benefits.

To turn to simpler examples, children are usually the focus of TV ads near Christmas, to the dismay of their parents. Not terribly subtle blackmail. The appeal is directed to users, not buyers.

Recent research has disclosed that even purchases for the home and car are influenced by your children – and holiday venues even more so. Advertisers should bear in mind that, for example, the *Sun* is read by 26 per cent of boys under the age of 16 (I wonder why) but only 4 per cent read the *Telegraph*. It won't be long before direct mail hits those in this age group, and because they don't get many letters at present, the attention span is likely to be high. At the same time they are perceived to be perceptive and cynical about marketing. The good salesperson takes this kind of thing into account.

Learn to listen

When you're talking you're not listening, when you're not listening you're not learning. A good salesperson is a good listener, not necessarily just a good talker as popular assumption has it. How many hear without listening? You listen to promote dialogue, for *buying indicators* and points you can pick up for leads and decisions.

Many salespeople have their set patter which defies interruption. They have to go through the routine, trotting out all the selling points regardless of the buyer's reaction.

Difficult buyers

Old hands at buying can sometimes floor you by repeatedly asking questions. Turn it back and answer a question with a question.

> *Buyer*: Why should I give up my existing supplier I've known for years?
>
> *You*: When did you last get another quote?
> *or*
> Don't you think some competition is good for everyone?

One of the hardest buyers to sell to must be the silent or 'grunt' type. Your spiel produces no interest. The only way to draw out such a person is to keep asking short open-ended questions. If you have a product that can be demonstrated, then encourage discussion by involving the prospect.

Buying indicators

All through your presentation you should be looking for buying indicators. If not green lights, then there are amber lights saying: 'Right, I'm interested, sell me some.' *Talk too much* and the buyer may change his or her mind or think of a good reason not to buy.

Examples of buying indicators are:

'What are your deliveries like?'
'Do you do them in red?'
'We've tried similar products in the past.'
'Do you do trial offers?'
'What's the minimum quantity?'
'How much does it cost?'

The new salesperson will not recognise these as intimations to buy but treat them as a series of questions and simply make the appropriate reply. He or she should be reaching for the order book.

Concessions

Never make a concession without asking for something in return.

'If I discount by 5 per cent will you order 1,000 instead of 900?'
'If I... will you...?'

Handling objections

Objections to buying are your *opportunity*. Quite simply they are reasons that you can fasten on to and turn to your advantage. Let's look at some common objections and ways of getting round them.

Buyer: It's too dear.
You: Are you sure you're comparing like with like? The benefits I mentioned will give longer service and save you money in the long term.

If price is the cause of objections, then switch from price to value. Rolls-Royces would never sell on price alone. They are bought because they last 30 years, everything works superbly, they have 30 coats of paint, are hand trimmed and sail through the traffic because of their status.
  If you are selling volume items it sometimes helps to quote unit costs or break the cost down to so much a week.

Buyer: You can't meet my delivery times.
You: How critical are those delivery dates? Can we part deliver and produce the rest at weekly intervals?
          or
          If we could meet your delivery how many would you like?
          or
          Let me ring the works and talk that over with my colleague and see what we can do.

> *Buyer*:   You're a small firm and we only deal with established contractors.
>
> *You*:   Everyone has to start from somewhere. Being small means that we can adapt more quickly to pressures and switch over to rush orders. You can pick up the phone and speak to me, the boss, with no difficulty. Our overheads are lower than large suppliers and the benefits are passed to you.

Ring the changes and find out if the objection is genuine or if you are simply being fobbed off. Buyers often raise objections on price because they are undecided. It is the easy way out. Move on to delivery or aftersales and other benefits and find out if cost is a genuine reason. If it still is, then you'll have to bring in other arguments and probe deeper.

Never *argue* over objections. Reason and put your point of view but don't lose control of the discussion. And never enter into a slanging match.

Always be on your guard not to disclose confidential information and never use derogatory tones about others. The buyer may well think, 'If s/he says that about them, what will s/he say about my firm?'

It's also easy to be unwittingly pumped about the buyer's competitors. Use discretion. The odd name dropped with care can sometimes help with clinching an order. Farmers in particular tend to imitate their more go-ahead neighbours and want to know what is happening on the other side of the hedge.

A final important reason why you get objections is that the buyer often has to convince superiors and perhaps a committee that his or her decision was the right one. The buyer is using you as a devil's advocate. The buyer's own integrity and judgement are at stake and he or she must be assured that all the possible objections are covered. It would amuse you to see the reversal of roles later on when the buyer argues the points to colleagues.

Second sourcing

Unless you have a genuinely unique product, the main objection presented to you will be an existing supplier firmly entrenched. Every firm has suppliers that you cannot budge, and for a new small business to oust existing loyalties, great patience and persistence are required. Several key points can be raised with the buyer:

1. How long would it take you to replace your major supplier if they had a fire, strike or merger? What would be the effect on your business?
2. Wouldn't it keep your other supplier on their toes if they knew there was someone else knocking on the door? Competition is a marvellous shatterer of complacency. It's an insurance policy.
3. What were the reasons for placing the business with them in the first place? Isn't the position similar now?
4. When did you last compare prices?
5. When did they last let you down on delivery or quality? (Every firm does at some time.)
6. Put 'suppose' questions. 'Suppose you landed that big contract, could they meet all your demands?' 'Suppose the pound drops again, do they have enough stocks to fulfil the quantity?'
7. Large companies often have several suppliers for identical components.

Closing the sale

Closing the sale simply means getting an *order* – the whole point of this exercise.

All through your presentation you should be alert to those buying indicators and looking for a quick close. You don't have to go through all the merits of your wonderful product if you're getting good signals. Close the sale there and then.

The techniques of asking for an order are many. Some salespeople claim to know and use over 100. I'll not pretend that you need to be fully conversant with all of these, but being prepared may open your eyes to what can be achieved. Having more than two means you do not continually have to steer the discussion around to your pet phrases.

Two vital points must be grasped.

1. A closing question is any question that you ask, the answer to which confirms that the buyer wishes to buy.
2. Whenever you ask a closing question – *shut up*!

If you keep quiet then only one of two things can happen: either the customer goes along with you and you have an order, or a reason is given that you can discuss.

The direct approach

Why not ask for an order? That is what you're there for, after all. They can either say 'yes' or 'no' and if it is 'no', then you have an objection you can get to work on.

An objection *can* be a buying signal. Some buyers are indecisive and want to be helped in making the decision. There might be a doubt on some detail that needs clearing up.

The order form close

This is the most well used of all. Get an order pad out on your knee and during your discussion ask the customer questions completing the answers on your form.

'What is the delivery address? Where should the invoices be sent?'

Unless you are stopped, they've bought, haven't they? The *assumption* is made that they are going to buy but you never actually ask the question.

Alternative choice close

There was a hamburger bar that wanted to increase sales of eggs. As customers walked in, they were asked, 'One egg or two?' Few stopped to consider whether they wanted an egg at all. Your closing questions give the *choice* of buying this colour or that, with wheels or not. The choice is not between whether you want any or not, but assumes that you are certainly going to have *some*, the only decision is what variety.

'When do your want delivery, before Christmas or after?'

Alternative choice questions are invariably prefaced with, 'Which do you prefer?' or related to those old friends when, what, where and how. The questions must always be assumptive.

Sharp angle close

The best salesman I know claims he first learnt this technique as a lad watching the Birmingham costermongers. He relates the story of a woman asking, 'Are those oranges sweet?' To which came the irrefutable reply, 'Would you like some if they were?'

Save this technique for when you are asked:

'Can it do this?'
'Will it run uphill?'
'Will it stay clean?'

Reply (sharp angle back) by saying, 'Do you want it if it does? Instead of tamely saying, 'Yes, it does.'

When you've agreed that the customer wants it if it does, then you've made your sale.

Secondary question close

The secondary question close goes like this: 'As I see it, the only decision you have to make today is whether you have the order this week or next. By the way, do you want to use your pen or mine?'

There is an alternative choice here, but the trick is splitting the decisions into major and minor. It is a distraction. When the prospect has made the minor decision, he has made the major as well.

Question closing

Question closing is a simple technique that is often missed. If you are asked, 'Can I get the delivery in seven days?' don't say, 'Yes' but close the sale by asking, 'Do you want delivery in seven days' time?' When the customer has said 'Yes' he's bought, hasn't he?

Call back close

We've all heard the line: 'I'll think it over. Call me next week.' It's a polite way of saying 'No!'

When you do call back, *never* start by saying, 'Well, did you think it over?' because the likely response will be, 'Yes I did; no thanks'. Instead, try: 'I am sorry but the last time I called I forgot to tell you...' It doesn't matter what it is. Continue by saying, 'Let's run over what we agreed last time,' and go through the whole presentation as before, the only difference being that you will now say, 'As you remember',

'You will recall', 'We said that' and then go into the normal closing techniques. *Never* ask whether the buyer has thought it over.

Objection close

If you come across a client who continually raises objections which you then defeat, ask: 'Tell me, is this the one final objection?' If it is, then you have made a sale.

Summary question close

To be used on the prospect who waffles and won't come to a decision. You allow the subject to use 'no' when they really mean 'yes'. An example:

Just to clear my thoughts, what is it that you're undecided on? Is it our delivery date?

If the prospect says, 'No', it means the delivery date is acceptable and that is not a valid objection. So continue with all your selling points one at a time.

'Is it this?' 'Is it that?'

Every time you get a 'No', you have got a 'Yes'. If you get 'No' to all of your 'Is its?', you have made a sale! If the prospect says, 'Yes', you have pinned him or her down to a definite objection that you can go to work on.

Endorsement close

Bring in a *true* story of someone who has used your product and benefited from its use. The knack is tying it in with someone the buyer can relate to. Alternatively, tell a tale of someone who *didn't* use you and suffered as a result. This close is widely used in the insurance field.

The fear close

The fear close should be used with discretion. The object is to plant a seed of doubt or fear in the prospect's mind: a fear that if he or she doesn't order today then the chance will not recur. If the prospect says he or she will order 'next time' then you have to say you will not be able to offer the same advantageous terms. That statement must be transparently accurate.

Examples

'Sign now and you'll get £100 off.' Much used by double glazing salesmen.

All the more suspect when used by itinerant tarmac gangs: 'We've just finished resurfacing the road round the corner and we've got a few barrows left. Not worth taking back. Shall we do your drive now, missus?'

The referral close

If you've failed to get an order, ask the buyer if he or she can recommend anyone else who may be worth tackling. Psychologically most people will want to be seen to be somewhat helpful, so you should get some referrals. Thank the buyer and say, 'Thanks for these but why not buy some yourself?' It has been known for a change of heart then to magically take place.

The phone close

If the prospect is arguing over detail, phone the works and pretend to discuss with your sales director or production supervisor. 'Yes, you can have that if you give me the order now.'

Agreement close

Work through your sales points with the client getting a 'yes' to each benefit, writing them down so that the client can see. Then gently lead on to delivery date or quantity, whichever seems most relevant. Without the client quite realising it, an order has been subtly introduced.

The briefcase close

Very unsporting, but I have heard of two closes that would fit under this label. The unscrupulous can buy briefcases with a hidden tape recorder that is set off by adjusting the handle. If a salesperson calls on you, makes his or her sales pitch and then leaves the room, you might feel inclined to discuss the proposition. The salesperson then reappears and takes the case to the car to get some papers. Lo and behold she returns with much more confidence and meets your wishes.

Number Two is even worse. Many contracts are placed by tender to be met by a certain date. You phone the buyer on the day and say you are dreadfully sorry but you will be late. You prepare three tenders at difference prices and turn up late asking the buyer, 'By the way, what was the lowest tender?' In a surprising number of cases you are told, whereupon you rummage in your case and produce an even lower tender. These sort of practices get selling a bad name.

Other products and other customers

Before you leave ask two questions:

'What other products are you interested in?'
'Do you know of other prospects that I could see?'

If you don't ask, you may not be aware that their buying patterns have changed or new processes have been installed. *They* may not be aware that you have other lines. But don't carry this to excess – leave something for your next visit.

Other prospects could be buyers at head office or another division that uses the same products. There's nothing like a referral from one buyer to get you into the magic sales office. Don't forget your stock in trade is *names*. If you're dealing with a big customer, don't forget the commitment that some expect. As one buyer said, 'We want a real commitment from you, not just a contribution. I had bacon and eggs for my breakfast this morning. The chicken made a contribution, but the pig made a commitment.'

The dangers of sale or return

SOR is a common practice among craft shops, garden centres and galleries, largely, I suspect, because most are under-capitalised and do not know their market. For the new producer the offer is tempting.

Everyone wants their goods on display in the high street so why worry? You haven't made a *sale* until the money comes in. The goods could very well be damaged or soiled and unsaleable if they come back to you. What check have you whether the goods have been sold anyway?

The whole areas is ripe for disputes, although it does have a genuine place for the experimental piece or single expensive sculpture or picture. It is entirely legitimate that the gallery owner should hang and display works of art on an SOR basic if they have a limited but defined appeal.

SOR goods must be the subject of a written agreement. You will need to cover:

1. Insurance – at whose risk are the goods on display?
2. Commission – at what rate?
3. Terms of payment.
4 Packaging and carriage – who pays for the return?
5. An agreement that the goods remain your property until paid for.

The art of demonstrating

Demonstrating a product requires its own technique. Practise first how and what points you are going to highlight. Check out all the components before you set up, each and every time. It is not sufficient to put it away and take it out next month without a dry run.

If it is an audio-visual (AV) presentation, run through the slides or video and check everything works. Take a spare bulb.

The art of demonstration should involve the following features:

1. While you are actually showing the product – keep quiet. The client can't listen to you and look at the features.
2. *Respect the product*; don't dump it on the table. Even if it's only a cheap item, bring it out of a decent box, remove the tissue and give it a polish. Handle with care and reverence – all part of the image.
3. *Involve the customer* and let him or her handle the goods. But if there is anything approaching a knack to any operation, keep the customer away. Encourage questions. Try to leave the goods for

the client to play with, if that is appropriate, on a trial basis. It gives you another selling opportunity when you call back.

4. Working demonstrations for plant and equipment can go down very well. Farmers love to try out a bit of new apparatus on their land. Get a group together with a chemical firm or your big local contractor and you've got the right atmosphere to generate some business. Don't forget a reasonable amount of food and drink.

Quotations, invoices and terms of trading

Gentlemen's agreements should have no place in your sales pitch. Although the law says that a contract can be made verbally, with or without a shake of the hand, if things go wrong it is awfully difficult to prove what was agreed. Some golden rules:

1. Never accept an order without confirmation in writing. A simple fax confirmation is often sufficient.
2. Never order materials before you get a written acceptance.
3. Don't accept an order over the phone without a written order.
4. Don't vary the order or accept additions without the same procedure. Each variation is a fresh order.

An *estimate* is a well-reasoned guess at what the job is likely to cost. You are allowed to alter the final figure.

A *quotation*, on the other hand, is a firm figure at which you undertake to complete the work. If that figure is accepted, you have made a contract. If you break that contract either by poor performance or non-delivery you could be sued.

Always put a *time limit* on your quote for acceptance: 'This figure holds good for 30 days,' or whatever. In days of high inflation it is folly to give either long fixed-price contracts or undated quotations. Some sectors use a known-cost-of-materials index – architects and builders, for example.

Make sure you get a signed *acceptance* in an approved form. The simplest method is to get back a signed copy of the quote or equip yourself with a duplicate book from any stationers.

References should be taken for new customers before committing yourself to large or special orders. Any professional trickster always keeps a couple of tame referees available so it helps to *ring* rather than write. Speak to the other firm's credit controller – you should be able to pick out the dubious characters. Credit agencies (page 55) and your own bank can also help with inside research. Ask your bank manager to explain the nuances of the reply as there are sometimes coded warning signals to the initiated. If you are uncertain, send a *pro forma* invoice that must be paid before any goods are delivered.

Always be suspicious of large orders dangled before you for no sound reason.

A *specification* should be given saying what you are supplying. You may need to supply drawings, dimensions, samples, and detail any special finish. Reference should be made to a British Standard colour chart and the relevant BS or Ministry of Defence standards if appropriate.

Your *invoice* must be addressed correctly as this is what passes title in the goods.

For small firms make sure you distinguish between sole proprietorships and those with limited status as invoicing in the wrong name could make later legal actions difficult. For large firms always quote their order number and any other detail required. Mark it for the attention of their authorising person. Include your VAT number. Don't give them any excuse to delay payment.

Terms of trading should be stated on the invoice. When is payment required? In 30 days? On delivery? And do you mean 30 days after delivery or after the date of the invoice? 'Monthly' could mean either the end of the month after the month of delivery or a month after delivery. Complicated, isn't it?

When you date the invoice is important. Many large firms regard the last day of the month as sacrosanct. If you deliver on the last day of the month and invoice religiously on the first you'll lose 30 days in your cash flow. Most firms like to pay at the end of the month after the month of delivery.

Many companies now close off the books on the 25th of each month or thereabouts. Miss that cut-off point and you'll have to wait a further month to get into the system. If you are dependent on several large firms, find out how their systems work. Fit your invoicing and deliveries to *their* scheduling – not yours. In the interests of cost cutting, many firms are no longer sending out *statements*. If you are following the trend make sure that your invoice is clearly stamped, 'Please pay on invoice – no statement will be sent.'

Delivery and *advice notes* should state after what period damage claims can no longer be entertained.

Deposits should always be taken with orders for specials or one-offs from unknown customers. The amount should preferably cover the cost of materials. If they object to paying a deposit in advance, open a trust account in the name of your solicitor to act as stakeholder.

Conditions of sale are the small print on the back of your order form. They should cover damage claims, dispute and arbitration procedures, suppliers' liability and payment terms, among others. One point to watch: by accepting an order you are bound by *the customer's* conditions of sale *unless* you point out the contrary. It is then up to the customer to accept your amended conditions or refuse the contract. It would be surprising if you managed to get a large firm to amend its conditions of sale unless it were for very minor reasons. If you are in the contracting industry you will be aware of the Palaeolithic contracts used there that in effect say, 'You'll be paid when I get paid.'

Many attempts to get statutory *overdue interest* on unpaid bills and quicker payment from large firms have failed dismally. You can write a clause into your conditions surcharging interest but whether you will ever get it is dubious. As an inducement to prompt payment some firms offer *discounts* of 2½ or even 7 per cent for settlement in seven days. The problem comes when large customers deduct the early discount and still pay in three months.

Satisfaction notes signed on completion of an order do not hold the force of law. The customer can still claim against you afterwards under the Sale of Goods Act 1971 for fitness of purpose. The mere signing of a note does not relieve liability.

Retention of title clauses mean that in the event of *insolvency* of a debtor company, your goods can be identified, and if payment has not been made, you, as the seller, can uplift the goods, provided that they have not been built or absorbed into other articles. You must have included an appropriate clause in your conditions of sale. Your claim will have preference over that of other creditors. In essence, the wording should run, 'Title to the goods does not pass until payment has been made.'

Using agents

Wholesalers/distributors purchase the goods and sell on. In return they expect a minimum of 30 per cent mark-up. To reduce the distribution cost an agent can be used.

- Agents usually work for a direct commission on volume only.
- Commission varies but is rarely less than 7½ per cent, and 15 per cent is not unknown.
- The goods are sold to the agent but invoiced direct to the stockist.
- The agent may not see the goods at all, apart from sales samples, as they are delivered direct to the buyer.

Few small firms can afford their own sales force and perhaps fewer still enjoy selling as a pastime. But someone has to do it. It is supposed to cost over £40,000 a year (2001) to keep a good salesperson on the road, including car and general travelling expenses. Inevitably there is a running-in period where the investment is awaiting some return. And you run the risk of picking the wrong person.

The logical sales route is via agents. A good agent will have *contacts* in your field, buyers personally known to him or her, with perhaps many years of detailed product knowledge. The important thing to remember all the time is that, like you, the agent is in business on his or her *own account* and stands or falls by his or her own efforts. If the agent doesn't sell he or she won't earn.

Agents are paid purely on commission. You, as principal, pay out directly on results. It is obviously in both your interests to develop a close working relationship and it is not a situation where you can shovel all the responsibility for sales on to someone else and forget about it. That will quickly lead to disillusionment. You will join the throng of firms who say, 'Agents don't work.'

How to find an agent

You can advertise in your specialist trade press or the *Daily Telegraph* (widely used for this purpose), or place a notice on your show stand. There are also agents' associations, but the only reliable method I have ever found is by approaching outlets where you wish to sell. They know the honest, competent and regular agents who call on them. Draw up a short-list and invite them to apply.

The success rate for matching good agents with small firms is not high. I have to confess that few succeed. Too many agents have hung on to a few lucrative long-lasting accounts and see no reason to extend themselves for a new struggling firm with an untried product. It is a very real problem to find professional representation in the field. Your product has to be first class, growth prospects exciting, with plenty of promotional material and back-up support.

Most agents work on their own, though partnerships of several individuals, or even limited companies, are not unknown. You should find out:

1. What other agencies he or she already has. They mustn't compete with yours, but should be complementary.
2. What is the agent's knowledge of the trade, geographical area covered.
3. What are the agent's contacts.
4. What is the agent's proven selling record.
5. Does the agent appear honest, reliable and a fit person to represent your business.
6. You will need to draw up an agreement to cover the main points including commission rates, when payable, retention of 'house' accounts, training and support given and periods of notice required to terminate.

Telephone sales

I've left the hardest to last. Next to face-to-face selling, using the telephone is the second most effective method of persuasion. Many more calls can be made as there is no lost travelling time, and cars and hotels are more expensive than a warm phone. It is also usually easier to reach the decision maker – if you put telephone selling in *skilled hands* (or should it be mouths?). A mailshot on average may reach perhaps half its audience, but few are read beyond the first line. With upwards of 20 million phones in the country (to say nothing of abroad) the audience is readily identified and approachable, unless you live in parts of London where the ex-directory rate is running at 40 per cent. But there are drawbacks. In many parts of the country telesales are becoming a bit of a pest.

Planning a telesales campaign

Names and research have to be gathered in the same way as for any other selling exercise. It helps to include a space for the phone number on your coupon replies and ads so that this goes into your system along with the address. Armed with lists you must then rehearse what you are going to say. Using the phone is a definite skill. Unlike face-to-face selling, you have *only* your voice to persuade. No reaction from the buyer in terms of expression, no demonstrations, no colourful leaflets – and no written order form to close the deal.

Setting objectives

The telephone can be used to:

1. Research the market, in all its implications.
2. Gather names for a mailshot.
3. Make appointments for interested parties.
4. Follow up on a previous marketing exercise, eg mailshot.
5. Secure sales.
6. Keep the customer happy. Follow up on after-sales service.
7. Service existing clients, avoiding expensive salespeople's visits.

Obviously, many items are too complex or need the personal touch to secure actual orders, so reasonably attainable objectives need to be set out. In most cases weeding out hopefuls to make best use of personal face-to-face selling can be done over the phone.

Training in this field is more important than ever. There are many courses available. Like others, you may well find that your female staff are more adept at telesales than the men. You must rehearse and record for self-improvement. Don't forget that for all telephone calls – incoming and outgoing – the person handling the phone is your company. A sloppy or indifferent manner will do you no good.

Voice techniques

Given that you can't see the other person, you can quickly form an impression of their personality: whether they are excitable, young or old, think before they speak, are bored or tired or just 'nice'.

As with all selling you sell yourself first. Your enthusiasm will be projected over the phone just as clearly as if you were sitting in the same room. The listener will form a mental image of you from your speed of delivery, mumbling or clear diction, forcefulness or tardiness.

Clear diction, meaning and sincerity are therefore vital points to practise. *Smile* on the phone. Have you ever heard a voice that isn't smiling? It's surly, discouraged and defeated. Why should you *buy* a voice like that?

Preparation

You will be working from a prepared list of prospects with the usual background details. Some practitioners go so far as to suggest a written script. That I find a bit extreme, but use one if it helps you. At the least you want a short list of the main selling benefits.

Getting past the switchboard

In a depressing number of companies the switchboard operators are trained to fight off salespeople like the plague, so avoid referring to selling or any other close relation like market research or surveys.

Describe the nature of your call: 'I'd like to discuss a new technique in adhesives', or 'I'm sure he'll be interested in profiting from a new discovery.'

There is no point in launching into a sales pitch with anyone other than the decision taker.

When you speak to the buyer

Good telephone selling revolves around bringing out an interest in the prospect's company.

> 'I notice that you won a nice order from Kuwait the other day.'
> 'I see that you are exhibiting at the next trade fair.'
> 'Your trading results had a good press on Sunday.'

Open out the client to get him or her talking and look for opportunities to inject some sales points. Use the regular techniques – what, when, where, how and who? *Why* tends to lead to rather abrupt remarks and may seem to be too probing. Telephone selling must always be the model of courtesy. No hard sell here.

Radio actors should make good telephone salesmen. They know how to sound interesting and convincing, when to pause and vary the pitch of the voice.

Other uses of the phone

Don't neglect *incoming* calls as a sales opportunity. They may be ringing up for lengths of timber. Ask about stains, fixing and cutters and the like. The idea may not have occurred to them. They may not even *know* that you stock such lines.

Take a hard look at your sales route. Could not those *regular* customers be just as easily serviced by phone? It could be easier for them and certainly cheaper for you. It would leave you more time to call on fresh prospects. Train other staff to handle all telephone sales. Pick a person with a bright cheery personality and more business may be developed than by yourself, the boss.

The most profitable way of expanding your sales is by selling more goods to your *existing* customers. That should be writ large in every sales office. You should be thinking all the time, 'What else can I sell them?' We are all creatures of habit and tend to go back to the same shop or supplier. If you keep up a smart service and look after people, it is far less time-consuming to sell to existing customers than chasing round looking for new faces. And the easiest way to do this is by phone.

... and abuses

1. Keeping the customer waiting without explanation while the extension or buyer is tracked down. If there is likely to be a delay, promise to ring back – and make sure you do.
2. How often do you ring a firm to hear, 'Abrgwtyrulifod Company'? The person is so used to answering the phone that the firm's name becomes incomprehensible.
3. A common fault in engineering firms is to locate the phone in the noisiest part of the works. At least that's how it seems. It's sometimes more interesting to listen to the conversation and hubbub in the background than the caller.
4. Good bosses tell someone when and for how long they will be out.

5. Try to avoid putting the phone down before the customer does. It's a subtle point but hearing the 'click' is somehow impolite and disconcerting. It sounds as though you are glad to be rid of him or her.

6. Anyone who answers the phone should have a basic grounding in what the firm does. Whoever answers the phone *is* the firm to the caller and an indifferent voice is no help or image builder.

7. Identify the caller before quoting a price. He or she could be a large trade customer who deserves the best price.

8. Chain a pad and pencil to the phone. How amateurish to be asked to 'Hold on a tick while I find a pen.'

9. Computer call-answering machines that leave enquirers hanging on for minutes do you no favours. For some sectors – the elderly – there is no substitute for the human voice, and you will lose business if you rely on an answering service. There are bureaux that will handle after-hours calls but the fee could be around £3 each, making low-cost items prohibitive – but useful for doctors and emergency building services.

If you have an answerphone you will know that many people (especially the older generation) refuse to leave a message. All you hear on playback is the click. Try *opening* your recorded message with a quip. Instead of, 'This is the Mayfair Widget Company on 234 67845', try 'Yes, I hate these things too', or 'I quite agree. These machines are dreadful.' It does work by breaking the ice with a human touch.

Customer care

Having made the sale, it should be obvious that looking after customers will not only ensure that they come back for more, but that there is a fair chance that they will tell their friends. It's called building a reputation. One of the acknowledged gurus in this field is Julian Richer, who, by the grand age of 35, had built up his chain of retail hi-fi shops, Richer Sounds, to be the busiest in the world. As he says in *The Richer Way*: 'You can play around with prices to push sales and turnover up. You can mess around with margins and hammer costs to make profits look good. But these are short term-tricks. Unless the customer is happy, the business will not last.'

Keeping the customer happy means, firstly, motivating all your staff so that they totally accept that the customer must be at the heart of the business, and, secondly, treating all your staff as important and valuable. Decent pay and conditions are one way; listening and acting on suggestions are almost as important. The objective is to raise morale. Sales targets need to be set to be within reach of all, yet recognising that even warehouse packers need acknowledgement and thanks. Recognition by the management should be mandatory. Your policy should be to catch them doing something *right*, not telling them off in times of failure.

Customer care in a selling situation means courteous, prompt attention without fawning or pressure. Make the premises warm, inviting and tuned to your audience. Encourage browsing and don't hassle people. Listen to the customer, don't switch sell and be honest at all times. If you don't know the answer, don't bullshit, but make sure you do find the right answer. Under promise, over deliver. If a repair, for example, is likely to take 10 days, caution 14 and the customer will be delighted when it arrives sooner. Acknowledge people queuing, be attentive and don't let them wander off.

No-quibble guarantees – like Marks & Spencer's – should be your avowed policy. The damage resulting from prevarication or nit-picking is never worth the hassle. At periodic intervals it can be helpful to ask customers what they think of the service and of any ways it can be improved. And probably most important of all, make your shop fun and pleasant to work in for staff and customers alike. Install a drink machine, offer mince pies at Christmas, hot cross buns at Easter, loan brollies in the rain. Be different...

Sales promotion

Sales promotion (SP) was a little-known science to the general public till the Hoover marketing people thought they would do their bit for the flagging airline industry. It would have been better if they had gone into aircraft in the first place. Well, it only cost the company £47 million to redeem the prizes. And they did sell a lot of Hoovers.

SP Techniques are a way of bringing forward sales, encouraging brand loyalty or manipulating the price levels to distort the sales graph. SP is invariably used in the fast-moving consumer goods (fmcg) sector, where differences between brands are slight and the market is well developed, if not overcrowded. Sales promotion is now a huge industry with some claiming that the spend is twice that of advertising. Unfortunately, there is little place here for the small firms so I shall not spend much time on the subject.

Price manipulation

1. Discounts can be used to even out off-season or quiet times in the trade, be it a hairdresser, theatre or caravan site. Dance halls, or should I say 'Nite Spots', often offer free entrance to girls before 9.00 pm to correct an imbalance of the sexes.
2. Seasonal businesses need to iron out cash flow problems where they can by offering easy credit for early delivery. These invoices can then often be placed with a factor.
3. Sales, if not overdone, can be used to clear stock before the next season's delivery arrives.
4. Firms that deal in a multitude of small lines can use a sale to reduce the chore of stocktaking.
5. For similar reasons a dead stock figure would look better on the balance sheet if turned into cash.
6. New lines are sometimes launched at an unrealistic price to get plenty out on to the market.
7. For the same reason spoiling tactics can be used to defeat a competitor's launch of a rival product.
8. Stockists left with last year's model need to clear the showrooms to make way for the new one.

There is a danger that too frequent sales will devalue the image of the business so that no one buys at all when there isn't a sale on. A bargain sale may also simply bring forward purchases, leaving a drop in subsequent turnover till consumer stocks need replenishing.

Loyalty schemes

Like much of marketing in this area, SP techniques come and go in cycles. A few years ago, money-off coupons were all the rage till many supermarkets decided that the hassle of matching the coupon with the product wasn't worth it. They gave money off at the checkout regardless – which wasn't what the manufacturer intended.

So the great cry at present is dreaming up schemes to retain customer loyalty. The usual way is by giving stamps based on the value of purchase to be redeemed against cash. Now didn't the Co-op do that 50 years ago? The runaway success in this field has of course been *Air Miles*, which combines the glamour and excitement of foreign places with building up expectations. Smart cards are becoming widely used by supermarkets that record all your purchases; they can then mail you with appropriate special offers. By analysing your purchases (Liebfraumilch or Bollinger) they can also form a pretty good idea of your disposable income, leading down all sorts of avenues. Maybe one day the capture cost will become more relevant for small firms. From a supplier's point of view the information they can provide is mouth-watering. A complete profile of the customer combined with tracking high-value activity opens up numerous doors. Until the cost of these smart cards diminishes, small firms can stay with more tried and tested coupons to encourage showroom traffic and measure advertising effectiveness. More boring, but within your means.

Competitions

Always popular as a crowd stopper at exhibitions, and with the National Lottery now a fact of life, the passion for a chance seems undiminished. Competitions must involve using some skill and judgement, otherwise you will come against the Lotteries and Amusements Act, whose rules are strictly enforced. (Don't defeat everybody though by leaving the ball still in frame as one 'Spot the Ball' promoter did. I regret to say that it was in Ireland: some entries still got it wrong.) The motor trade is fond of competitions to draw old customers back into the showroom to test-drive the latest model.

Anyone in doubt should contact the Institute of Sales Promotion at 66–68 Pentonville Road, London N1 9HS; tel: 020 7837 5340, for a copy of its code of sales promotion practice. Alternatively, you can visit its Web site at www.isp.org.uk.

Figure 7.2   Eye-catching sales promotion

Figure 7.3   A shelf-seller for grocers

Promotional gifts

This is a vast field and includes everything from personalised pens, scrap-pads and calendars to T-shirts, watches and mousemats. That is the cheap end of the market. Moving up the scale some offer champagne balloon trips, boxes at Ascot and trips to Nassau. The reason for all this largesse is either to reward loyal staff or, more likely, to influence good customers, buyers and prospects in the nicest possible way. The promotional gift industry, for that is now what it is, supports several magazines and two trade shows.

It is an ideal market for small firms to supply, as the big customers are looking for quality, individuality, imagination and fresh ideas. Many services are featured – travel, leisure and entertainment (corporate hospitality is the grand word) – while manufactured items must usually be capable of bearing the giver's name. Personalisation. No point in giving something if the recipient forgets who gave it away. To source this sector, try the British Promotional Merchandise Association. Telephone them on 01932 35560 or visit their Web site at www.bpma.org.

Finally, here is an old sales joke that is worth a wider audience. Grocer Goldberg was showing his new junior round the stock room.

'My, what a lot of cheese you must sell!'

'Not me,' said Goldberg, 'But you should meet the man who sells *me* cheese!'

Summary

- Recognise that selling is a vital skill to survival. If you really can't do it, employ someone who can.
- Study the psychology of why people buy.
- Set reasonable selling objectives.
- Plan your campaign. Decide on 10 key accounts that you would really like to do business with.
- Organise a system that is simple, informative and one that you will use.
- Practise your presentation, check any audio-visual aids and make sure that any demonstration of your product will be fool-proof.
- Aim to be a good listener. Nod, respond and maintain eye contact. Look for buying signals.
- Be prepared to close at any time.
- Rehearse likely objections and learn to turn them to your advantage.
- Don't forget to ask who else in the company could be interested, and look for other lines to sell. Never underestimate the potential purchasing power of your prospect.
- Widen the use of the telephone both to make better use of your own time and involve your own team.
- If you can use agents, take great care in selection, training and motivation. Hang onto the good ones. They are a rare breed.
- Make sure your paperwork is as professional as your selling effort. Always follow up quotes promptly and diary forward to review.
- Establish an efficient complaints procedure: a satisfied customer could be one for life.

8 *Exhibitions and shows*

You can mess around with margins and hammer costs to make profits
look good. But these are short-term tricks. Unless the customer is happy,
the business will not last.

Julian Richer

Buyers learn of new products in three equal ways: from representatives, advertising – and attending exhibitions.

Trade exhibitions and local shows are an important part of many
small firms' marketing efforts. At one leap you can be in a major
selling arena alongside giants of your industry. The visitors may have
set out to meet their customers, but it is your job to make the best of
that opportunity to lure them on to your stand as well. The exhibition
calendar splits into a number of different sectors. There are the well-
known public (consumer) shows such as *Ideal Home*, *The Motor Show*,
Boat Show, etc, that can run for weeks. But by far the biggest number
of exhibitions is in the trade show sector where the public is generally
not admitted, but where serious selling is done within that trade sector.
So for the motor trade there are such shows as *Forecourt Marketing &
Equipment Show*, and *International Commercial Vehicle Bodywork
Show*. Lastly there are the local agricultural, balloon festival, steam
rally and craft shows held in every county where the biggest (*The
Royal* at Stoneleigh) attracts some 300,000 people. Before booking
space, there are a number of questions to be answered.

1. What is the audience? Trade only, consumer, general or
    specialist?
2. Venue. Can you visit beforehand?

3. What is provided by the organiser.
4. Cost, length of show.
5. Why are you going to exhibit?

If you do your homework properly a high proportion of the right audience will have been selected for you. Choose the wrong show and you may waste a few thousand pounds (if you exhibit at the National Exhibition Centre or other major venue) as well as all your time.

It should be obvious that the main reason to exhibit is to meet a large number of buyers under one roof within the space of a few days. The average salesperson will be lucky to see more than six prospects a day. An exhibitor can manage a couple of hundred in the usual four- or five-day show.

You should appreciate that the psychology has subtly shifted. From being the wooer calling at *the purchaser's* door, and wheedling past the protective secretary, you are setting out your stall to lure the punter on to your stand. But make no mistake: taking a stand at a show is a significant and expensive step that needs considerable planning to make the most of the opportunity.

How to choose the right show

There are around 3,000 trade fairs held each year in the UK alone ranging from motor cars to fur and feather. They are listed in *Exhibition Bulletin* (see page 52). With so many to choose from, care must be taken to pick the right one. Fair promoters are keen to push the merits of their own efforts and are fond of launching new concepts to fill alleged fresh gaps in the market. In general, stick to tried and proven shows. Ask for last year's catalogue and if possible visit the actual show before becoming a paying exhibitor. You can quickly form an idea of the merits of the show by picking out the brand leaders in your trade. Show organisers may also send you a list of exhibitors who have actually booked space in advance. The better shows will provide a visitor breakdown of the previous year's attendance – how many plant managers or specifiers, etc. The figures should be audited.

General shows have vague titles – Spring Fair – while the more specialised shows will only attract visitors of that interest.

The more popular shows will be booked up perhaps six months

ahead, with preference on position given to previous exhibitors. Some literally have a waiting list from one year to the next.

Objectives

I frequently ask why small firms go to shows and depressingly often I get two answers: 'To show the flag' and 'Because I always do'.

Shows are very expensive. Any reasonably major show will cost upwards of £1,200 for the bare minimum of space and a shell stand (see Figure 8.1 on page 227). On top of that will go travel and hotel bills (which can be ruinous in London or near the Birmingham NEC).

So your marketing objectives need to be clearly thought through. These could be:

1. To sell more product.
2. To launch a new line.
3. To find distributors or outlets in a new territory. (Many northern firms put this as number one when exhibiting in London.)
4. To find overseas agents. Major shows attract many overseas buyers and if you find someone you can work with you avoid the expense of going abroad yourself.
5. To attack a new market.
6. To reposition your company in the market.
7. To give support to field agents.
8. To get quick feedback on a projected new range. You can see a lot of prospects in a short time.
9. To re-establish links with clients whom you perhaps do not see often. This can be overdone but is nevertheless a quite valid way of cementing relationships. Shows are good gathering places.
10. And last but not least, pure PR to strengthen the company's position in the marketplace. This should be used as an internal PR exercise as well. Take shopfloor workers and loyal over-worked secretaries along to meet some real clients and let them see the competition.

Cost

Remember that whether 20 or 200 square metres are rented, the fair organiser can only provide the same audience. You won't get any more people through the turnstile by having an enormous stand.

Space rental is just that: whatever is placed on that space is at additional cost. *A shell stand* provided by the organiser is usually three plain white walls, a fascia board with your name, common lighting, and sometimes floor covering and a front desk. Extras you *may* need are power points (sometimes amazingly expensive), spotlights, chairs (you will want to rest occasionally), coat rack, reception desk, leaflet and display racks, a better floor covering, muslin ceiling to hide all the cables and beams, and a waste-paper basket. You may well want to improve the lighting by extra spots and bring colour to the walls by drapes, tiles or display stands.

Your stand design may be governed by restrictions on height and often weight. Unusual exhibits must be cleared with the organiser first. They are all careful about flame retardant materials. Heavy or bulky exhibits must be moved in early during the setting-up phase.

Although the show organisers often specify approved stand contractors, this *doesn't* preclude bringing in your own designs. Prior submission is usually required. Everything to do with exhibitions tends to be expensive. If you happen to be a joiner or in display, or have other practical skills, build your own stand fittings. Design them so you can use them again – and again. But, and it's a big one, if you are at a major exhibition venue, be wary of doing any part of the erection on site. Entire shows have been stopped by exhibitors hammering in a nail or even changing a bulb, when such work was the prerogative of one or more unions. This is usually spelt out in the exhibition contract. Tempers tend to be frayed before a show and getting hold of the organiser's tradespeople to fit your stand together is a very frustrating business. I haven't yet been to a show where someone isn't still painting the walls on the first open day.

A final thought on cost: use carpet tiles and lay them back in the office ready again for next year.

Stand design

This is the most obvious area where the first-time exhibitor stands out like a sore thumb from more seasoned professionals. You have three choices:

- Go to a professional exhibition designer, who will doubtless produce an excellent design – if you can afford it.
- Take the organiser's standard shell scheme (Figure 8.1). This is the preferred route, allowing you to be there with the minimum of fuss.
- Make your own additions to that or simply rent space and put your own stand on it.

Looking at the last option, you must study the exhibitor's regulations very closely; rarely will any deviations be permitted. Ideally you should attend the show, as a visitor, the year before taking a stand, to get the feel of what succeeds and where the aisles and traffic flow go.

If that is impossible, visiting any show at the same *venue* can also be revealing. Because of service points and the sheer construction of the hall (pillars and exits, etc), each show will tend to follow the same layout regardless of whether it is the Motor Show or Show for Menswear. You will get an idea of dead corners and balcony appeal.

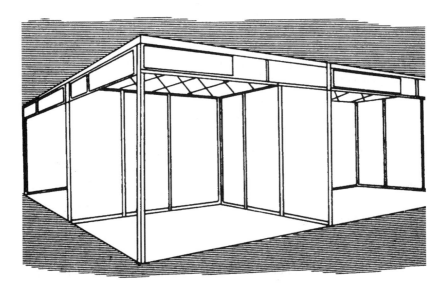

Figure 8.1   Exhibition shell stand

There are 10 main objectives to bear in mind.

1. You must get people to *stop* in front of the stand (what goes on here?).
2. You are in an advertising environment and must *sell a benefit.*
3. There must be no psychological barrier to getting on your stand.
4. Leave enough room for *people* on the stand. Frequently overlooked.
5. Design a cubbyhole for your hats and coats, rubbish and spare literature – and probably the obligatory fire extinguisher.
6. How can you show your product to best effect?
7. Display literature on your product.
8. Have attractive and effective lighting.
9. Contrive some movement or interest on the stand.
10. Can you use part or all of the stand later?

The stand design will depend first of all on what position you have been able to secure. All the best spots will usually have been taken by the regular (and larger) exhibitors and you may have to make do with a very inferior slot. By researching the venue you may decide that the cost is unlikely to offer sufficient returns in view of the poor location. Ideally, choose a position where visitors are approaching you face on so that the full benefit of your magic design can be obtained. Corner sites also offer two frontages. Draw the layout of the stand and make card cut-outs to show the position of the front desk, literature stands, product displays, etc. Better than that is a 3D model, if you're up to it. Make a cardboard man of the right scale and move him around. Then tape up the dimensioned stand and build a full-size mock-up.

Many exhibitors seem to think it is sufficient just to be there. It is most important to grasp that you still have to get visitors to stop and come on to the stand for a *selling situation* to arise. What is known as the 'hover point' is about three feet in front of your stand. You can watch people look at a stand, puzzle through their mind (anything of interest here?) and come to an instant decision to move on or be attracted. It is rather like direct mail, which I talked about in Chapter 5. You have about two seconds at most to influence the right decision.

There are a number of ways you can do this.

1. There must be an immediate, loudly proclaimed benefit. It is not sufficient, for example, just to stick up your name and product as so many exhibitors do. There could well be a hundred other exhibitors all competing in roughly the same field. Write a compelling headline in text large enough to be visible from the 'hover point'.

2. Get some movement onto your stand, as there is nothing worse than a static display. If your product can be demonstrated – a craft worker actually producing – this is always a good pull. However, don't expect this craft worker to sell as well. An audio-visual display, either video or changing slides, can be effective. Beware of a loud continuous commentary that may drive you to distraction by the end of the first day. A turntable can be a simple method of imparting some life, available in size from a simple jeweller's stand to one big enough for a car. A water fountain can be a good draw, perhaps with table tennis balls bouncing in it. Try to involve all the senses. In a slightly different vein, the Jorvik Viking museum at York uses not only lights and sounds but the *smell* of an open cesspit!

3. Run a competition or draw. Few can resist giving up their business card to take part in winning one of your treasured products or bottles of bubbly. Also good for services. One recent show I attended invited visitors to have a free pull at a fruit machine conveniently placed at the front of their stand. Who could resist?

4. Don't neglect other stand exhibitors, who could well be important clients. I designed the 'caption competition' illustrated in Figure 8.2 that was dropped on every stand as well as given to visitors (see page 230). It served to highlight the main selling point of my client, and the same theme was used before and after the show in trade magazines.

5. Novelty knows no bounds in exhibitions. American shows I have attended have included a stand-up comedian giving half-hour performances and Polaroid photos of visitors embracing pretty girls. A recent building exhibition made the national papers when one firm displayed girls taking showers on its stand.

Avoid having to *step* onto your stand. Ideally your carpet should merge into that of the aisle so there is no psychological barrier to moving into

Caption competition

Think of a better caption and win a bottle of
10 year old vintage Somerset Cider Brandy.

My caption is:

From:

Tel number

MIDDLETON ENGINEERING Ltd
Meare · Glastonbury · BA6 9SU
Tel 01458 860264 · fax 01458 860311
website · www.middletonengineering.co.uk

Figure 8.2 This caption competition was run as an advert before an NEC show to draw visitors; it was also run at the show and delivered to stands. The result was pushed out as a press release after – a lot of publicity for little expense

a different environment. There is a change between the neutral territory of the aisle and the more pressurising atmosphere of a stand.

Lighting should illuminate your product and text panels, not your staff. Create pools of interest. It is common practice, because it is convenient, to fix spotlights on the back of the fascia. This means that you will be looking *into* the light for the week. Tiring and unflattering. Fix the lights to point at the walls where your text and products are likely to be. You must also be careful not to create reflections that could make your display illegible. Inevitably a small stand will mean that you have to put your graphic displays on the walls. Make sure that the most important parts of your message are at eye level with the headlines – the eye-catching messages – above head level in large type. Don't forget to visualise the stand with a crowd who may obscure parts of your display.

If space permits, design a quiet area to the rear where serious discussion can take place. This can also be used for moderate staff relaxation and making a cup of tea. (No alcohol.)

Literature

This is always a tricky subject for firms with limited budgets. Depending on the show, it sometimes pays to have two levels of brochure: one cheap for casual enquirers, and the other full colour, multi-paged for serious prospects. There is nothing more depressing than seeing your expensive brochures blowing round the carpark at the end of the day. Some shows are a magnet for schoolchildren who collect freebies or who are doing a project. Nothing wrong with that, but they are hardly serious specifiers who warrant your best leaflets.

Numbers are often a problem and it may help to work on no more than 5 per cent of the expected gate. But it all depends on what sort of show and what your objectives are. Don't arrange your leaflets in too geometrical a display as visitors will be reluctant to disarrange it by taking one.

Product display

The exhibits you show, with rare exceptions, must be spot on. No prototypes or sticky tape or scratches must mar your professional presentation. Ensure they match your literature. There is nothing more calculated to deter a buyer than to say, 'Of course, this is only the

Figure 8.3 Maybe a little over the top? But it certainly pulls in the punters

prototype. The final item will be much better.' I would accept prototypes if they were from an R & D consultancy – that is the nature of their business. Another exception? Ex-rally cars at motor shows, with the obligatory gash down the roof and mud over the doors.

Don't put your most interesting exhibit at the back of the stand. Place it where people can see it from the gangway. If you are using moving items make sure they don't trap visitors or get dislodged. Tie down small and valuable items or put them in a locked display case. Arrange your display so that a glance will disclose a missing item. Leave free passage for visitors – around 60 per cent of the stand.

Signs and labels must *always* be properly printed. Handwritten or even typed product labels look awful. Most printers will set and dry-mount text to give that professional finish. Cut-out display letters can be bought in a variety of styles and materials from mirror glass to polystyrene. Paint the polystyrene in your house colour.

Pre-show publicity

It is important to make the most of your presence by alerting prospects and old clients that you will be there. Most shows are large and busy, and the better buyers draw up a list of people they must see before they go. Telling them you will be there makes your chances better.

The most underused resource of most exhibition organisers is their publicity department. It is there as a *free* service to exhibitors and to promote the exhibition. The best way for organisers to promote exhibitions is to feed the trade and consumer press with a regular flow of interesting stories of firms that will be exhibiting. But if exhibitors don't supply them with enough live stories, inevitably the organisers will tend to go to the regular old firms that they know.

Apart from putting out press releases, the organisers will be producing the show catalogue, and sometimes for the larger shows a newspaper that is given away each day. Most small firms just don't bother to make the most of these opportunities.

The better shows provide stickers with your stand number that can be affixed to every letter you send out as a reminder. Extra invitations are also often given to post to your own prospects.

Staff training and selling

Exhibitions are serious and expensive operations that demand pre-planning from everyone involved to have maximum effect. Planning and training falls into two phases – before and during the show. It helps if there is a common dress code for all the staff. A smart blazer for the men and a suit for the women can be most effective. Small firms will say, 'I can't afford all that!' I would say think ahead and tell your staff that a show is coming up in six months. It could be agreed that a common colour is worn so that next time someone buys a skirt or shirt it matches. Also make sure that whatever colour is chosen it doesn't clash with the stand. Lapel badges must be worn to identify staff.

New exhibitors frequently fail to understand how exhausting exhibitions can be. You need to plan to take enough staff – even roping in spouses and friends if you don't have enough on the payroll. Staff need to get away and relax apart from the stand so work out a rota. Two hours on duty is usually the maximum for efficiency. When they are not on duty, make sure you know roughly where they've gone and when they are due back. Use part of this period to evaluate the competition and seek new ideas.

While most of the visitors who come through the door should vaguely be within your sector of activity, you will still have to weed out specific prospects from the leaflet gatherers, the time-wasters and the *spies*. You rarely have the luxury of long discussions at trade shows, so you must establish a standard routine to:

● Identify the visitor, by name, company and position.
● Establish his or her interest.
● Ask open-ended questions to explore the visitor's depth of intentions.
● If necessary, pass on to a colleague who can handle the enquiry more suitably.
● Record full details, supplying literature if required.
● Mark for any action required later.

Showing the welcome mat

Manning a stand is like being at the zoo – only this time you are the animals. You're there to be peered at, poked and to provide the entertainment. You must never look bored, tired or drunk but always welcoming without being effusive, knowledgeable and a good advertisement for your firm. Most organisers frown on your giving out leaflets or 'accosting' people in the aisle. You have to be more subtle than that, using the techniques outlined earlier, allied to good stand design.

Even the way you stand can affect potential visitors. Some seem to adopt a threatening, arms-folded stance, daring you to come on the stand. Others block the entrance. A common mistake is for staff to huddle in a group at the back at though as a private party. No one wants to break in.

When prospects do venture on, give them time to settle and get their bearings, unless directly approached. Don't pounce or hover at their shoulder: it makes for an unsettling atmosphere. *Never* say 'Can I help you?' There is an even chance that the answer will be 'No', so where do you go from there? It is more fruitful to start a discussion with:

'What interests you in this range?'
'Have you used our product before?'

'Let me show you how this works.'

'The main benefit of this is…'

'This has just been launched at the show…'

Identify prospects and if they have a casual or nil interest, get rid of them as politely as possible. If the conversation looks like getting long-winded you'll have to invent an acceptable excuse – appointment, phone call to make, etc. Most serious enquirers will either want a quotation or follow-up visit later. Record visits with action required in a proper visitors' book or on printed sheets, *but* ensure that this is kept under control, preferably under a desk. Loss of this could negate a week's work.

If you take a *new* product to the show, make sure a large sticker says so. That's the most important word in the exhibitor's dictionary. As the show progresses, put some 'sold' stickers on your exhibits. It impresses the visitors and depresses the opposition.

Sales literature

Never give out sales literature wholesale without an exchange of address. Never display it at the edge of the stand where it can be purloined with no commitment. My favourite method of distributing high-quality literature is to keep a word processor on the stand, type address labels and post them first class to visitors' offices. Explain that you don't want to burden the client at the show, but it will arrive on his or her desk next morning. It looks professional, avoids waste and gets to the recipient.

Stay smart

After the first enthusiasm wears off, many stands get that lived-in look. Make sure that yours is kept neat and tidy, no drink visible, no dirty glasses or ashtrays overflowing or display racks left empty. Keep the spirits of your staff high by varying the routine and sending them off on spec 'spying' trips around the show. It never ceases to amaze me what useful information is offered free to innocent questions.

It shouldn't need saying but I've seen it happen too often – *never* leave the stand unattended. There's usually a lot of tempting merchandise around and exhibitions are not noted for their honesty, sad to say. The danger time is when the show closes. All hell breaks loose with everyone desperate to get out. Trucks and lifting gear struggle to get in. Many busy men with overalls wander round with obvious intent. You're too busy dismantling your own stand to wonder who those efficient folk are next door. I have heard of whole stands disappearing into the wrong lorry.

After the show

Follow up all enquiries promptly – most don't. Book appointments and get those orders. Hold a post-mortem with other staff and learn.

Don't forget to tell the press what a wonderful show you've had, to keep the name in view. Hold onto the show catalogue, which will be useful for contacts and a mailing list afterwards.

It is unfair to judge results on the attendance of one year's show. You will undoubtedly learn and adapt from your first effort. Major visiting buyers also are a little wary of brand-new names but will renew acquaintance in succeeding years. If you have met potential agents at the show, don't sign them up then and there, but take time to investigate their background.

Summary

- Find an exhibition for your speciality and research whether it represents effective use of your time and money.
- Ideally attend the show first as an observant visitor, or failing that go to the hall and get an idea of the layout.
- Decide on your objectives.
- Do a budget, and add 10 per cent for contingencies.
- Book the stand and local accommodation if necessary.
- Design a stand from mock-ups.
- How are you going to get visitors to stop?
- Get some life and excitement into the stand.
- Organise your literature.
- Make use of the organiser's publicity machine, early and often.
- Train all your staff.

- Allow ample time to set up.
- Get a good night's sleep beforehand – leave the junketing (if any) to the end.
- During the show keep the stand pristine and keep the staff alert by sending them off at regular intervals to explore, spy and learn.
- Record all your visitors.
- Keep a tight eye on security, especially at break down.
- Follow up all enquiries promptly and hold a post-mortem.

Sources

Exhibition Bulletin
The Showman's Directory
(see page 52)

9 *Starting in exports*

The customer is always right.

Gordon Selfridge

Despite all the exhortations of HM Government, 90 per cent of our export trade is still carried out by under 50 companies. The arrival of the EU has made some tasks simpler, but exporting is still a formidable task for many small firms. The reasons are not hard to find. Distance from overseas markets and customs, new packaging, labelling, safety and electrical standards, freight and customs requirements, to say nothing of currency and language confusion. Fortunately, English is increasingly the international language of commerce, so that problem has lessened, though it is often polite to reply in customers' native tongue (by letter). The fax and e-mail have greatly simplified communications, and as the world shrinks, you can find native speakers close by to translate the more obscure languages.

Air freight costs have come down, allowing much quicker deliver and sophistication of handling, and if you are fortunate to live near a conurbation there is probably an active Chamber of Trade with helpful members to give practical advice. Exporting is very much a practical skill that can best be learnt from other practitioners – not, I regret to say, from the official or semi-official bodies, the DTI or banks.

Some firms start exporting in one of two ways, either by deliberate policy, or often, in my experience, as the result of an unsolicited request from abroad. If it is the latter you need to quickly establish:

1. The status of the enquirer, unless that is obvious. Your bank can carry out a status check using its overseas agents for a modest

fee. It is better to find out whether an enquirer is a time-waster early, before spending time on frequent quotes and correspondence.

2. How the enquirer intends to pay.
3. Delivery dates and any special requirements.
4. Costs of shipping the goods. (You should contact a freight forwarder to establish these.) An ex-works price is not a lot of use to a client in New York.

If you intend to embark on exporting as a means of expanding the business, then there are some steps you can take without going through *le Chunnel*. Around 20 per cent of UK trade is concluded through buying houses or agents based in this country. Delivery is made to a nominated shipper and payment made in sterling. Most of these buying houses are of long standing.

Why export anyway? There is no intrinsic merit in exporting – often quite the reverse. It is important to develop a strong home base first, then move on to what can be gained abroad. Do not regard export as a means of disposing of your domestic surplus. There must be solid objectives in taking that route, which could be one of the following:

1. To spread the risk of tying yourself to one domestic market. A recession here is not necessarily mirrored abroad.
2. More profit in selling abroad. Not so long ago we were equals in Europe in terms of living standards. Today, in a frighteningly short space of time, the UK is becoming the poor man of Europe. Some luxury goods may command a wider market in the European Union.
3. Our professional services – design, consultancy, engineering, financial, computer software, etc – are in great demand throughout the world. The developing nations, both oil-rich and impoverished, can make very good use of experts willing to travel.
4. Growth. As world standards rise, the possible markets for your goods expand at an accelerating rate.
5. To improve the product. Many products, once exposed to the harsher conditions overseas, take on innovations that result in a better article.

Staying in this country

Let's look at my first option and chase export business from this country.

There are hundreds of confirming houses, export merchants and buying offices which act for overseas principals in selecting and procuring goods for export. Most of them are based in London, many around Tottenham Court Road and Regent Street. Look in the *Directory of Export Buyers* (Trade Research Publications, Berkhamsted; copies in the bigger reference libraries) for a detailed breakdown of who deals in what. You will find buyers for industrial and consumer goods and agents for department stores in the United States, Canada, Japan, South Africa and throughout the Commonwealth. Do the rounds. Dealing with export houses can be a lengthy business with sometimes endless requests for samples. Persevere: when the orders do come they can be worthwhile. Payment is invariably in sterling and delivery to a named shipper. Paperwork is minimal.

Some will not reveal their principal as they would not wish you to go direct and cut them out, and it is unlikely you will know what price is charged. Some technical products are obviously not suited to dealing through UK-based intermediaries, so you will have to source distributors and end-users based in your target countries. Many of the names listed will be members of the *British Exporters Association* (Broadway House, Tothill Street, London SW1H 9NQ; tel: 020 7222 5419; fax: 020 7799 2468; e-mail: bexamail@aol.com; Web site: www.bexa.co.uk) which could help to put you in touch with an active exporter.

The National Exporters Database is a largely free service, based on the Internet, run by the DTI. Once the simple entry form is completed (0800 783 2394, or visit www.tradeuk.com), details of your company and products will be available to anyone on the Web. Export sales leads that match your abilities will be e-mailed to you that cover:

- Private-sector opportunities from overseas agents and distributors.
- Tenders and public-sector opportunities.
- Joint ventures, licences, cooperative opportunities.
- Market pointers, successful tender bidders.
- Public interest information, changes in legislation, custom controls, etc.

You are entitled to five free downloads per month for the first three headings, then charged at £20 per shot.

Direct exporting

If you wish to be more energetic – and initiate an export drive – there is a number of reference sources you can start with.

Your first call should be to your nearest office of British Trade International (BTI), formerly called Overseas Trade Services, part of the DTI. Most information by far is held at the information centre of Trade Partners UK, 66–74 Victoria Street, London SW1E 6FE; 020 7215 5444; Web site: www.tradepartners.gov.uk. Much of its information may be accessed on the Web site, including country-by country guides to dealing with overseas markets. Among the services offered by BTI are:

1. The *Export Intelligence Service*. For details see www. tradeuk.com.
2. *Scatter missions* are organised subsidised trips of groups of business people to specific countries. Brief the consulate abroad on your interests and it will try to line up appointments and a suggested itinerary for you. The groups are usually members of a Chamber of Commerce or trade association. They can be a very useful way of learning from other, perhaps more experienced, members of the business community.
3. The *Fairs and Promotions* branch mounts a British presence at over 300 shows overseas. It usually rents a large block space and partitions it out to UK exhibitors. There is great advantage in a small firm being part of a large national stand. Buyers come to visit the well-known large firms and must pass their smaller brethren. There is usually a common colour scheme and layout which pulls it all together. There is a subsidy on stand space, transport of exhibits and travel, depending on the venue. Much of the hassle is removed by being part of a well-organised operation of this sort. Little things like a common pool for publicity and advertising can help a lot in getting over the message. Demand is keen for the major shows and early booking is essential.

4. They will put you in touch with organisations which will attempt to investigate the particular sector for your product using the local knowledge of the commercial consuls in the countries concerned (for one such company, visit www.eirene.com). A report can be given on the competition, price, pattern of demand and methods of selling. The section also suggests local agents who may be worth approaching to represent you. Full status reports can be obtained. Unfortunately, it is not a cheap exercise and costs several hundred pounds.

5. Probably of most use is the scheme whereby *Export Development Advisers* – business people with practical experience of exporting – are attached to the larger Chambers of Commerce or Business Link to help on a personal basis.

Regrettably I have to add that I hear mixed reports about BTI's performance on the practical side. Some consulates are excellent in producing agencies and market research but other countries fall down. I suspect it depends simply on the motivation and length of stay of individuals in our embassies abroad whether you get competent service. Happily I can recommend the Fairs and Promotions branch (part of Support for Exhibitions and Seminars Abroad (SESA), based in Scotland), market research expertise in London, and publicity through using the Central Office of Information (see pages 245–46).

Other sources of information

You should join your nearest large *Chamber of Commerce*. Most towns have chambers of trade but they tend to be composed of retailers and have no expertise in exporting. The biggest are those of London and Birmingham but all the conurbations have chambers to help you. The more efficient will be able to offer regular sponsored group selling, or fact finding, trips abroad, documentation advice, carnets, certificates of origin and all the new impedimenta to smooth your sales efforts. The more progressive hold regular meetings to enable firms to discuss common problems.

Export clubs are another informal way of meeting fellow marketing people and learning about the pitfalls of selling abroad. They tend to be *ad hoc* groups of small business people perhaps sponsored by local councils and trade associations.

There are a variety of overseas Chambers of Commerce, embassy libraries (the US embassy in Grosvenor Square in particular) and joint trade bodies to foster links with overseas countries. Not all are too keen to help with exports as many are more geared to selling *you* something, but the sources of information are invariably there in great detail.

All the major banks offer free literature and guidance. You will inevitably be using them a great deal for arranging payment, perhaps for obtaining status reports via their agents abroad, exchange control and currency. Try to get one of their staff from the overseas branch to visit. The smaller branches will probably not have many dealings with export documentation and it may pay you to move your account if much export is contemplated.

Exporting can sweeten the bank's relationship with you as priority has always been given to lending to those so engaged.

Overseas Trade is a monthly magazine produced by the Department of Trade and Industry that keeps you up to date on tariff changes and opportunities. There are quarterly trade fair supplements.

Freight forwarders

Another source of guidance is the freight forwarder – one of those people who will ship your valued goods all over the world to the port of destination. The paperwork involved in export probably causes more headaches to small firms than anything else. Every country seems to require different forms and there are changes every week. Unless you are engaged in a very stable part of the world and regularly ship items of the same character, I would urge you to pass all the paperwork over to a friendly freight forwarder. Certainly, you will be charged for the privilege, and small consignments may bear an uneconomic charge, but they are dealing with it every day. In general, don't look to your bank or the BTI for matters of detail such as commercial invoices or certificates of origin. I have found a good freight forwarder far more practical and knowledgeable.

Where to export

You will probably find it simpler to export to English-speaking countries first – the old Commonwealth and United States, depending on the worth of the dollar. Many retain our customs and style of life. Financial links are still strong, with many British banks having subsidiaries and agents in those countries.

The European Union takes 60 per cent of Britain's trade, and when (or if) the euro arrives, trade will increase. Travel costs in money and time are less and their standards of living are equal to (or ahead of) ours. There are few restrictions on trade and no customs barriers, in theory! Small firms seem to do well in Holland and Germany, with France traditionally a difficult market to break into. It is, of course, a highly developed, sophisticated and competitive market where quality, premium products will always sell if correctly presented. Japan takes much perseverance and you should be wary of quick results. You should approach *JETRO*, the Japanese former export, now import, agency for help. It can be found at Leconfield House, Curzon Street, London W1J 5HZ; 020 7470 4700; Web site: www.jetro.go.jp.

Third World and Eastern European countries pose special problems. Payment is rarely simple and finding the right channel of distribution difficult. You are probably better dealing with a government or United Nations agency already working in the field help with specification requirements and methods of payment.

Commitment

It is a sad fact that in most countries now Britain's share of the market is decreasing. Former strongholds of British produce have been over-taken by the Japanese, Germans or French. They seem to have put more effort into tackling the market. Close study of each individual market has been undertaken, modifications made to take account of the local conditions, languages learnt and perhaps most important, hard investment made with distributors in other countries. It is this constant back-up to the selling operation that has paid dividends. Japanese busi-nessmen travel abroad 20 times more often than ours. Unless you take a long-term view, are prepared to make frequent trips to see what is happening on the ground and support the local man with promotion and exhibitions, direct exporting is not for you. Getting established abroad is a long, costly exercise and requires a great commitment to see it through.

Getting paid

One of the main attractions of dealing with export houses or buying agents in this country is the certainty of getting paid reasonably promptly and in sterling. Extended credit is not usually a sales requirement. Once you start dealing direct you come against two problems: how to ensure getting payment and avoiding exchange risks.

A surprising amount of trade is carried on open account, ie invoices are raised, the goods delivered and payment made by bank transfer. A large element of trust has built up. There is really no difference here between home and export business. Most of the Continent deals in this way and will expect you to do the same. Outside Europe you will probably have to draw up Bills of Exchange and get involved with Letters of Credit, which the overseas branch of your bank should be able to help with. Overseas factoring can be useful – where you discount the invoice with a factoring company and get paid in sterling. The largest company in this field is GMAC Commercial Credit Limited (part of Lloyds Bank), which can be found at PO Box 240, Sovereign House, Church Street, Brighton BN1 3WX; tel: 01273 321211.

The Web

One of the trumpeted virtues of having a Web site is the ability to deal worldwide but till we all deal in one currency, exporters are faced with the problems of quoting a delivered price and getting paid. Small items – books, CDs, etc – can be quoted with a carriage price based on a percentage increase of the value to cover yourself. Ask enquirers to complete an e-mail order form from which a precise sales figure including carriage can be quoted. The key is rapid response, as we have become conditioned to regarding the Web as an instant resource. Taking days to reply will kill any edge you may have over your competition. An automatically generated response is helpful – 'Thank you for your enquiry; it will be dealt with within the next 24 hours.'

Publicity

The *Central Office of Information (COI)* is the government's main propaganda agency for pushing out news items all round the world. It collects news about British products, new inventions, large contracts, etc, and sends them out to our consulates abroad. They in turn feed their local press. Something like 50,000 stories and 20,000 photographs a year are sent out. If the story warrants it the COI will send its own photographer to your firm to get the best job. Many of the staff are ex-Fleet Street and in my experience provide a first-class service. On occasions they will also produce film and video to slot into news programmes overseas. They will write scripts and do 'voice overs'. It is particularly appropriate to use the COI if you are exhibiting abroad as it will be able to tie in the story with your presence. The charge is £80 for the first article, £40 thereafter.

The COI works closely with the BTI and contact should be made through the regional offices.

There are also a number of press agency services that will write a story, translate here and abroad with a native speaker, and send out to the appropriate journal overseas. It can be very effective if you have the right story and go to a top agency and is particularly good for engineering and technical products. The cost can be several hundred pounds for a story translated into, say, three languages. The skill lies in the expert translation as the wrong nuance can be devastating.

Some export terminology

The most casual reader will soon come up against some jargon of the export trade. A few major terms are:

Bill of lading. The document given to you by the shipping line as a receipt and title (ownership) for the goods carried. A valuable document that tends to have several copies, some of which are sent to the importer and paying bank as evidence of compliance with your terms of trading.

Certificate of origin means what it says – an authenticated statement by the exporter backed by a Chamber of Commerce, and sometimes by an embassy, to state where the goods emanate.

Commercial invoices are more detailed than domestic invoices. They usually contain a full description of the goods, packing marks, weights, insurance, and transport routes. Every country seems to require different methods of spelling out the same thing – some require consular and Chamber of Commerce authentication, some want declarations if not the whole invoice in their own language. Commercial invoices are also of major interest to the Customs in both countries as a means of checking exports, imports and any duties to be levied.

FOB (free on board) is the usual method of quoting export prices. Added to your price will be the cost of transport to the specified port, dock charges, etc, up to placing on board ship (or aircraft). As the cost depends on which exit port is used, it is best to add the name of the port as well – FOB Harwich, for example.

CIF (cost, insurance, freight) takes it one stage further. Added to the FOB price is the actual shipping charge to a named port and the cost of insurance on board.

Spot and forward rates of exchange. Spot rates are currency deals struck at once, while forward rates are those at which a bargain may be struck at some time in the future. You can protect the amount of currency you are going to receive by contracting to sell at the time that your deal is made.

SITPRO (Simplification of International Trade Procedures) is an attempt to reduce the complexities of export documentation. The basis of it is a master document from which, by using a copier and different overlays, the various other documents can be run off, avoiding constant retyping. Many freight forwarders and large companies are now using this scheme.

There are also various PC software packages that remove a lot of the tedium.

Reference sources

Croner's Reference Book for Exporters (Croner Publications Ltd, Croner House, 145 London Road, Kingston upon Thames; 020 8547 3333) is one in a large series of loose-leaf, hand reference books on specialist subjects – loose-leaf because you get a regular update as part of your annual subscription.

The Export Handbook is a good source of export information produced by the London Chamber of Commerce/Kogan Page (3rd edn, 1998).

10 New products: innovation, patents, licensing and design

For God's sake Clive, I don't care if they have rubber bands in as long as
they work.
*Alan Sugar to Clive Sinclair on attempting to understand the intricacies
of Sinclair's latest gadget*

Just when you think you've made it, along comes someone with a
product that's half the size and a quarter the price. Complacency has
been the death of much of British industry, and its services as well. As
the world shrinks and you can e-mail a design to Taiwan and have the
sample back in a week or two, so we must all be aware of changes.

Innovative or die. It doesn't matter whether you supplied milk to the
Milk Marketing board or jewellery to Ratners, you must never assume
that customers will always be there. To be semantic, *innovation* is
usually regarded as a change, a novel approach rather than pure invention, a somewhat rarer occurrence that creates a truly new product. In
other words, many can be innovative, without necessarily being inven-
tive. I've met quite a few hopeful inventors, both individuals and
established businesses, but extremely few have ever made any money
out of their ideas. As this area is even more full of sharks than many
others – and dispassionate advice elusive – I will spend a little time on
the subject.

So what's the big idea?

Try to forget about the wonders of your brainwave and look at the market first. Is there a need for the product? Who needs it? Is it simpler or more complicated than the item it may replace? What is the size of the market – general or exclusive? Is the market likely to grow or reduce? What is the competition? Why hasn't anyone thought of it before? Well over 90 per cent of ideas have been invented before. Sad but true. Patents may have been taken out, they may have expired or lapsed. The product may have reached the market and failed.

Many engineers and other perfectionists have spent small fortunes on perfecting the product before looking at the market. They have been so caught up in the excitement and their own convictions that they have not accepted that just because they liked it, not everyone else would buy one. Much money and anguish could have been saved if they had reversed the timetable. So re-read Chapter 2, do your basic research and satisfy yourself as objectively as you can that there is indeed a need for your product, and that there is a way of making money out of it.

Be realistic

Unless you are already in business in that line of country, my advice is invariably to try to sell (license) the idea on to someone who may already have the engineering capability to turn it into a productive object and who has access to markets. The difficulty is that selling just an idea is rarely fruitful. In this complicated world most ideas have been thought of before, so any potential investor or developer would need proof that it works. Prototypes and preferably production models need to be developed, which can consume a great deal of money. On the assumption that you hope to get a return from your invention, your bargaining position is strengthened the further along the road you go. Paper ideas are cheap, working prototypes, market analysis and even orders are worth considerably more.

Keep it confidential

Approaches to outside parties immediately throw up the problem of confidentiality. You don't want them to run off with your idea, but some will not be able to help unless they know what you are talking about. If you reveal the secret – or publish it – before lodging a patent application, without a confidentiality agreement, you run the risk of the patent being challenged. It will then be in the public domain, as the lawyers say. A simple specimen agreement is shown in Figure 10.1. However, I must warn you that actions for breach of confidence are both rare and extremely difficult to prove.

Approaches to companies to take up your invention may also be met with a refusal to sign any confidentiality agreement. They could argue that they are working on a similar project, and would not want to reveal that fact or risk any confidentiality infringement at a later date. They would normally suggest that you lodge a patent before disclosing your invention.

Intellectual property

This is the fancy name given to patents, copyright, design right, trade and service marks, know-how agreements – anything in a legally enforceable form that protects innovations.

There are two schools of thought about patents. The first (I have to say generally promoted by patent agents) is that you should patent first to protect your idea, then rush around developing the product. Once you have lodged the first application with the Patent Office (now free), which will give you a priority date, not a patent, you have just a year to decide what to do. At the end of that time you pay a fee (£130) and request preliminary search and examination. The claims are made at this stage. About 18 months after the priority date it is made public. A year is rarely long enough, and the only way to prolong it is by allowing the first application to lapse and lodging a fresh application. But this *must* involve a significant fresh development over what you lodged before – otherwise you could carry on for ever. Unless the object is simple and you are happy that:

(a) you have ironed out all the problems;
(b) a licensee is lined up to take it on;

my choice would be to wait as long as you can, then lodge the application.

Confidential Disclosure Agreement

THIS AGREEMENT is made the   day of
between

of

(hereinafter called the 'Supplier') of the one part and of

(hereinafter called the 'Receiver') of the other part.
WHEREAS
The Receiver is interested in the following project

and the Supplier is the owner of the said project and has in his possession confidential information (Information) which the Receiver is interested to receive in confidence for the sole purpose
of assessing the commercial practicability (viability) of the said Project ('Objective').

NOW IT IS HEREBY AGREED:

1. The Receiver undertakes to keep any and all information supplied by the Supplier strictly
    confidential and not to disclose it to any person, firm or individual without the express written
    consent of the Supplier. Such information may be technical, commercial, market or other-
    wise (and is detailed in the annexe hereto).
2. The Receiver shall not use information supplied by the Supplier for any purpose other than
    the aforementioned Objective.
3. The Receiver shall restrict all such information to those responsible employees whose
    knowledge of the same is necessary for the aforementioned Objective. In addition, the
    Receiver undertakes that employees, advisers and consultants to whom such information is
    disclosed are bound by the same commitment of confidentiality.
4. In the event that no business arrangements resulting in an Agreement in regard to the
    Project matures within a period of   months the Receiver undertakes to return to
    the Supplier immediately all such information and any copies thereof and to provide the
    Supplier forthwith with a full report and his reasons, and the supporting evidence, for such
    conclusion of decision.
5. The undertakings required in accordance with Clauses 1, 2, and 3 and 4 of this Agreement
    shall not apply to information which:
    (a) Can be shown to have been in the possession of the Receiver prior to disclosure.
    (b) Is in the public domain at the time of such disclosure or subsequently enters the public
        domain other than through any default of the Receiver.
    (c) Subsequently becomes available to the Receiver from any legitimate source without
        obligation of confidentiality or non-use.
6. The termination of this Agreement for any reason shall not affect the obligations of confi-
    dentiality and non-use contained herein.
7. This agreement is subject to the Laws of England.

Signed for an on behalf of   Signed for and on behalf of
(Supplier)   (Receiver)

Director   Date   Director   Date

Figure 10.1   Sample confidential disclosure agreement form

There are other ways whereby you can protect your idea to a limited extent. *Copyright* will automatically offer some protection to drawings or photographs and is well recognised among impoverished authors and painters. It will also cover intentions at the drawing stage if you can prove that you thought of the idea first. You will need to provide authentication. The simplest way is either to post a drawing back to yourself using the post office receipt (leave the envelope unopened) or get a solicitor to sign and date the drawings as having seen them. All you have done is claim originality in the drawings – and of course the process is free. Copyright lasts till 50 years after your death. Use the © sign on printed matter as notice to others.

Design registration will protect the outward appearance of the object, not the mechanical ingenuity. The Designs Registry, which is part of the Patent Office (address on page 52), will send you details. The fee is relatively modest and you could lodge it yourself. The Registry can be searched. *Design right* is similar to copyright in that there is no register to search and it is automatically created. On all your drawings and communications it helps to put 'Design Right' and the date. Go through the same procedure as copyright to establish a priority date. Protection theoretically lasts for 15 years.

None of these are as strong protection as a patent, which the state guarantees, subject to your purse being deep enough to fight any infringers. While there are many people who claim to have filed their own patents, the only test is when it comes to court. For serious projects, in my view, you must use the services of a patent agent, which will probably cost about £1,500 for a UK patent. There is no such thing as a world patent, but a number of countries have formed cooperation treaties that make filing a little simpler. A European Patent Convention application, for example, will cost over £5,000 so there is little point in proceeding without serious investors. Patents last for 20 years provided the annually increasing fees are paid.

Licensing

The only sensible route for the vast majority of small firms is to interest a bigger player. The costs of infringement actions can then be passed on, though insurance can be obtained to cover the risk. Use the standard reference books mentioned in Chapter 2 to identify players, advertise in trade journals or use technology exchanges (databases) that are around. The *Licensing Executives Society* is the little-known association of those with particular expertise in negotiating these contracts and with patent knowledge. Many tend to specialise in specific areas – electronics, pharmaceuticals, etc – and have worldwide contacts. Try visiting its Web site at www.les-europe.org/gb-ireland.

If you make the approach yourself, it often proves to be better to target No 2 in the sector rather than the market leader. The runners-up tend to be the hungry ones: No 1 often is imbued with the 'Not Invented Here' psychology that still permeates much of British industry.

What are the rewards?

The rewards are far less than you might think. Royalty rates paid are rarely more than 5 per cent of sales, often much less. Remember that unless you are a fully fledged R & D company the licensee still has an enormous amount of work to do – not least market the thing. Invention is often the easy part. You have the theoretical choice of outright sale, part-sale to cover expenses and periodic royalties as they proceed, or probably just royalties some time in the future. Always go for as much money upfront as you can secure.

Other help

Despite the often repeated cry that Britain is a nation of inventors, HM Government has diminished its help almost to vanishing point – unless you can make a bigger bang. The DTI trumpets its *SMART* schemes that offer £45,000 and above to help develop high-tech products, but you have to match their input. These schemes are run on the basis of a competition, which is a silly way to encourage a vital resource. The Design Centre has closed, BP and other players have stopped funding and almost all we have left is dear, brave *Tomorrow's World*, which is often the kiss of death to products that appear on the programme.

A strong warning. Be very wary of the number of invention brokerage agencies (some American) that offer vast riches, but have no knowledge of new product development. They will swiftly remove

£2,000 or more from your wallet and replace it with copies of *Yellow Pages* for you to follow up.

Try your local Business Link, which should be in a better position to advise. The long-established *Institute of Patentees and Inventors* has regular meetings, publishes a magazine and will be able to offer some advice. Membership fee is modest. Contact the Institute at Triumph House, 189 Regent St, London W1R 7WF; tel: 020 7434 1818.

The Patent Office (address on page 52) will send a good pack of leaflets, but it cannot advise on the suitability or merit of your proposed patent in the marketplace.

Reference sources

By some distance the most readable and useful booklet in this field for the lone inventor or small firm is *A Better Mousetrap* (Third Edition) by Peter Bissell and Graham Barker. Only 36 pages long and now, alas, out of print, a copy may be tracked down at Business Link.

Understanding Commercial & Industrial Licensing by Brendan
Fowlston is for the serious student (Waterlow).
Eureka is a good magazine for engineering designers.

A moral tale

If you've managed to get this far and are a little bewildered and disheartened that innovation is not for you, then let me tell you the tale of Pip Hills and the Scotch whisky industry.

One of the bigger grumbles among marketing folk is that 'The accountant's in charge, now.' Well, one Edinburgh accountant, Mr Pip Hills, thought he saw an opening for premier single malts. Yes, a marketing opening. Fifteen years ago he approached the major distillers and proposed they bottle single barrel malts and sell them at a premium price to connoisseurs. And what were the replies from these expensively trained marketing experts from the cream of Scottish industry? 'Can't be done. No market. It would have been done before if there were.' Universal derision.

So Pip Hills formed the Scotch Malt Whisky Society and bought selected aged casks and promoted worldwide. Today the Society has 15,000 members and is highly respected, especially in Japan. Some bottles sell for over £60 each. And what has been the reaction of the traditional Scotch whisky distillers? Need you ask?

If an accountant with vision can do it, so can we all.

And finally – my 12 golden rules

1. Identify your market segment.
2. Where are the gaps?
3. Where is there growth and profit?
4. Looks for needs and translate the benefits.
5. Always answer the question: what's in it for me?
6. How can you differentiate your product or service?
7. What else can you sell them and who else needs your product?
8. Look after the customer.
9. Be professional at all times.
10. Plan your objectives.
11. Think!
12. And make your business fun – life is not a rehearsal.

Index

Page references in italics indicate figures or illustrations